First World War
and Army of Occupation
War Diary
France, Belgium and Germany

66 DIVISION
Divisional Troops
Royal Army Medical Corps
2/3 East Lancashire Field Ambulance
27 February 1917 - 26 May 1919

WO95/3132/2

The Naval & Military Press Ltd
www.nmarchive.com
Published in association with The National Archives

Published by

The Naval & Military Press Ltd

Unit 10 Ridgewood Industrial Park,

Uckfield, East Sussex,

TN22 5QE England

Tel: +44 (0) 1825 749494

www.naval-military-press.com

www.nmarchive.com

This diary has been reprinted in facsimile from the original. Any imperfections are inevitably reproduced and the quality may fall short of modern type and cartographic standards.

© Crown Copyright
Images reproduced by permission of The National Archives, London, England, 2015.

Contents

Document type	Place/Title	Date From	Date To
Heading	WO95/3132/2		
Heading	66th Division 2-3rd (E. Lancs) Fd Amb 1915 Sep-1916 Feb 1917 Mar-1919 May		
Heading	66th Div 2/3rd R L Field Ambulance		
Heading	Army Medical Service R.A.M.C. T. War Diary 2/3 (East Lancs) Field Ambulance From 27/2/1917 To 31/3/1917 Vol. I		
War Diary	Colchester	27/02/1917	27/02/1917
War Diary	Southampton	28/02/1917	01/03/1917
War Diary	Le Havre France	02/03/1917	03/03/1917
War Diary	Berguette	04/03/1917	04/03/1917
War Diary	Lambres	05/03/1917	07/03/1917
War Diary	St. Venant	07/03/1917	14/03/1917
War Diary	Zelobes	14/03/1917	16/03/1917
War Diary	Bethune	17/03/1917	26/03/1917
War Diary	Lone Farm A.D.S	27/03/1917	28/03/1917
War Diary	Bethune	28/03/1917	31/03/1917
Miscellaneous	2/3rd East Lancs Field Amb War Diary Appendix "A" Relief Of 14th Field Ambulance	01/02/1917	01/02/1917
Miscellaneous	2/3rd East Lancs Field Ambulance War Diary Appendix "B"	01/04/1917	01/04/1917
Map	2/3 East Lancs Field Amb.		
Heading	War Diary 2/3rd East Lancashire Field Ambulance Volume 2 April 1917		
Heading	B.E.F. Summary Of Medical War Diaries For 2/3rd E Lancs /66th Divn 11th Corps 1st Army Western Front April-May 17		
Miscellaneous	2/3rd E. Lancs/66th Divn 11th Corps O.C. Lt Col L.H. Cox 1st Army		
War Diary	Bethune	01/04/1917	30/04/1917
Operation(al) Order(s)	Operation Order No. 18 By Colonel H.G. Falkner T.D. Commanding R.A.M.C. 66th Div	07/04/1917	07/04/1917
Miscellaneous	66th Division Stragglers Posts	16/04/1917	16/04/1917
Operation(al) Order(s)	Operation Order No. 19 By Colonel H.G. Falkner T.D. Commanding R.A.M.C. 66th Division	23/04/1917	23/04/1917
Heading	Volume III War Diary 2/3rd East Lancashire Field Ambulance From May 1st To May 31st 1917		
Heading	B.E.F. Summary Of Medical War Diaries For 2/3rd Lancs/ 66th Divn. 11th Corps 1st Army Western Front April-May 17		
Miscellaneous	2/3rd E. Lancs/66th Divn 11th Corps O.C. Lt. Col L.H. Cox 1st Army		
Miscellaneous	From Officer Commanding 2/3rd. East Lancs. Field Ambulance	02/05/1917	02/05/1917
War Diary	Bethune	01/05/1917	10/05/1917
War Diary	Locon	11/05/1917	24/05/1917
War Diary	Bethune	25/05/1917	31/05/1917
Operation(al) Order(s)	Operation Order No. 20 By Colonel H.G. Falkner T.D. Assistant Director Of Medical Services 66th Division	08/05/1917	08/05/1917

Type	Description	Start	End
Miscellaneous	Officer Commanding 2/3rd East Lancs Field Ambulance	18/05/1917	18/05/1917
Operation(al) Order(s)	Operation Order No. 22 By Colonel H.G. Falkner T.D. Commanding R.A.M.C. 66th Division	21/05/1917	21/05/1917
Heading	War Diary Vol. T 2/3rd East Lancashire Field Ambulance June 1917		
War Diary	Bethune	01/06/1917	22/06/1917
War Diary	Marles-les-Mines	23/06/1917	26/06/1917
War Diary	Petite Synthe	27/06/1917	30/06/1917
Miscellaneous	2/3rd East Lancashire Field Ambulance for W/ending June 2nd 1917	02/06/1917	02/06/1917
Miscellaneous	Programme of Training 2/3rd East Lancs Field Ambulance for Week Endg June 16th 1917	16/06/1917	16/06/1917
Operation(al) Order(s)	Operation Order No. 24 By Colonel H.G. Falkner T.D. A.D.M.S. 66th Division	11/06/1917	11/06/1917
Miscellaneous	A.D.M.S. 66th Div. Ref.-O.O.25	17/06/1917	17/06/1917
Miscellaneous	Programme of Training 2/3rd East Lancs Field Amb. for Week Endg. June 23rd 1917	23/06/1917	23/06/1917
Operation(al) Order(s)	Operation Order No. 27 By Colonel H.G. Falkner A.D.M.S. 66th Division	19/06/1917	19/06/1917
Operation(al) Order(s)	199th Infantry Brigade Operation Order No. 31	20/06/1917	20/06/1917
Miscellaneous	199th Infantry Brigade		
Operation(al) Order(s)	199th Infantry Brigade Operation Order No. 32		
Miscellaneous	2/3rd East Lancashire Field Ambulance Programme of Training Week Commencing 29th June 1917	29/06/1917	29/06/1917
Heading	War Diary of 2/3rd East Lancs Field Ambulance From 1st July 1917 To 31st July 1917 (Volume 1)		
War Diary	Petite Synthe (G 18 To Central Belgium Sheet 19)	01/07/1917	07/07/1917
War Diary	Petite Synthe	08/07/1917	09/07/1917
War Diary	Teteghem (I 7a19)	10/07/1917	12/07/1917
War Diary	Gbybelde	13/07/1917	14/07/1917
War Diary	Teteghem	15/07/1917	18/07/1917
War Diary	Teteghem	20/07/1917	22/07/1917
War Diary	Bray Dunes	25/07/1917	29/07/1917
War Diary	Zuydcoote	29/07/1917	31/07/1917
Operation(al) Order(s)	199th Infantry Brigade Operation Order No. 34		
Miscellaneous	Telegramme From 199th Infantry Brigade	11/07/1917	11/07/1917
Operation(al) Order(s)	Operation Order No. 37	11/07/1917	11/07/1917
Operation(al) Order(s)	Operation Order No. 28 By Colonel H.G. Falkner T.D. Assistant Director Of Medical Services 66th Division	14/07/1917	14/07/1917
Miscellaneous	A.D.M.S.2/130/P.14	22/07/1917	22/07/1917
Miscellaneous	A.D.M.S.66th Div. Ref.-2/130/P.14	23/07/1917	23/07/1917
Heading	War Diary of 2/3rd East Lancs Field Ambulance For The Month Of August 1917 Volume No. 6		
Miscellaneous	Officer Commanding 2/3rd East Lancs Field Ambulance	01/09/1917	01/09/1917
War Diary	Braydunes	01/08/1917	31/08/1917
Heading	War Diary of 2/3rd East Lancs Field Ambulance For The Month Of September 1917 Volume No. I		
War Diary	Braydunes	01/09/1917	28/09/1917
War Diary	Wardrecques	29/09/1917	30/09/1917
Operation(al) Order(s)	Operation Order No. 32 By Colonel H.G. Falkner T.D. A.D.M.S. 66th Division	23/09/1917	23/09/1917
Miscellaneous	199th Infantry Brigade Order (in so far as it effects this unit)	24/09/1917	24/09/1917
Operation(al) Order(s)	199th Infantry Brigade Administrative Order No. 21	23/09/1917	23/09/1917

Type	Description	Date From	Date To
Operation(al) Order(s)	199th Infantry Brigade Order No. 57	25/09/1917	25/09/1917
Miscellaneous	Table A	25/09/1917	25/09/1917
Heading	War Diary of 2/3rd East Lancs Field Ambulance From Oct 1st 1917 To Oct 31st 1917 (Volume 1)		
War Diary	Wardrecques Ref. Map 1/100,000 Sheet 5a. E.4	01/10/1917	02/10/1917
War Diary	Brandhoek Ref. Map 1/40,000 Sheet 28 G.6.d.5.1	03/10/1917	05/10/1917
War Diary	Ypres Prison Map Ref Sheet 28 I. 7.b.5.5	06/10/1917	06/10/1917
War Diary	Ypres Prison	07/10/1917	11/10/1917
War Diary	Brandhoek	12/10/1917	13/10/1917
War Diary	Arques	14/10/1917	31/10/1917
Miscellaneous	Addendum To 199th Infantry Brigade Operation Order No. 58	02/10/1917	02/10/1917
Miscellaneous	Correction To 199th Brigade Order No. 58	01/10/1917	01/10/1917
Operation(al) Order(s)	199th Infantry Brigade Order No. 58	01/10/1917	01/10/1917
Miscellaneous	March Table To Accompany 199th Infantry Bde. Order No. 58		
Operation(al) Order(s)	199th Infantry Brigade Administration Order No. 22	01/10/1917	01/10/1917
Miscellaneous	II Anzac Corps Medical Arrangements No. 4	02/10/1917	02/10/1917
Operation(al) Order(s)	Operation Order No. 34 By Colonel H.G. Falkner T.D. Assistant Director Of Medical Services 66th Division		
Operation(al) Order(s)	Operation Order No. 35 By Colonel H.G. Falkner T.D. Assistant Director Of Medical Services 66th Division	07/10/1917	07/10/1917
Miscellaneous	Addendum To Operation Order No. 36	10/10/1917	10/10/1917
Operation(al) Order(s)	Operation Order No. 36 By Colonel H.G. Falkner T.D. Assistant Director Of Medical Services 66th Division	10/10/1917	10/10/1917
Operation(al) Order(s)	199th Infantry Brigade Order No. 61	12/10/1917	12/10/1917
Miscellaneous	Report On Recent Active Operations	15/10/1917	15/10/1917
Miscellaneous	The Prison		
Miscellaneous	Instruction for The Disposal of Cases Treated at Advanced Dressing Stations		
Heading	War Diary of 2/3rd East Lancs Field Ambulance From Nov 1st 1917 To Nov 30th 1917 Vol. I		
War Diary	Arques	01/11/1917	01/11/1917
War Diary	Queue D Oxelaere Map Ref Sheet 27 O 34 B 6.7	02/11/1917	09/11/1917
War Diary	Westoutre Map Ref. Sheet 28 M.9.c.2.7	10/11/1917	11/11/1917
War Diary	Wippenhoek Map Ref. Sheet 27 L.28 D.4.8	12/11/1917	26/11/1917
War Diary	Caestre Map. Ref. Sheet 27 Q.33.c.2.6	26/11/1917	30/11/1917
Operation(al) Order(s)	199th Infantry Brigade Administrative Order No. 23	31/10/1917	31/10/1917
Operation(al) Order(s)	199th Infantry Brigade Order No. 64	31/10/1917	31/10/1917
Miscellaneous	March Table To Accompany 199th Infantry Bde Order No. 64		
Operation(al) Order(s)	199th Infantry Brigade Group Administrative Order No. 24		
Operation(al) Order(s)	Operation Order No. 37 By Colonel H.G. Falkner T.D. Assistant Director Of Medical Services 66th Division	07/11/1917	07/11/1917
Miscellaneous	199th Infantry Brigade Addendum To Administrative Order No. 24	08/11/1917	08/11/1917
Operation(al) Order(s)	199th Infantry Brigade Order No. 65	08/11/1917	08/11/1917
Miscellaneous	Move Table		
Operation(al) Order(s)	199th Infantry Brigade Group Administrative Order No. 25		
Operation(al) Order(s)	199th Infantry Brigade Administrative Order No. 31		
Operation(al) Order(s)	199th Infantry Brigade Administrative Order No. 32	25/11/1917	25/11/1917
Operation(al) Order(s)	199th Infantry Brigade Order No. 70		
Miscellaneous	March Table To Accompany 199 Infantry Bde Order No. 70		

Heading	War Diary of 2/3rd Lancs Field Ambulance From 1st Dec 1917 To 31st Dec 1917 Vol I		
War Diary	Caestre Map Ref. (Sheet 27) Q.33 C. 2.4	01/12/1917	20/12/1917
War Diary	Hazebrouck Map Ref. Sheet 27 V 27 D 1.2	21/12/1917	31/12/1917
Miscellaneous	II Anzac Corps Medical Arrangements No. 8	05/12/1917	05/12/1917
Miscellaneous	Second Anzac Medical Arrangement No. 8	16/12/1917	16/12/1917
Miscellaneous	Second Anzac Medical Arrangements No.8	07/12/1917	07/12/1917
Heading	War Diary From Jan 1st To Jan 31st 1918 2/3rd East Lancs Field Amb Vol II		
War Diary	Hazebrouck Sheet 27 V 27.d.1.2	01/01/1918	11/01/1918
War Diary	Waratah Camp Map Ref Sheet 28 G 15 C 2.9	11/01/1918	31/01/1918
Operation(al) Order(s)	Operation Order No. 40 By Colonel H.G. Falkner T.D. Assistant Director Of Medical Services 66th Division	05/01/1918	05/01/1918
Miscellaneous	199th Infantry Brigade Preliminary Order	05/01/1918	05/01/1918
Miscellaneous	Corrigendum To Operation Order No. 40	06/01/1918	06/01/1918
Operation(al) Order(s)	199th Infantry Brigade Operation Order No.73	07/01/1918	07/01/1918
Operation(al) Order(s)	199Th Infantry Brigade Administrative Order No. 34	08/01/1918	08/01/1918
Operation(al) Order(s)	199th Infantry Brigade Operation Order No. 74	08/01/1918	08/01/1918
Miscellaneous	Movement Table-199th Infantry Brigade		
Operation(al) Order(s)	199th Infantry Brigade Operation Order No. 75	10/01/1918	10/01/1918
Heading	War Diary of 2/3rd Lancashire Field Amb From 1st February 1918 To 28th February 1918 (Volume II)		
War Diary	Waratah Camp Poperinghe Sheet 28 G. 15.c.2.9	01/02/1918	11/02/1918
War Diary	School Camp Map Ref Sheet 27 (L 3a.8.4)	12/02/1918	17/02/1918
War Diary	Harbonniers Map. Ref Sheet 62 D W.11.d. Cent	18/02/1918	28/02/1918
Miscellaneous	Reference A.D.M.S. O.O. No 41 Dated 3.2.18	05/02/1918	05/02/1918
Miscellaneous	Medical Arrangements 66th Division	03/02/1918	03/02/1918
Operation(al) Order(s)	Operation Order No. 41 By Colonel H.G. Faulkner T.D. Assistant Director Of Medical Services 66th Division	03/02/1918	03/02/1918
Operation(al) Order(s)	199th Infantry Brigade Operation Order No.80	05/02/1918	05/02/1918
Miscellaneous	Copy in So far as it Effects 2/3rd Field Ambulance	05/02/1918	05/02/1918
Operation(al) Order(s)	199 Infantry Brigade Administrative Order No. 37	06/02/1918	06/02/1918
Miscellaneous	Move To Fifth Army Area	14/02/1918	14/02/1918
Operation(al) Order(s)	197 Infantry Brigade Administrative Order No. 38	23/02/1918	23/02/1918
Operation(al) Order(s)	Operation Order No. 42 By Lieut Colonel J.Bruce R.A.M.C. T. Acting A.D.M.S. 66th Division	23/02/1918	23/02/1918
Miscellaneous	2/3rd East Lancs Field Ambulance	24/02/1918	24/02/1918
Operation(al) Order(s)	197 Infantry Brigade Operation Order No.75	26/02/1918	26/02/1918
Miscellaneous	Table "A" To Accompany 197 Infantry Brigade Operation Order No. 75	28/02/1918	28/02/1918
Miscellaneous	Lorries		
Miscellaneous	Table "G" (To Accompany 199 Infantry Brigade Order No. 80) March Table For February 11th 1918	11/02/1918	11/02/1918
Heading	War Diary of 2/3rd East Lancashire Field Ambulance From March 1st 1918 To March 31st 1918 Vol II		
War Diary	Bernes	01/03/1918	22/03/1918
War Diary	Beaumetz	22/03/1918	22/03/1918
War Diary	Le Mesnil	23/03/1918	23/03/1918
War Diary	Barleux	23/03/1918	23/03/1918
War Diary	Assevillers	23/03/1918	24/03/1918
War Diary	Chuignes	25/03/1918	25/03/1918
War Diary	Chuignolles	26/03/1918	26/03/1918
War Diary	La Motte	27/03/1918	27/03/1918
War Diary	Gentelles	27/03/1918	28/03/1918
War Diary	Cottenchy	28/03/1918	30/03/1918

War Diary	Boutillerie	31/03/1918	31/03/1918
Heading	War Diary of 2/3rd East Lancashire Field Ambulance From April 1st To April 30th 1918		
War Diary	Pont De Metz	01/04/1918	02/04/1918
War Diary	Fluy	03/04/1918	03/04/1918
War Diary	Ailly Le Haut Clocher	04/04/1918	05/04/1918
War Diary	Neuville	06/04/1918	06/04/1918
War Diary	Candas	10/04/1918	11/04/1918
War Diary	Drucat	12/04/1918	22/04/1918
War Diary	Etrehem	23/04/1918	23/04/1918
War Diary	Vieil Moutier	26/04/1918	30/04/1918
Heading	War Diary of 2/3rd East Lancashire Field Ambulance From May 1st To May 31st 1918 (Volume II)		
War Diary	Vieil Moutier	01/05/1918	02/05/1918
War Diary	Vaudricourt	03/05/1918	31/05/1918
Heading	War Diary of 2/3rd East Lancashire Field Ambulance From June 1st To June 30th 1918 (Volume 2)		
War Diary	Vaudricourt	01/06/1918	03/06/1918
War Diary	Ochancourt	06/06/1918	16/06/1918
War Diary	Pierregot	21/06/1918	30/06/1918
Heading	War Diary of 2/3rd East Lancs Field Amb From July 1st To July 31st 1918 (Volume 2)		
War Diary	Pierregot	01/07/1918	17/07/1918
War Diary	Pont Remy	19/07/1918	31/07/1918
Heading	War Diary of 2/3rd East Lancashire Field Ambulance From 1st August 1918 To 31st August 1918 Volume II		
War Diary	Pont Remy (Somme)	01/08/1918	30/08/1918
War Diary	Pont Remy	30/08/1918	31/08/1918
Heading	War Diary of 2/3rd East Lancs Field Amb From Sep 1st To Sep 30th 1918 (Volume 2)		
War Diary	Etaples	01/09/1918	01/09/1918
War Diary	Abbeville	20/09/1918	21/09/1918
War Diary	Grand Laviers	21/09/1918	21/09/1918
War Diary	Prouville	24/09/1918	24/09/1918
War Diary	Bouquemaison	25/09/1918	25/09/1918
War Diary	Izel-Les-Hameaux	26/09/1918	28/09/1918
War Diary	Corbie	28/09/1918	28/09/1918
War Diary	Proyart	29/09/1918	29/09/1918
Heading	War Diary of 2/3rd East Lancashire Field Ambulance Oct 1st To Oct 31st 1918 (Volume 2)		
War Diary	Proyart	01/10/1918	01/10/1918
War Diary	Maricourt	04/10/1918	04/10/1918
War Diary	Moislains	04/10/1918	04/10/1918
War Diary	Templeux-La-Fosse	06/10/1918	07/10/1918
War Diary	Ronssoy	08/10/1918	09/10/1918
War Diary	Beaurevoir	09/10/1918	10/10/1918
War Diary	Serain	10/10/1918	11/10/1918
War Diary	Maretz	13/10/1918	14/10/1918
War Diary	Maurois	15/10/1918	31/10/1918
Heading	War Diary of 2/3rd East Lancs Field Ambulance Vol II		
War Diary	Le Cateau (Sheet 57b K 34.a.8.3)	01/11/1918	09/11/1918
War Diary	Taisnieres (Sheet Namur)	09/11/1918	10/11/1918
War Diary	St Hilaire Sur-Helpe (Sheet Namur)	11/11/1918	14/11/1918
War Diary	Solre-Le-Chateau (Sheet Namur)	15/11/1918	16/11/1918
War Diary	Montrliart	16/11/1918	18/11/1918
War Diary	Cerfontaine	18/11/1918	23/11/1918

War Diary	Morville	24/11/1918	29/11/1918
Heading	War Diary of 2/3rd East Lancashire Field Ambulance From December 1st 1918 To December 31st 1918 (Volume II)		
War Diary	Morville	01/12/1918	13/12/1918
War Diary	Dinant	14/12/1918	14/12/1918
War Diary	Champion	15/12/1918	15/12/1918
War Diary	Huy	16/12/1918	31/12/1918
Heading	War Diary of 2/3rd East Lancashire Field Ambulance From 1st Jany 1919 To 31st Jany 1919 (Volume III)		
War Diary	Huy (Liege Map)	01/01/1919	10/01/1919
War Diary	Huy S Meuse	11/01/1919	28/01/1919
Heading	War Diary Original 2/3 East Lancs Field Ambulance February 1919 Vol III		
War Diary	Huy	01/02/1919	17/02/1919
War Diary	Sorinne-La-Longue	18/02/1919	28/02/1919
Heading	War Diary 2/3 East Lancs Field Ambulance March 1919 Vol III		
War Diary	Sorinne-La-Longue	01/03/1919	03/03/1919
War Diary	Halloy	04/03/1919	27/03/1919
War Diary	Taviet	28/03/1919	31/03/1919
Heading	War Diary 2/3rd East Lancashire Field Ambulance April 1919 Vol III		
War Diary	Taviet	01/04/1919	30/04/1919
Heading	War Diary 2/3rd East Lancashire Field Ambl. Vol III May 1919		
War Diary	Taviet	01/05/1919	05/05/1919
War Diary	Giney	06/05/1919	21/05/1919
War Diary	Antwerp	22/05/1919	26/05/1919

WO 95/31321/2

66TH DIVISION

2-3RD (E.LANCS) FD AMB.

~~MAR 1917-DEC 1918~~

1915 SEP — 1916 FEB
1917 MAR — 1919 MAY

COMMITTEE FOR THE
MEDICAL HISTORY OF THE WAR
Date 11 MAY 1917

Army Form C. 2118.

WAR DIARY
or
INTELLIGENCE SUMMARY

(Erase heading not required.)

ARMY MEDICAL SERVICE, R.A.M.C.T.

CONFIDENTIAL WAR DIARY

2/3 (East Lancs) Field Ambulance

From 27/2/1917 to 31/3/1917

Vol. I

WAR DIARY or INTELLIGENCE SUMMARY

Army Form C. 2118.

SECRET

Instructions regarding War Diaries and Intelligence Summaries are contained in F. S. Regs., Part II. and the Staff Manual respectively. Title pages will be prepared in manuscript.

(Erase heading not required.)

Place	Date	Hour	Summary of Events and Information	Remarks and references to Appendices
COLCHESTER	27/3/17		Unit embarked for Port of Embarkation. SOUTHAMPTON. Strength Officers - 9. Other Ranks - 183. Horses - 53. Vehicles Ambulances Ford - 3. W.A.S. motor - 7.	ack4
			R.A.M.C. (MT) - 27. Limbered Water Carts - 3. Cycles - 1.	
			NOTE: Includes 1 Barrel Cob, 2 Draught Horses and 1 Waggon G.S. Motor Z-approved of. Sack Spares	
SOUTHAMPTON	28/3	0800	Arrived at Port of Embarkation. R.A.M.C personnel (marched) proceeded at REST CAMP Strength 1 Pte (R.A.M.C) admitted to Hospital at REST CAMP.	ack4
			Transport (under R.E.C. Personnel) proceeded on DOCKS.	
			RECEPTION AT REST CAMP.	
"	1/4/17	18:00	Embarked for FRANCE on board S.S. "G.W. MILLER". Good passage. No casualties. CAPT. W. FERGUSON R.A.M.C. (O.C. unit) as medical charge of other units and in charge of funds. Arrangements carried for troops on board - Other Units on BOARD. ALS SEE O.R.E. (TF) 66th DIVL MOBILE VET SECTION, 66th DIVL SANITARY SECTION.	ack4 ack4
LE HAVRE FRANCE	2/4/17	12:00	Arrived at Le Havre.	ack4
"	"	07:00	Disembarked. Unit proceeded at No.1 REST CAMP for night.	ack4
"	3/4/17	15:20	Entrained in charge of Embarkation (OTHER TROOPS ON TRAIN - 66 DIVL MOB VET SECTION, 66th DIVL SANITARY SECTION).	ack4 ack4
BERGUETTE	4/4/17	07:20	Detrained. Marched to LAMBRES where unit was billeted on Route Boulangeur. Company arrangements for into meal - motor transport.	ack4
LAMBRES	5/4/17	—	Duty.	ack4
"	7/4/17	08:30	Motor ambulance garrison unit (3 DAIMLER CARS, 1 FORD Personnel - 9 other ranks)	ack4
"	7/4/17		under Capt. Morris proceeded to ST. VENANT.	ack4

Army Form C. 2118.

Sheet No 2.

WAR DIARY
or
INTELLIGENCE SUMMARY.
(Erase heading not required.)

Instructions regarding War Diaries and Intelligence Summaries are contained in F.S. Regs., Part II. and the Staff Manual respectively. Title pages will be prepared in manuscript.

Place	Date	Hour	Summary of Events and Information	Remarks and references to Appendices
ST VENANT.	7/3/17		Unit arrived and billeted in barn & outbuildings of doubtful quality - all water except for drinking had to be taken from showers, (one under supply (ie from shower) food obtained in enough amount.	W.M.
"	8/3/17		2nd unit from ENGLAND arrived.	W.M.
"	"	19.30	2nd unit of motor transport from unit (1 FORD AMB CAR, 2 BICYCLES, 2 PERSONNEL 4 OTHER RANKS)	W.M.
"	9/3/17	08.00	2 Officers 40 other Ranks proceeded to BETHUNE 14th FIELD AMB. for instruction.	W.M.
"	10/3/17			
"	11/3/17			
"	12/3/17	08.00	Second Party (Strength 3 OFFICERS, 40 OTHER RANKS) proceeded to BETHUNE, 14th F.D. AMB. for instruction. First party returned to unit. LIEUT. J.M. BOUNDS JH. proceeded to OFFICERS REST STATION, CHATEAU BUSNES. Suffering from neuralgia.	Ref.
"	13/3/17			
"	14/3/17	09.00	Departed by road for ZELOBES.	W.M.
ZELOBES	"		Arrived. Unit very in a divisional DRESSING STATION.	W.M.
"	14/3/17	15.00	Third Party (Strength 40 OTHER RANKS) left for training with 14th FIELD AMB.	
"	15/3/17		2nd party arriving with the second reinforcements at BETHUNE. The party no ready to go to 14th FD. AMB. and acted as the advance party of the 3rd BDE LANCS FIELD AMB.	W.M.
"	16/3/17	12.00	Unit left by road for BETHUNE.	W.M.
"	"	15.00	Unit arrived and billeted at the CINEMA used as the 14th FIELD AMB reported.	W.M.
BETHUNE	"		here sick.	W.M.
"	"	16.00	14th FIELD AMB. relieved by 3rd BDE LANCS FD. AMB.	"A" W.M.
"	17/3/17	19.00	No. 390. G.M.B., COLLINSON, S.L. accidentally killed by motor car. Admitted to No 33. C.C.S. BETHUNE where he died shortly afterwards.	W.M.

Army Form C. 2118.

Sheet No. 3

WAR DIARY
or
INTELLIGENCE SUMMARY.

(Erase heading not required.)

Instructions regarding War Diaries and Intelligence Summaries are contained in F.S. Regs., Part II and the Staff Manual respectively. Title pages will be prepared in manuscript.

Place	Date	Hour	Summary of Events and Information	Remarks and references to Appendices
BETHUNE.			WEEK END STATISTICS.	
	18/3/17	—		
	19/3/17	—		
	20/3/17	—		
	21/3/17	—		
			WOUNDED SICK.	
			ADMITTED DURING WEEK — 18.	
			TRANSFERRED FROM 4th FLD AMB. 2. 65.	
			EVACUATED OUTSIDE } — 12.	
			DIVISIONAL AREA }	
			RETURNED TO DUTY. — 1.	
"	23/3/17	11.30	Inspection of MAIN DRESSING STATION by D.D.M.S. XI CORPS. LIEUT. COL. M. BOUNDS, T.H.	WM
"	28/3/17	10.00	Inspection of ADVANCED DRESSING STATIONS and R.A.P's by A.D.M.S. 66th DIVISION.	WM
"	24/3/17	—	WEEK END STATISTICS.	
			WOUNDED SICK	
			ADMITTED DURING WEEK 32. 209.	
			EVACUATED 32. 152.	
			DIVL AREA	
			RETURNED TO DUTY. 1. 36.	
"	25/3/17	13.10 / 21.0	Aeroplanes over 1 hour - Cameron & SUMNER hurt	WM
				WM
"	26/3/17	—	ADVANCED DRESSING STATION under shell fire for 15 minutes - 9 shells dropped in the immediate proximity of A.D.S. each one passed through its EAST end of ADS Station in a covered part by 15' SOUTH wall of its General Officer's room. NO CASUALTIES.	WM
LONE FARM 27/3/17 No. 6 ADS				

Army Form C. 2118.

Sheet No 4.

WAR DIARY
or
INTELLIGENCE SUMMARY.
(Erase heading not required.)

Instructions regarding War Diaries and Intelligence Summaries are contained in F. S. Regs., Part II and the Staff Manual respectively. Title pages will be prepared in manuscript.

Place	Date	Hour	Summary of Events and Information	Remarks and references to Appendices
LONE FARM A.D.S.	29/3/17	17.00	ADVANCED DRESSING STATION against enemy shell fire. 5 shells dropped in the immediate vicinity - 2 of which passed through the EAST corner wall. NO CASUALTIES. NOTE: the whole of remaining no. bearing etc at the A.D.S. were put to shell and gas test on arrival.	Lt.M
BETHUNE	"	24.00	Reinforcement of 3 other Ranks arrived. Frame and 2000 sandbags received - issued to rebuild call. room of field ambce has been unstructed in the use of the Primus B.C. Respirator.	Lt.M
"	"			Lt.M
"	19/3/17	-	three men instructed in the use and repair of the Tissot Box Respirator.	
"	20/3/17	-		
"	21/3/17	-		
			WEEK END STATISTICS	
			ADMITTED DURING WEEK	WOUNDED	SICK
				22	135
			EVACUATED OUTSIDE DIVL. AREA	22	40
			RETURNED TO DUTY	-	13
			BATHS - Stopped on account of		Lt.M
B E F				B
1 APRIL 1917			Ew.G.Terryman Capt OFFICER commanding 7/0-10 EAST LANCS, FLD. AMB.	

Map reference:
FRANCE, BETHUNE (COMBINED SHEET)

2/3rd. East Lancs. Field Amb.

WAR DIARY ... Appendix "A".

Relief of 14th. FIELD AMBULANCE.

MAIN DRESSING STATION. Ecole MATERNELLE (E.5.a.40).

Headquarters consists of School Buildings and few outhouses. The main building is used for wards- of which there are 5 and 1 for Officers. Receiving Room, Dressing Room, Dispensary, Pack Store and Q.M. stores. The outhouses are ..

In "A" Compound. .. Bath House (Armstrong Huts).
Wash House.
Dining Room, Patients'
Latrines,
Coal Store.

In "B" Compound. .. 3 covered in verandahs - mortuary,
police Room.
Equipment stores.
Dining Room for Personnel.
Carpenters' Shop.
Three tents for Infectious cases and 1 for Orderlies.

In "C" Compound. .. Cookhouse.
Lamproom.
Equipment Stores.
Barber's shop.
Shoemaker's shop.
Medical Inspection Room (Armstrong Hut).
Sergeant Major's Office.   do.
Latrines, Personnel.

C.O's office is in Rue Catorive, opposite to Main Dressing Stn.
Water Supply - from Stand Pipe in street, good quality.
Orderly Officer - sleeps in hospital.

Transport Lines - (E.4.c.9½.6), all under cover on good standings
Water trough on opposite side of road from the standings. There is a good harness room near.
Waggons are kept on open ground just N. of Headquarters and motor ambulances on space just S. of Headquarters.

Billets. Personnel are billeted in houses close to Headquarters. (without subsistence).

Advanced Dressing Stations.

TUNING FORM - (F.5.a.4.0) - In farm buildings consisting of Dressing Room, 3 dug outs, total accomodation for 38 stretcher cases. ~~or sitting cases.~~
Billets for M.O., and personnel.
Cookhouse.

Personnel. - 1 M.O., 1 Sergt. 1Cpl. Pvtes.22. Daimler Car 1.

R.A.M.C. Post at R.A.P. BARNTON ROAD with 4 Pvtes. who are relieved every 48 hours from A.D.S.,
This A.D.S. clears 1 R.A.P.,
Casualties are brought down from R.A.P. by
1. Trolley which passes in front of the A.D.S.
2. By hand, carrying along Barnton Avenue trench to FESTUBERT-GIVENCHY ROAD, thence to A.D.S. by wheeled stretcher as far as ESTAMINET DUMP, and ambulance car from there to A.D.S. by day or night.

A.T.S. is given at A.D.S. . Cases from A.D.S. are disposed of as follows . If urgent straight to 33rd. C.C.S. - all particulars having been taken and forwarded to Headquarters , other than urgent to H.Qrs. for ultimate disposal. Field Medical Cards are made out. A Horse Ambulance Wagon leaves Hdqrs. at 18.30 o'clock with rations for Tuning Fork, and on return brings back any sick cases from the A.D.S. and GORRE. Some local sick are seen at Tuning Fork . M.O. relieved weekly , personnel fortnightly.
Water Supply. From Local Pump. Chlorinated or boiled before use.

LONE FARM. - (A.7.d.2.3.)
In building consisting of ground floor used for Billets for M.O. and personnel. Cellar used for Dressing Station. Accommodation for 18 Stretcher Cases and 20 sitting. Cookhouse.
Personnel. One M.O., one sergeant, one Lance Corporal, 22 privates one Ford Car and One Water Cart. One Motor Cyclist Orderly.
R.A.M.C. POSTS.
    1. HERTS REDOUBT.
    2. QUEENS ROAD
    Each with two R.A.M.C. privates.
This A.D.S. clears R.A.Ps.
    1. HERTS REDOUBT.
    2. WINDY CORNER.
    2 S. QUEENS ROAD.
Cases are brought to A.D.S. by trolleys, which run right up to the door of the Dressing Room, or by hand and wheeled stretchers - by day or night.
A.T.S. is given here and Field Medical Cards made out. Cases are disposed of to 33rd. C.C.S., if urgent, or to HDQRS. if not urgent. Horse Ambulance Wagon leaves Hdqrs. 18.30 o'clock with rations for Lone Farm, as far as WESTMINSTER BRIDGE, and on return this wagon brings back any casualties.
No Transport, except Motor Ambulance Cars, is allowed across WESTMINSTER BRIDGE , by daylight.
Water Supply. A loaded water Cart leaves HDQRS. daily with 24 hours supply. This cart remains at A.D.S. - the empty one being brought back to HDQRS.
Reliefs as for TUNING FORK.

    (W.30. a.8.9.)
WHITE HOUSE. This is used as a Convalescent Depot, which only men nearly fit for duty are sent from HDQRS., when there are few or no places available at C.R.S. Accommodation available,
    1. On Ground Floor.
        One large room used for Dining and Recreation.
        One Office and Dispensary.
        One Kitchen and Small Pantry.
        One Covered in verandah used as Pack Store.
    2. One First Floor.
        Three Rooms each taking four or five stretcher or trestle beds.
    3. Outhouses which could be used.
    4. Latrine accommodation.

2/3rd. EAST LANCS. FIELD AMBULANCE.

WAR DIARY.......... APPENDIX "b".

BATHS.

BETHUNE. ECOLE DE JEUNES FILLES. In basement of Divisional School, capable of Bathing 120 men per hour. One Slipper bath for Officers. Shower baths for Men.
Personnel. One Sergeant, 10 Privates.
Water Supply. Good.
Clean Clothing. The question of Clean Clothing is serious. There has not been a regular supply for some time, before this Unit took over from the 14th. Field Ambulance. Urgent representations have been made to the O.i/c Xl Corps Laundry, GORRE, who explains that there has been difficulty with the machinery, but he hopes that he will be in a position to make a regular supply of Clean Clothing soon. Every man bathing should get a clean change of underclothing.

ANNEQUIN. FARM BUILDINGS. CONVERTED. Capable of bathing 40 men per hour. Separate Bathing facilities for Officers and Sergeants.
Personnel. One Sergeant and 9 privates.
Water Supply. Good.
Clean Clothing. The same remarks, as for BETHUNE, Baths, apply here.

                                                                                 Ferguson Capt

In the Field . B.E.F.   Officer Commanding,
1st. April 1917.   2/3rd. East Lancs. Field Amb.

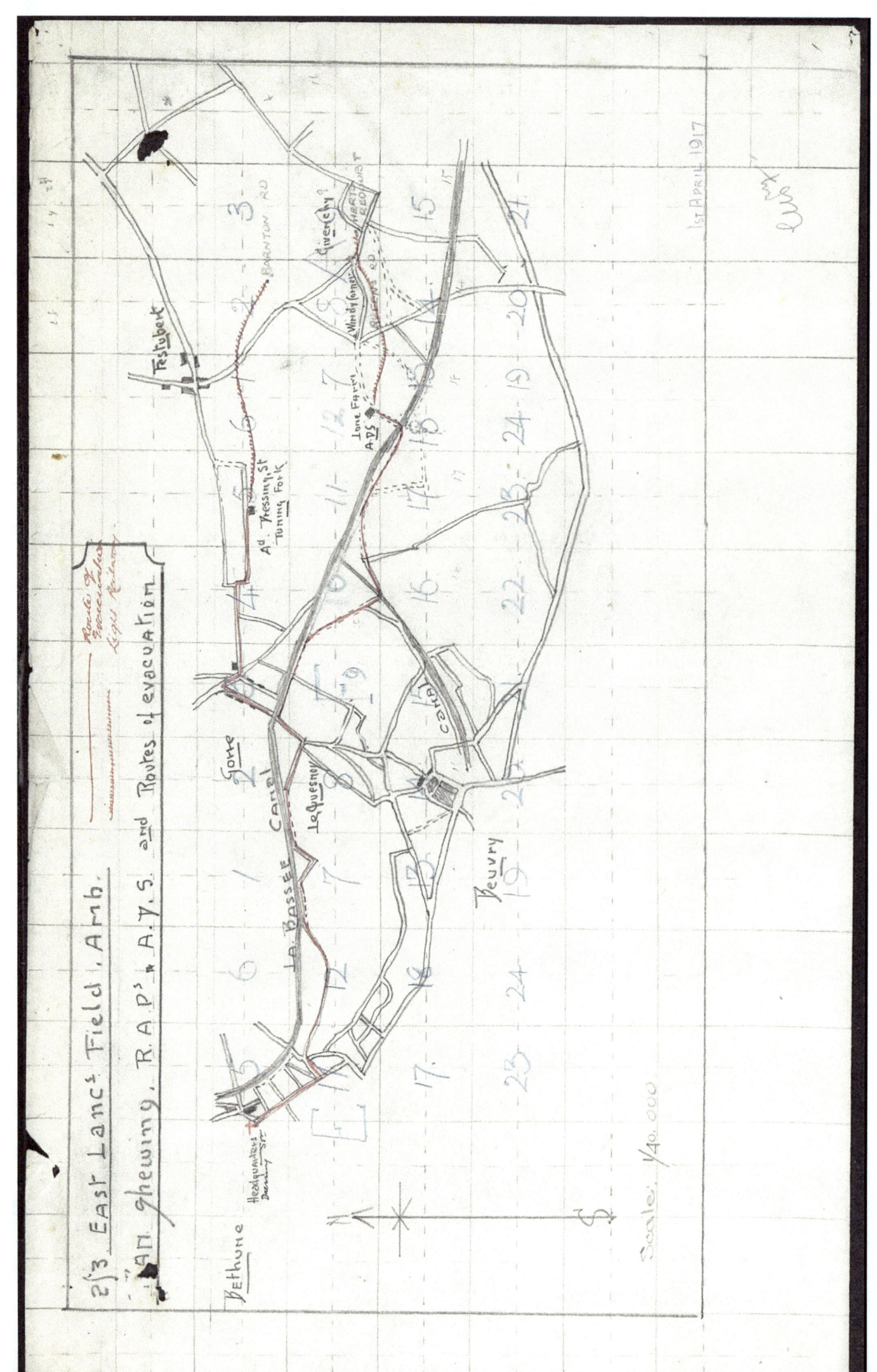

WAR DIARY

2/3rd East Lancashire Field Ambulance.

VOLUME II.

April 1917.

B.E.F.

F.A.
SUMMARY OF MEDICAL WAR DIARIES FOR 2/3rd E. Lancs / 66th Divn. 11th Corps
1st Army.

WESTERN FRONT April-May. '17.

O.C. Lt. Col. L.H. Cox.

SUMMARISED UNDER THE FOLLOWING HEADINGS.

Phase "B" Battle of Arras - April-May. '17.

1st period Attack on Vimy Ridge April.
2nd Period Captue of Siegfried Line May.

B.E.F.

F.A.
2/3rd E. Lancs./66th Divn. 11th Corps. WESTERN FRONT.
O.C. Lt. Col. L.H. Cox.   April. '17.
1st Army.

Phase "B" Battle of Arras- April- May. '17.

1st Period Attack on Vimy Ridge April.

1917.   Headquarters. at Bethune.

April. 4th. Moves Detachment: O and 6 to No. 1 C.C.S.

7th.   Sanitation: Gorre Baths and Foden Disinfector taken
             over from 66th Divisional San. Sect.

             Casualties. Preceding week:- 159 Sick admitted.
             77 sick evacuated, 24 wounded admitted 20 wounded
             evacuated.

9th.   Medical Arrangements: White House (1,40,000 W.30.a.
             8.8.) opened as a temp. R.P. closed 15th.

14th.   Casualties.:- Preceding week :- 145 sick admitted,
             79 sick evacuated, 46 wounded admitted 43 wounded
             evacuated, 2 died of wounds.

21st.   Preceding Week 130 sick admitted, 98 sick evacuated,
             25 wounded admitted, 18 wounded evacuated.

28th.   Preceding week:- 131 sick admitted, 101 sick evacuated,
             39 wounded admitted, 38 wounded evacuated.

             Scabies. 23 cases of Scabies admitted during the week
             from 10 Units,

B.E.F.

F.A.
2/3rd E. Lancs./66th Divn. 11th Corps. WESTERN FRONT.
O.C. Lt. Col. L.H. Cox.   April. '17.
1st Army.

Phase "B" Battle of Arras- April- May. '17.

1st Period Attack on Vimy Ridge April.

1917.	Headquarters. at Bethune.
April. 4th.	Moves Detachment: O and 6 to No. 1 C.C.S.
7th.	Sanitation: GORRE Baths and Foden Disinfector taken over from 66th Divisional San. Sect.
	Casualties. Preceding week:- 159 sick admitted 77 sick evacuated, 24 wounded admitted 20 wounded evacuated.
9th.	Medical Arrangements: White House (1,40,000 W.30.a. 8.8.) opened as a temp. R.P. closed 15th.
16th.	Casualties. Preceding week:- 145 sick admitted. 79 sick evacuated, 46 wounded admitted 43 wounded evacuated, 2 died of wounds.
21st.	Preceding Week 130 sick admitted 98 sick evacuated 25 wounded admitted 18 wounded evacuated.
28th.	Preceding week:- 131 sick admitted 101 sick evacuated, 39 wounded admitted, 38 wounded evacuated.
	Scabies. 23 cases of Scabies admitted during the week from 10 Units.

Army Form C. 2118.

Page 1.

WAR DIARY
INTELLIGENCE SUMMARY.
(Erase heading not required.)

Place	Date	Hour	Summary of Events and Information	Remarks and references to Appendices
Béthune	1/4/17	2000	Major E. H. Cox, R.A.M.C. (T.F.) arrives from England and takes over command of the field Ambulance. Transferred by war office from 1/3rd East Lancashire Field Ambulance, 42nd Division. The disposition of the Field Ambulance is precisely the same as stated in Appendix "A" Vol. 1 for March. The strength of the unit, including officers attached is 10 officers; 181 R. & F.; 35 A.S.C. (attached) H.T. 3rd A.S.C. (M.T.) attached.	A.T.C.
"	2/4/17	0900	Inspection tour of Main Dressing Station made by officer commanding, also of Horse Lines. Inspected by Arrival of A.D.M.S. 66th Division followed Dressing Station inspected by A.D.M.S. 66th Division.	A.T.C.
"	3/4/17	1000	Proceeded to Advanced Dressing Station, Rue Douin, + inspected it. This Dressing Station is located in an old farmhouse. The cookers and officers house is in the course of being protected by sand-bag walls + on the top floor of the house. This is being carried out by the personnel of the station.	A.T.C.

2353 Wt. W2511/1454 700,000 5/15 D.D.& L. A.D.S.S./Forms/C. 2118.

Army Form C. 2118.

Page 2 -

WAR DIARY
or
INTELLIGENCE SUMMARY.
(Erase heading not required.)

Instructions regarding War Diaries and Intelligence
Summaries are contained in F. S. Regs., Part II.
and the Staff Manual respectively. Title pages
will be prepared in manuscript.

Place	Date	Hour	Summary of Events and Information	Remarks and references to Appendices
Bethune	4/4/17	11.00	Proceeded to Advanced Dressing Station. Turning Park, on a tour of inspection. Everything working satisfactorily. The dug-outs (or rather elaborate dug-outs) are being re-inforced with sand bags. The dressing room dug-outs have been fitted with blankets, sprayed with vermorel solution in the event of drift gas coming over. Stretchers proceeded to the Regimental Aid Post at Beuvry Gare Road. Found everything satisfactory - factory. 1 N.C.O. + 5 men endorsed by D.D.M.S. XI Army Corps. Went out to a.i.l.l.s. They were struck off the strength of the unit - Inspected Bethune Baths - found everything satisfactory -	S.A.C. S.A.C.
"	5/4/17	10.00		
"	8/4/17	11.00	Proceeded to Lone Farm Dressing Station + inspected same. Considerable progress has been made with sand-bag protections. Afterwards went up to the Regimental Aid Posts at Queens Road + Herts Redoubt + inspected the working of these posts. Also inspected the S.A.P. at Herts Redoubt -	S.A.C.

2353 Wt. W2,314/1454 700,000 5/15 D. D. & L. A.D.S.S./Form/C. 2118.

Army Form C. 2118.

page 3

WAR DIARY
or
INTELLIGENCE SUMMARY.
(Erase heading not required.)

Place	Date	Hour	Summary of Events and Information	Remarks and references to Appendices
Béthune	7/4/17	10.00	Took over charge of Corps Baths & Mr Follen & Disinfector from the 66th Divisional Sanitary Section. 1 N.C.O. i/c & 6 men were stationed at the Baths, for working same. 1 N.C.O. & 7 men were detailed to assist with the working of the Foden Disinfector. The Baths will accommodate 60 men per hour. There are no arrangements for cleansing men's coats & clothing. 6 men found to be infected with lice. The returns for the week ending today shews:— Sick admitted 159 wounded " 24 Sick evacuated to area 77 wounded " " 20 Sick returned to duty 36 wounded " " nil.	E.H.B.
"	8/4/17	10.00	Lecture given by D.A.D.M.S. XI Army Corps on Army Organization. also lecture by Captain Allen on Gas poisoning & treatment. Operation Order No. 128 received from A.D.M.S. (See Appendix I)	E.H.B. Appx. I.

WAR DIARY
or
INTELLIGENCE SUMMARY.

Army Form C. 2118.

page 4.

Place	Date	Hour	Summary of Events and Information	Remarks and references to Appendices
Béthune	9/4/17	1000	White House (Location – N. 20.a.8.c.) Opened as a temporary Rest Post (vide Operation Order No: 18).	SAR
"	10/4/17	1000	Lectures by Major P.D.S. (D.A.D.M.S. XI Army Corps) they had Captain Allen repeated for those medical officers of the 68th Div. who were not able to attend the lecture on Sunday last.	SAR
"	11/4/17	1000	Routine.	SAR
"	12/4/17	1000	Routine.	SAR
"	13/4/17	1000	Routine.	SAR
"	14/4/17	1000	Weekly returns: Sick admitted 145 wounded " 2 wounded " 46 died 2 Sick evacuated to C.C.S. 79 Sick transferred wounded " " 43 to Corps Rest Stat. 20 Sick returned to duty 46 wounded " " 2	SAR Appen. I

WAR DIARY
or
INTELLIGENCE SUMMARY.

(Erase heading not required.)

Army Form C. 2118.

page 5.

Place	Date	Hour	Summary of Events and Information	Remarks and references to Appendices
Béthune	15/4/17	16:00	Operation Order No. 16 cancelled. The situation returns to normal	SAR
"	16/4/17	12:00	Instructions received for the formation of Straggler Posts during active Operations.	SAR Appen. II SAR
"	17/4/17	10:00	Received instruction that the Officer of A.P. in S. in S. is to be closed on the 18th and to reopen at Loeon on the 18th.	SAR
"	18/4/17	17:00	One Man sent to water duties with the 2/6th Batt. Duke of Wel. Reg.	SAR
"	19/4/17	10:00	One M.T. man evacuated to No. 33 C.C.S.	SAR
"	20/4/17	11:00	Inspection of Main Dressing Station by D.D. in M.S. 66th Div. Captain 15/4 N. Ditz details for temporary duty with the 2/6th Batt Lancs. Fusiliers. One detailed to 203 M.G. Co. for water duties.	SAR
"	21/4/17	10:00	Weekly return –	SAR

Sick   Wounded
AD [illegible]   130   25
Evac. to C.C.S.   52   17
  "   " C.R.S.   [illegible]   [illegible]
  "   " C.D.S.   37   2
To duty   Died

Army Form C. 2118.

Page 6

WAR DIARY
INTELLIGENCE SUMMARY.
(Erase heading not required.)

Instructions regarding War Diaries and Intelligence Summaries are contained in F. S. Regs., Part II. and the Staff Manual respectively. Title pages will be prepared in manuscript.

Place	Date	Hour	Summary of Events and Information	Remarks and references to Appendices
Bethune	22/4/17	1000	Routine.	SDB.
"	23/4/17	1100	Inspected the Baths at Béthune.	
		2030	Received Operation Order No. 19.	See Appen. III & Appen. IV.
		2100	Received orders from A.D.M.S. to open White House (W.30.a.8.8.) as a refreshment post for men passing through. 1 N.C.O. & two men placed in charge.	
			Received from Town Major, Béthune, "Scheme for the evacuation of Béthune in the event of a bombardment. This unit on receipt of orders from him is to move to billets at MESPLAUX (X.14.a.9.6.).	
	24/4/17	1600	Reinforcement draft of 10 men arrived & reported to this unit. This draft brings the unit up to full strength with the exception of 2 men.	SDB.
	25/4/17	1630	Operation Order No. 19 comes into effect. 8 men ordered to report	SDB.

Army Form C. 2118.

Page 7

WAR DIARY
or
INTELLIGENCE SUMMARY.
(Erase heading not required.)

Place	Date	Hour	Summary of Events and Information	Remarks and references to Appendices
Bethune	26/4/17	1630	(cont:) to Lone Farm A.D.S., & also 8 men to Tunnyforts A.D.S.	MR
		1720	One Motor Lister Ambulance Wagon sent to each A.D.S.	
		2330	Received intimation that the operations detailed in Operation Order no: 19, were cancelled for the night 25/26th.	
"	26/4/17	1000	Orders received from A.D.M.S. that arrangements detailed in Operation No: 19 are to remain unchanged.	MR
"	27/4/17	0900	Captain J.H. Paul ordered to relieve Captain Crawshaw - R.M.O. 2/5th Batt: East Lancs. Reg. I inspected the Baths at Annequin & found everything satisfactory.	
"	28/4/17	1000	Operation Order no: 19 (dated 23-4-17) Cancelled. The extra personnel from both Advanced Dressing Stations were reverted to m.D.S. White House was closed in the afternoon & personnel returned to m.D.S.	
		1150	Capt. Chapman was ordered to proceed to no: 56 C.C.S., Lillers to be attached for temporary duty.	

Army Form C. 2118.

Page 8.

WAR DIARY
or
INTELLIGENCE SUMMARY.
(Erase heading not required.)

Place	Date	Hour	Summary of Events and Information	Remarks and references to Appendices
Béthune	28/4/17	1500	No: M2/237256 Pte Loxton, C.B., A.S.C. (M.T.) ordered to proceed to England on duty for admission to Officers Cadet Corps. week end returns — Sick Wounded Admitted 131 39 Sent to C.C.S. 39 34 To C.R.S. } C.S.T.S. } 6 4 To duty 23 2 Died 1 2	A large number of cases of Scabies were admitted during the week — 22 (from 10 units).
	29/4/17	1000	Routine.	
	30/4/17	1000	Routine.	

E.M.McK. Major.
R.A.M.C. (T.F.)
D.A.D.M.S. 2/3rd 2nd Lowland Div. Art.

Appendix T.

SECRET.

OPERATION ORDER. No.18.
by
COLONEL H.G. FALKNER.T.D.
COMMANDING. R.A.M.C.66th.Div.

Reference.1/10.000. Secret Trench Map.

WHITE HOUSE. (W.30.a.88) will be opened for a short period as a Temporary Rest Post for men passing through.

The O.C.2/3rd.East Lancs Field Ambulance will detail the following.-

      1.Medical Officer.
      1.Good N.C.O.
      2.Nursing Orderlies.
      1.Cook.
     10.General Duty Men.

to proceed to WHITE HOUSE (W.30.a.8.8) by 10.am. on April. 9th.1917.

The R.A.M.C. personnel will take all their equipment, blankets, and the un-expended rations for the day, and the rations will be sent to WHITE HOUSE afterwards in the usual way.

He will arrange for Cookhouses and Latrines being erected if not already in existance.

Tinned food if necessary and stews, hot tea, bovril, etc, will be prepared for cases passing through this post.

The following will be required.-

    4 Tents (of which 3 are to be pitched, and one
        kept in reserve). These tents will be
        used as a cover for the men in case of rain.
   30.Blankets. If more are required the O.i/c will
        send for and obtain them from your Field Amb.
   Small supply of drugs, dressings, etc.

No Admission and Discharge book will be kept. The Officer i/c will keep a Record Book giving particulars of groups of men passing through, time they arrive, time they are sent off, and destination.

Instructions regarding the evacuation of these cases will be forwarded later.

When the M.O. i/c has 100 cases, he will immediately notify the A.D.M.S. 66th.Division.

The Officer Commanding. 2/3rd.East Lancs Field Ambulance will also send the following.-

3.Motor Ambulance Cars (9 Cars in all will be allotted) to be at the Office of A.D.M.S. (E.XI.a.2.7) at 11.am.April.9th.

The Drivers and Orderlies of the 9 Cars allotted, will be rationed by you.

ACKNOWLEDGE.

D.H.Q.
7th.April.1917.

(sgd) H.G.FALKNER.Colonel.
A.D.M.S. 66th.Division.

SECRET.

66th. Division.

STRAGGLERS POSTS.

Appendix II-

	Position.	Strength.	R.P. Found by.
1.	S.25.d.5.2.	1.Provost Serg 4.R.P.	197th. Inf Bde.
2.	A.8.b.1.5.	1. : : :	:
3.	A.8.c.7.3.	1. M.F.P. :	:
4.	A.14.d.2.9.	1.Provost Sergt :	198th. Inf Bde.
5.	A.14.d.2.6.	1. M.F.P. :	:
6.	A.20.b.2.7.	1.Provost Serg. :	:
7.	A.20.c.4.3.	1.M.F.P. :	:
8.	A.25.d.2.4.	1.Provost Serg. :	:
9.	A.25.d.1.1.	1.M.F.P. :	199th.inf Bde.
10.	G.2.d.5.3.	1.Provost Serg. :	:
11.	G.8.b.3.2.	1.M.F.P. :	:

STRAGGLERS COLLECTING STATIONS GORRE
    AND   and
PRISONERS CAGES.   F.22.c.8.4.

A.P.M. and remainder of M.M.P. at Gorre.

TRAFFIC CONTROL POSTS.

GORRE... 4.M.F.P.
BEUVRY...... (2 Posts) .... 7.M.F.P.
CARTER'S POST............................. 5.M.F.P.
CORPS H.Q.HINGES........................ 4.M.F.P.
ESSARS & LOCON ROAD JUNCTION.E.6.a.4.9. 4.M.F.P.
BULLY KEEP CROSS ROADS.......L.6.c.5.6. 3.M.F.P.

ABOVE STRAGGLERS POSTS WILL IMMEDIATELY TAKE UP POSITIONS
AS ALLOTTED DURING OPERATIONS.

D.H.Q.   (sgd) W.H.ROWELL. D.A.D.M.S.
16-4-17.   for A.D.M.S. 66th.Division.

SECRET.   23rd. April. 1917.

OPERATION ORDER. No. 19.
By.
COLONEL. H.G. FALKNER. T.D.
Commanding. R.A.M.C. 66th. Division.

Reference.- Trench Maps.

1. INTENTION.- No. 4.(S) Coy. R.E. and F.(S) Co. R.E. will make an attack N. & S. of the LA BASSEE CANAL on the night 25/26th. April. 1917.

   Zero hour will be 12 Midnight.

2. DETAIL.
   (a) The C.R.A. will arrange to bring shrapnel fire upon "Tender Spots" commencing at Zero plus ten minutes, especially in the vicinity of AUCHY, the "RAILWAY TRIANGLE", SAXON WAY, SUNKEN ROAD, CH110 St ROCH, and S.28.b. also for counter battery work when the enemy commences his retaliation.
   (b) Gas Alert will be put "ON" at 11.45.pm, and will remain on until ordered "OFF" by Infantry Brigadiers.
   (c) Should weather conditions not be favourable at midnight all troops will stand by until the operation is carried out or orders for its postponment are received from D.H.Q.
   (d) Full use id to be made of this opportunity for indirect M.G. fire.
   (e) During operations the manning of trenches will be modified in consultation with the Officers Commanding (S) Coys R.E.

3. Additional Personnel for Advanced Dressing Stations will be detailed as follows.-

   By. O.C. 2/2nd. East Lancs Field Ambulance.

   CAMBRIN.   (2. Nursing Orderlies.
                   (8. Stretcher Bearers.

   HARLEY STREET. (2. Nursing Orderlies.
                   (4. Stretcher Bearers.

   By O.C. 2/3rd. East Lancs Field Ambulance.

   TUNING FORK.   (2. Nursing Orderlies.
                   (6. Stretcher Bearers.

   LONE FARM.   (2. Nursing Orderlies.
                   (6. Stretcher Bearers.

4. An additional Motor Ambulance will be stationed at each Advanced Dressing Station.
5. Officers Commanding Field Ambulances will see that all Advanced Dressing Stations have an ample supply of amonia ampoules, and that oxygen cylinders at Main Dressing Stations are fully charged.
6. Moves to be completed by 6.pm. 25th. April. 1917, and on conclusion of present operations extra presonnel and Motor Ambulances will return to their Main Dressing Stations.

ACKNOWLEDGE.

D.H.Q.   (sgd) H.G. FALKNER. Colonel.
                                A.D.M.S. 66th. Division.

Secret.

VOLUME III.

WAR DIARY

2/3rd East Lancashire Field Ambulance.

From May 1st to May 31st 1917.

COMMITTEE FOR THE MEDICAL HISTORY OF THE WAR
Date 10 JUL. 1917

B.E.F.

F.A.

SUMMARY OF MEDICAL WAR DIARIES FOR 2/3rd E. Lancs./66th Divn. 11th Corps
1st Army.

WESTERN FRONT April-May.'17.

O.C. Lt. Col. L.H. Cox.

SUMMARISED UNDER THE FOLLOWING HEADINGS.

Phase "B" Battle of Arras - April-May. '17.

1st period Attack on Vimy Ridge April.
2nd Period Captue of Siegfried Line May.

B.E.F. 1.
F.A.
2/3rd E.Lancs/66th Divn. 11th Corps.   WESTERN FRONT.
O.C. Lt. Col. L.H. Cox.   April. '17.
1st Army.

Phase "B" Battle of Arras- April-May. 1917.
2nd Period Capture of Siegfried Line May.

1917.

May. 5th.   15 cases of Scabies admitted during the week from 6 Units.

10th.   Moves: To Mesplaux- Sheet 36A 1,40,000 X.14.a.9.4. Took over from 1/2nd W.R. Field Ambulance.

11th.   Operations Enemy. Baths at Annequin shelled during afternoon.

12th.   Scabies. 22 cases from 6 Units.

13th.   Operations Enemy. 1 and 15 admitted gas poisoning (Shell) Gas.

15th.   Medical Arrangements: White House reopened as R.P. closed 16th.

19th.   Scabies. 29 cases from 11 Units admitted during preceding week.

24th.   Moves: Ambulance site taken over by 2/1st E. Lancs.

F.A. 2/3rd F.A. to Ferme due ROI:- (Combined Sheet, Bethune: E.6.C.7.3.)

25th.   Moves Detachment: 1 and 89 and 6 G.S. Wagons and pairs to Gorre as working party.

2/3rd Field Ambulance in rest.

1.

B.E.F.　　　　　　　　　　　　　　　　　　　1.
　　　F.A.
2/3rd E.Lancs./66th Divn. 11th Corps.　　　WESTERN FRONT.
O.C. Lt. Col. L.H. Cox.　　　　　　　　　　April. '17.
　　1st Army.

Phase "B" Battle of Arras. April-May. 1917.
2nd Period Capture of Siegfried Line May.

1917.

May. 5th.　15 cases of Scabies admitted during the week from 6 Units.

10th.　Moves: To Mesplaux- Sheet 36A 1,40,000 X.14.a.9.4. Took over from 1/2nd W.R. Field Ambulance.

11th.　Operations Enemy. Baths at Annequin shelled during afternoon.

12th.　Scabies. 22 cases from 6 Units.

13th.　Operations Enemy. 1 and 15 admitted gas poisoning (Shell) Gas.

15th.　Medical Arrangements: White House reopened as R.P. closed 16th.

19th.　Scabies. 29 cases from 11 Units admitted during preceding week.

24th.　Moves: Ambulance site taken over by 2/1st E. Lancs. F.A. 2/3rd F.A. to Ferme dur R.OI. (Combined Sheet, Bethung: E.6.C.7.3.)

25th.　Moves Detachment: 1 and 89 and 6 G.S. Wagons and pairs to Gorre as working party.

　　2/3rd Field Ambulance in rest.

SECRET.

From Officer Commanding,
    2/3rd. East Lancs. Field Ambulance.

To D. A. G.,
    3rd. Echelon.

WAR DIARY.

Herewith War Diary, of this Unit, for the month ending 31st. May 1917.

                      Lieut. Colonel R.A.M.C. (T.F.)
                      Commanding, 2/3rd. East Lancs. Field Amb..

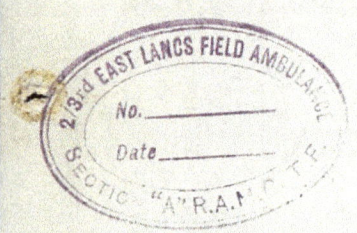

2nd. June 1917.

WAR DIARY
INTELLIGENCE SUMMARY
(Erase heading not required.)

Army Form C. 2118.

Part I.

Place	Date	Hour	Summary of Events and Information	Remarks and references to Appendices
Béthune	1/5/17	4 pm	Two reinforcements reported from Base.	EMR
"	2/5/17	10 am	N.C.O. i/c Baths at Gare reports that supply Proctor is bad study.	EMR
	3/5/17	10 am	Routine.	EMR
	4/5/17	10 am	Reported to office of D.D.M.S. XI Corps, re cells in ambulance site at the Rue de Laborive. As officer commanding receiving from G.O.C. 66th Division permission to assume badges of rank of Lieut. Colonel.	EMR
	5/5/17	Noon	Cases admitted during the week— Sick — admitted 152 wounded — ditto 34 To C.C.S. 66 to C.C.S. 26 " C.R.S. 71 " C.R.S. 4 " C.S.D. 23 " C.S.D. " " duty " duty 2 Principal disease — 15 cases of Scabies from 6 units.	EMR

Army Form C. 2118.

Page 2.

WAR DIARY
INTELLIGENCE SUMMARY.
(Erase heading not required.)

Place	Date	Hour	Summary of Events and Information	Remarks and references to Appendices
Béthune	6/5/17	11.30 am	Made an inspection of Baths at Gorre, and Advanced dressing at Tuning Station; found everything satisfactory.	
	7/5/17	11.30 am	A.D.M.S. called & made an inspection with regard to arrangement made for dealing with equipment. Letter received from A.D.M.S. stating that it has been decided to move this Field Ambulance to a site at Mesplaux Farm (Béthune continued sheet — X. 14. a. 9. 8.) — Field Ambulance were dressing station to be closed from tonight; all cases to be sent up to 2/2 East Lancs Field Ambulance at Annezin.	SAR
	8/5/17	11.30 am	Lt Capt. G.G. Wray, R. Ame. (T.F.) eleventh sick to Lines of Communication.	SAR
		4.00 am	Operation order no: 20 received from A.D.M.S.	SAR afternoon
	9/5/17	3.30 pm	Captain Porter Smith, R. Ame (T.F.) reported for temporary duty with the Field Ambulance	SAR

Army Form C. 2118.

Page 3

WAR DIARY
INTELLIGENCE SUMMARY.
(Erase heading not required.)

Place	Date	Hour	Summary of Events and Information	Remarks and references to Appendices
Bethune	14/5/17	1000	Field Ambulance moved to Ambulance site at sunflower Farm by road. The site was taken from 1/2nd West Riding Field Ambulance. 1 Officer + 36 O-Ranks were left at site in Bethune to continue the work of the Dressing Station, Chiefly for morning sick parades for units in Bethune, and also civilian sick.	
		5:30 pm	Orders received from A.D.M.S. to open site at sunflower Farm as Main Dressing Station for receiving Patients.	S/R
Locon	14/5/17 8pm		Report received that Baths at Annezin had been shelled at 4pm. this afternoon.	S/R
Locon	15/5/17 12 noon		Statistics for week ending 15/5 –	

Sick – admitted 96   Wounded – admitted 13
To C.C.S.   42   To C.C.S.   7
" E.R.S.   56   " E.R.S.   2
" C.S.D.S.   16   " Duty   3
" Duty   –   " Died   1
" Died   –   (cont.)

WAR DIARY
INTELLIGENCE SUMMARY.
(Erase heading not required.)

Army Form C. 2118.

Page 4.

Instructions regarding War Diaries and Intelligence Summaries are contained in F. S. Regs., Part II. and the Staff Manual respectively. Title pages will be prepared in manuscript.

Place	Date	Hour	Summary of Events and Information	Remarks and references to Appendices
Loos	13/5/17	Noon 12	Principal diseases admitted during the week: Scabies 22 cases from 6 units – 12 coming from 2/8th James. Fusiliers.	
"		P.m. 4.00	Capt. R.T. Chapman returned to unit after completion of temporary duty with No: 58 C.C.S.	
"		P.m. 7.10	Capt. T.H. Paul returned to unit from 2/5th Batt. East Lancs. Rey. after completion of that duty. M.O.	2/8R
"	13/5	Noon	One officer and 15 other ranks admitted to H.T.O. Sanatorium (Shell) –	2/8R
"	14/5/17	a.m. 10	In company with Capt. Braytin, in accordance with instructions received from A.D.M.S., 66th Div., at 9 searches the district between Loos and Hayes for a possible site for a main Dressing Station. A report was prepared and sent in to D.D.M.S.	
"		P.m. 9.10	Capt. 15 H.N. White returned to unit, on completion of duty with 2/6th Batt. Lancs. Fusiliers.	2/8R

WAR DIARY
or
INTELLIGENCE SUMMARY.
(Erase heading not required.)

Army Form C. 2118.

Page 5.

Place	Date	Hour	Summary of Events and Information	Remarks and references to Appendices
Locon	15/5/17	12.30 pm	under instructions from A.D.M.S., White House Rest Post were re-opened.	Appendix III
		2.30 pm	In company with Capt. Barton, under instructions from A.D.M.S., I made a thorough search for suitable sites for walking wounded Rest Posts at Gorre & Hamel. Report rendered to A.D.M.S. Have recommended that posts be established.	S.M.C. S.M.C.
"	16/5/17	4 pm	White Rest Post closed by orders of A.D.M.S.	
"	17/5/17	2 pm – 4 pm	Ordinary duties. Men attached to 2/6th Batt: Manchester Regt.	S.M.C.
	18/5/17	11.00	D.D.M.S., XI Army Corps, inspected the Dressing Station in the School at Rue du Catoure, Béthune. Inspection of Transport and main Dressing Station by G.O.C. 66th Division, accompanied by A.D.M.S., & A.A. & Q.M.G., 66 Div.	S.M.C. S.M.C.
	19/5/17	15 Noon	Inspected Dressing Station at Rue du Catoure, Béthune. (Cont.)	S.M.C.

Army Form C. 2118.

page #6.

WAR DIARY
or
INTELLIGENCE SUMMARY.
(Erase heading not required.)

Place	Date	Hour	Summary of Events and Information	Remarks and references to Appendices
Locon	18/9/17	12 Noon	Weekly Statistics –	
			Sick – admitted 157 wounded admitted 27	
			to C.C.S. 45 to C.C.S. 23	
			" C.R.S. } 75 " C.R.S. 4	
			" C.S.D. } Died 1	ESM
			" Duty 18	ESM
			Principal Disease – Scabies: 29 cases from 11 units.	
"	20/9/17	1000	Routine.	
"	21/9/17	1045	Inspection of A.D.S., Touringhem, by A.D.M.S.	
		2100	Operation Order No: 22 received from A.D.M.S.	appdx iii
"	27/5/17	1145	Advance party of 1 officer and 40 O.R. arrived from 2/1st East Lancs:	ESM
		430	Fd. Amb. to take over site at Herfeaux Farm. Two officers arrived from 2/1st E. L. Fd. Amb. were instructed to proceed direct to the Advance Dressing Stations at Tunney	ESM

Army Form C. 2118.

Page 7.

WAR DIARY
or
INTELLIGENCE SUMMARY.
(Erase heading not required.)

Place	Date	Hour	Summary of Events and Information	Remarks and references to Appendices
Lozon	27/9/17	15.30	Inspection of Main Dressing Station at Mazingarbe Farm by D.M.S., 1st First Army	SMO
"	29/9/17	12.15	The taking over 57th Ambulance site at Mazingarbe Farm began by 2/Lt E. Davies. 3rd Amb. The Troolhs & Ambulances Dressing Stations were handed over.	SMO
		14.00	The personnel of this unit proceeded by road to take over the site at the Ferme du Roi (Location — Combined Sheet Bethune: E.b.c. 73). Captain A. Royston, R. Muir. (T.F) Transferred to 2/15 2nd Lancs. Field Ambulance by orders of A.D.M.S.	SMO
Bethune	25/9/17	7 am 9.0	A working party of 1 Officer, 89 O.R., & 6 G.S. wagons proceeded to serve & report to C.R.E., 66th Division.	SMO

Army Form C. 2118.

Page 2.

WAR DIARY
or
INTELLIGENCE SUMMARY.
(Erase heading not required.)

Instructions regarding War Diaries and Intelligence Summaries are contained in F. S. Regs., Part II. and the Staff Manual respectively. Title pages will be prepared in manuscript.

Place	Date	Hour	Summary of Events and Information	Remarks and references to Appendices
Bethune	26/5/17	12 noon	Week-end Statistics -	
			Sick - admitted 100 wounded - admitted 9	
			to C.C.S. 43 to C.C.S. 8	
			" C.R.S.} 56 " C.R.S. 1	
			" C.S.D.} - 2/Lt S. J to Auxb. 2	
			" duty 8	
			" 2/Lt E.Jones to April 24	
"	27/5/17	15.40	Inspection of Farm at E.6.c.7.3. by D.D.M.S., XI Army Corps.	SMR
"	28/5/17	10.00	Lecture by A.D.M.S. to Officers of this unit on the organisation of the Medical Services with Field during active Operations.	SMR
"	29/5/17	11.00	Inspected transport & personnel & billets of working party at Gorre.	
	30/5/17	10.00	Routine.	
	31/5/17	10.45	Routine. Photo reinforcement returned from A.S.S.	SMR A.R. M.S. O.C. 2/3 W. St James St Bank

Appendix I

SECRET.   Copy.No.4.

Operation Order No.20.
by
Colonel.H.G.Falkner.T.D.
Assistant Director of Medical Services
66th, Division.

Reference Map. Sheet.36A. 1/40000.

      The 2/3rd, East Lancashire Field Ambulance will take over the Ambulance site at MESPLAUX X.14.a.9.4. from the 1/2nd, West Riding Field Ambulance 49th, Division.

      Transfer will be effected on the morning of May, 10th, 1917.

      Copies of receipted handing over certificates will be forwarded to this office.

      Two Medical Officers with a Section of the Field Ambulance and equipment will remain at the present site of the 2/3rd East Lancs Field Ambulance. Patients remaining in Ecole Catorive, BETHUNE, will be under the charge of this Section.

      Officers Commanding the two Field Ambulances concerned will mutually arrange the handing over.

      Completion to be reported to this Office.

Acknowledge.

D.H.Q,   (Signed)   H.G.FALKNER. Colonel.
May, 8th, 1917.   A.D.M.S. 66th, Division.

Appendix II

SECRET.

From: Officer Commanding,
2/3rd East Lancs Field Ambulance.

To: A.D.M.S,
66th, Division.

---

(1) With reference to the provision of Walking Wounded Rest Posts, I suggest, for the Southern Area of the Sector, the baths almost completed by the Engineers at the Estaminet DE LA GARRE (Billet No.3), just by the Southern side of GORRE Bridge.(Map Reference.- F.3.c.3.3).

There is ample accommodation in the Baths in the yard and also in the rooms of the Estaminet.

Of course the baths would not be in use on the occasion of the necessity for a Walking Wounded Rest Post.

(2) For the Northern Area of the Sector, I suggest the Grocery Store situated on the main Essars Road (Map Reference.-X.20.b.6.1). The following is the accommodation.-

(a) Three huts. 108-ft X 45-ft, with a second deck all round.
(b) One shed divided into a small apartment, 75-ft X 10-ft, containing bunks, an orderly room and a kitchen.

These would be very useful for cases or for the offices in connection with a Walking Wounded Rest Post.

There is also a barn (in poor repair) 45-ft X 15-ft, on the site.

None of these buildings are at present occupied.

(Note.- This place might be taken into consideration for a Main Dressing Station.)

Alternative to (2) above.
As an alternative to No.2 above, I suggest the Estaminet (a la chef des champs au HAMEL), Map Reference.- X.27.a.6.8.

There is a barn 40-ft X 15-ft. Also, there are several rooms in the Estaminet, including a cellar.

The premises are occupied.

The house occupies a conspicuous position at Cross Roads, and might therefore be easily recognised.

(signed) E.H.COX. Lt-Colonel.R.A.M.C(T.F
Commanding 2/3rd East Lancs Field Ambulance.

18-5-17.

Appendix III SECRET. Copy.No.5.

Operation Order No.22. by Colonel.H.G.FALKNER.T.D.
Commanding R.A.M.C. 66th,Division.

1. The 2/1st,East Lancashire Field Ambulance will move to MESPLAUX Farm (X.14.a.9.5) on 24th,May,1917,and take over the duties of the 2/3rd,East Lancs Field Ambulance.

2. The 2/1st,East Lancs Field Ambulance will be opened to receive patients from 24th,instant.

3. An advance party of 2 Officers and 40 other ranks will proceed to Mesplaux on the morning of the 22nd.instant,to take over the M.D.S. and the A.D.Ss.

4. The move will be arranged between the O.Cs of the respective Field Ambulances.

5. The 2/3rd East Lancs Field Ambulance will,on relief,move to E.6.c.7.3. and occupy the buildings on this site. Their horse lines will be E.6.c.7.3.

6. The 2/3rd.East Lancs Field Ambulance will cease to receive patients from the handing hour of handing over to the 2/1st, East Lancs Field Ambulance on the 24th,instant.

7. Whilst closed,the 2/3rd,East Lancs Field Ambulance will be in rest and undergo a course of training.

8. The Field Ambulance site is to be handed over to the relieving unit as a "going concern". The 2/3rd,East Lancs Field Ambulance will move taking with them only their authorised Mobilization Equipment,handing over any surplus fittings,equipment,and stores,to the relieving unit as a part of the site.

9. Articles should be checked on handing over,and a receipt obtained.

10. Completion to be reported to this Office.

11. Acknowledge.

(Signed) H.G.FALKNER.Colonel.
D.H.Q,   A.D.M.S,
21-5-17.   66th,Division.

ARMY MEDICAL SERVICE
RAMC

Secret.

original

Vol 4
(40/2250)

WAR DIARY.

VOL. I.

2/3rd East Lancashire Field Ambulance.

June 1917.

COMMITTEE FOR THE
MEDICAL HISTORY OF THE WAR
Date -7 AUG. 1917

COMMITTEE FOR THE
MEDICAL HISTORY OF THE WAR
Date -7 AUG. 1917

Army Form C. 2118.

page 1.

WAR DIARY

INTELLIGENCE SUMMARY.

(Erase heading not required.)

Instructions regarding War Diaries and Intelligence Summaries are contained in F. S. Regs., Part II. and the Staff Manual respectively. Title pages will be prepared in manuscript.

Place	Date	Hour	Summary of Events and Information	Remarks and references to Appendices
Bethune	1917 June 1	1000	The unit is located in billets at la ferme du Roi (map. ref: Y/9000: E.6.C.7.3.) —	sic
"	" 2	1000	The working party have returned from 2nd Field Amb. Routine.	sic Appx. 1.
"	" 3	1000	Routine. Programme of training for week ending June 9th submitted.	sic
"	" 4	1500	Lecture by A.D.M.S. at Hesdigneux Farm on medical Services in the field during active operations.	sic
"	" 5	1000	Routine.	sic
"	" 6	1000	One man evacuated sick to C.C.S.	sic
"	" 7	1000	Routine.	sic
"	" 8	1000	One man evacuated sick to C.C.S.	sic

WAR DIARY

INTELLIGENCE SUMMARY

Army Form C. 2118.
Page 2.

Place	Date	Hour	Summary of Events and Information	Remarks and references to Appendices
Bethune	June 9th 1917	1000	One A.S.C. man & one R-Bruce returned to duty from 54 C.C.S. Routine.	S/R.
"	10 "	1000	Routine. Three Daimler Motor Ambulance Cars attached to 2/2nd S. Lanc. Fd. Amb. (2 members of AP.M.S. Programme of Training for week ending June 16th submitted)	S/R. After III
"	11 "	1430	Inspection of Field Ambulance with Transport by D.D.M.S. XI Corps.	S/R.
		2000	Operation Order No: 24 by A.D.M.S., 66th Div. received	Appen III
"	12 "	1000	Routine.	S/R.
		1730	Ref: O.O. No: 24, 3 Daimler Motor Ambulance Wagons des- patched to report	S/R.
"	13 "	1000	Routine (See weekly programme of Training)	S/R.
"	14 "	1000	Routine (" ")	S/R.

Army Form C. 2118.

page 3.

WAR DIARY
INTELLIGENCE SUMMARY
(Erase heading not required.)

Place	Date	Hour	Summary of Events and Information	Remarks and references to Appendices
Bethune	1917 15 June	1000	Routine. (See programme of Training) -	ADMS
"	16 "	1000	Routine. "	ADMS
			Preliminary notice received from A.D.M.S. to hold unit in readiness to take over XI Corps Rest Station from the 49th Div.	ADMS
"	17 "	1000	Routine.	
		2200	Operation Order No. 25 received from A.D.M.S. Programme of Training for week ending June 23rd submitted to ADMS.	Appen. IV & V
"	18 "	1000	Routine.	ADMS
		1700	One Officer, one sergeant + two privates arrived from 5th Field Ambulance, 2nd Division, to take over the ambulance site at la Ferme du Roi.	
		1900	Operation Order No. 47 received from A.D.M.S., 6th Division.	ADMS

Army Form C. 2118.

Page 4.

WAR DIARY
INTELLIGENCE SUMMARY.
(Erase heading not required.)

Place	Date	Hour	Summary of Events and Information	Remarks and references to Appendices
Béthune	1917 Jan 19	1030	The C.O. Revd. from 5th Field Ambulance arrived.	s/lc
		1400	The main body of 5th Field Ambulance arrived.	
"	" 20	0035	Operation Order No: 47, by A.D.M.S., 6th Division, Cancelled.	
			Operation Order No: 27, by A.D.M.S., 66th Division, received.	Appen. VI.
"	" 21	1000	Routine.	s/lc
"		1700	Ambulance site at le Jeune du Roi officially handed over to 5th Field Ambulance, A.D.M.S., 66th Div., notified.	
		1730	Wagons & horses returned from working party, Gorre.	
"	"	1930	The men forming the working party at Gorre, returned to H.Q.	
		2000	Operation Order No: 31 received from 199th Infantry Brigade.	s/lc

Army Form C. 2118.

Page 5.

WAR DIARY
INTELLIGENCE SUMMARY.
(Erase heading not required.)

Place	Date	Hour	Summary of Events and Information	Remarks and references to Appendices
Béthune	22 Jun	1000	The Field Ambulance moved from la Serve du Roi to billets at Verquin-lès-mines (map ref: Bethune Columbia Sheet 44C; D.19.c.5.7. The unit moved by road arrived at billets at 11pm. Report of arrived sent to 199th Infantry Brigade + A.D.M.S.	
		1630	Administrative Order No.8 received from 199th Infantry Brigade.	Appen. 8.
		2100	Operation Order No.32 received from 199th Infantry Brigade.	" 9. see
Verquin-les-mines	23"	1800	Routine.	see
"	24"	1800	Routine.	see
"	25"	1800	Routine.	see

Army Form C. 2118.

Page 6.

WAR DIARY
INTELLIGENCE SUMMARY.
(Erase heading not required.)

Place	Date	Hour	Summary of Events and Information	Remarks and references to Appendices
Marles-les-Mines	26 June	0400	Transport moved off from Marles-les-Mines for entraining at Fouquereuil.	
		0530	The Field Ambulance moved off for entraining at the same station by train.	
		1020	All transport & personnel entrained. Train moved off.	
		1330	Arrival at Pont Plage – place for detraining. Unit detrained by 8 p.m. Moved off to billets at Petite Synthe (Map ref: 1/40,000, Sheet 19; H.19.A.3.6.). The unit with transport marched by road to billets, a distance of 12 miles.	
		1730	Arrived at billets in Petite Synthe at the chateau for Cures from 199th Infantry Brigade. Reception Post Reports of arrival with location sent to A.D.M.S. & 199th Inf. Brigade.	EWR

Army Form C. 2118.

Page 7.

WAR DIARY
INTELLIGENCE SUMMARY.
(Erase heading not required.)

Instructions regarding War Diaries and Intelligence Summaries are contained in F. S. Regs., Part II. and the Staff Manual respectively. Title pages will be prepared in manuscript.

Place	Date	Hour	Summary of Events and Information	Remarks and references to Appendices
Little Sypthe	1917 June 27	1000	Routine.	
		1400	Medical arrangements for XV Army Corps review.	s/W
	"28	1000	Programme of training for week ending July 5th submitted to A.D.M.S.	s/W. AK Anno.
		1400	Two N.C.O.s evacuated sick to No.1 Canadian C.C.S.	
	"29	1000	Routine (See programme of training). One to have transferred to 2nd Field Ambulance.	s/W.
		1400	Routine.	s/W.
	"30	1000	Statistics for week ending Noon the 30th: admitted sick — Officers 2; O.R. 30. remaining 8.	
		1400	One man attached to 209 Machine Gun Corps for weekly duties.	

2353 Wt. W2511/1454 700,000 5/15 D.D.&L. A.D.S.S./Forms/C. 2118.

2/3rd East Lancashire Field Ambulance for W/ending June.2nd. *
1917.

Daily Routine.

    5-30.am.   Reveille.
    6- 0.am.   Physical Drill.
    9-15.am.   Commanding Officer's Parade.

Day	Time	Activity
Monday. May.28.	9-30.am. to 12-30.pm. 2-0.pm. to 3-0.pm.	Route March. Instruction in First Aid.
Tuesday. May.29.	9-30.am. to 12-30.pm. 2-0.pm. to 3-0.pm.	Company Drill. Gas Drill. Stretcher Drill. Lecture on "First Field & Shell Dressings."
Wednesday. May.30.	9-30.am. to 12-30.pm. 2-0.pm. to 3-0.pm.	Route March. Lecture on "Revised Field Medical Cards."
Thursday. May.31st.	9-30.am. to 12-30.pm. 2-0.pm. to 3-0.pm.	Company Drill. Gas Drill. Stretcher Drill. Carriage of Patients by Improvised Methods. Erection of Bivouacs.
Friday. June.1.	9-30.am. to 12-30.pm. 2-0.pm. to 3-0.pm.	Route March. Practice in Bandaging.
Saturday. June.2.	9-30.am. to 12-30.pm.	Kit Inspection.

* Owing to return of men returning from employment outside unit, the above program of training was repeated for week ending June.9th. 1917.

Lt-Colonel.R.A.M.C.(T.F),
Commanding 2/3rd East Lancs Field Amb.

Programme of Training. 2/3rd East Lancs Field Ambulance. For week endg June.16th.1917.

Daily Routine.

5-30.am. Reveille.
6- 0.am. Physical Drill.
9-15.am. Commanding Officer's Parade.

Day	Time	Activity
Monday. June.11.	9-30.am.to 12-30.pm. 2-30.pm.	Instruction by Section Commanders on the Equipment carried by Pack Transport for an A.D.S. Inspection by D.D.M.S.
Tuesday. June.12.	9-30.am.to 12-30.pm. 2-0.pm.to 3-0.pm. 3-0.pm.to 4-0.pm.	Instruction by Section Commanders on the Formation of Bivouacs. Lecture by Section Commanders on "Sanitation in Bivouacs." Lecture by Commanding Officer on "Procedure for taking a summary of Evidence and the preparation of Papers required for a Field General Court Martial."
Wednesday. June.13.	9-30.am.to 12-30.pm. 2-0.pm.to 3-0.pm. 3-0.pm.to 4-0.pm.	Route March. Lecture by Section Commanders on "Supply and Purification of Water in the event of a rapid forward move." Lecture (Part.I) by Commanding Officer on "The formation of a table of Medical and Surgical Equipment and Ordnance Stores required for an A.D.S.during a rapid forward move."
Thursday. June.14.	9-30.am.to 12-30.pm. 2-0.pm.to 3-0.pm. 3-0.pm.to 4-0.pm.	Instruction by Section Commanders on the care and treatment of cases of Gas Poisoning. Instruction of Nursing Orderlies. Lecture (Part.II) by Commanding Officer on "The formation of a table of Medical and Surgical Equipment and Ordnance Stores required for an A.D.S. during a rapid forward move."
Friday. June.15.	9-30.am.to 12-30.pm. 2-0.pm.to 3-0.pm. 3-0.pm.to 4-0.pm.	Field Training. Instruction by Section Commanders on the best mode of treatment and care of cases of fracture of the thigh. Lecture by Commanding Officer (Part.III) on "The preparation of a table of Medical and Surgical Equipment and Ordnance Stores required for an A.D.S. during a rapid forward move."
Saturday. June.16.	9-30.am.to 12-30.pm.	Kit Inspection.

Lt-Colonel.R.A.M.C.(T.F),
Commanding 2/3rd East Lancs Field Amb.

SECRET.   Copy.No.3.

Operation Order
No.24.
By
Colonel.H.G.FALKNER. T.D.
A.D.M.S. 66th. Division.
===============================

1. Certain Operation will be undertaken on the night of 12/13th instant.

2. Barnton Road.R.A.P. (A.2.b.4.9)

    One Medical Officer will be detailed by the O.C. 2/1st.East Lancs Field Ambulance to report to this R.A.P. at 5-0.pm.12th.to take over duty in this R.A.P.

3. TUNING FORK A.D.S.(F.5.a.6.0.)

    The Officer Commanding 2/1st.East Lancs Field Ambulance will detail the following additional personnel for the above A.D.S.on 12th.instant,-
        3 Nursing Orderlies.
        16.Stretcher Bearers.

4. Two additional Motor Ambulance Cars will be stationed at the above A.D.S.

5. The Officer Commanding 2/1st.East Lancs Field Ambulance will see that there is an ample supply of Ammonia Ampoules,Dressings, Aplints,and Stretchers at this A.D.S.

6. Moves to be completed by 5-0.pm.on 12th.instant.

7. The Officer Commanding 2/3rd East Lancs Field Ambulance will detail three Daimler Motor Ambulances to report to Officer Commanding 2/1st.East Lancs Field Ambulance at MESPLAUX (X.14.a.9,6) at 6-0.pm.on 12th.instant,to be at his disposal.

8. On the conclusion of these Operations personnel and Motor Ambulance Cars will return to their respective M.D.S's.

9.Acknowledge.

                        (Signed) H.G.FALKNER.Colonel.
11th.June.1917.   A.D.M.S. 66th.Division.

C O P Y.

A.D.M.S.66th.Div.Ref.- O.O.25.

S E C R E T.

TO:- Officer Commanding,
    2/3rd East Lancs Field Ambulance.

Preliminary Order.-

(1) 2nd.Division will relieve the 66th.Division, relief to be completed by 6-0.am. 23rd.June.

(2) 66th.Division will proceed to training area by rail, commencing 24th.instant.

(3) Arrangements for move will be put in hand forthwith.

(4) Details will be issued later.

(5) Acknowledge.

D.H.Q.
17-6-17.

(Signed) H.S.FALKNER. Colonel.
A.D.M.S.
66th.Division.

5.

Appen. V.

Program of Training. 2/3rd East Lancs Field Amb. For Week endg. June.23rd. 1917.

Daily Routine.

  5-30.am.   Reveille.
  6-0.am.   Physical Drill.
  9-15.am.   Commanding Officer's Parade.

Sunday. June.17.	Church Parades.	
Monday. June.18.	9-30.am.to 12-30.pm.	Instruction by Section Commanders on the Equipment carried by Pack Transport during a forward move.
	2-0.pm.to 3-0.pm.	Gas Drill.
	3-0.pm.to 4-0.pm.	Lecture by Commanding Officer on "Military Law."
Tuesday. June.19.	9-30.am. to 12-30.pm.	Erection of Bivouacs.
	2-0.pm. to 3-0.pm.	Lecture by Section Commanders on "Sanitation in Bivouacs."
Wednesday. June.20.	9-30.am.to 12-30.pm.	Route March.
	2-0.pm.to 3-0.pm.	Lecture by Section Commanders on "Supply and Purification of water during a forward move."
	3-0.pm.to 4-0.pm.	Discussion on the best treatment of fractures in the Field."
Thursday. June.21.	9-30.am.to 12-30.pm.	Instruction by Section Commanders on the treatment and care of cases of Gas Poisoning.
	2-0.pm.to 3-0.pm.	Instruction of Nursing Orderlies.
Friday. June.22.	9-30.am.to 12-30.pm.	Field Training.
	2-0.pm.to 3-0.pm.	Instruction by Section Commanders on the best mode of treatment and care of fractures of the thigh.
	3-0.pm.to 4-0.pm.	Lecture by Commanding Officer.
Saturday. June.23.	9-30.am.to 12-30.pm.	Kit Inspection.

Lt-Colonel.R.A.M.C.(T.F),
Commanding 2/3rd East Lancs Field Amb.

SECRET.   Copy No. 13.

                        Operation Order No. 27.
                        By Colonel H.G. FALKNER,
                        A.D.M.S.   66th. Division.
                        ─────────────────────────

1. The 66th. Division will be relieved by the 2nd. Division during the
   period 21st. to 23rd. June. 1917.

2. On the relief the Field Ambulances will act and move in conjunction
   with their Brigade Group and will be billetted in their Brigade areas.

3. The 100th. Field Ambulance will arrive on 20th. instant, and be billeted
   in Ecole Catorive that night, and they will take over from the 2/1st.
   East Lancs Field Ambulance on the 21st. instant the M.D.S. and A.D.Ss
   run by this Field Ambulance. This move to be completed by 12 Noon
   21st. instant.

4. The 5th. Field Ambulance who arrived on the 19th. instant will take
   over from the 2/3rd Field Ambulance at Ferme du Roi. Handing over
   will be completed by 5-0.pm. 21st. instant. The 2/3rd East Lancs Field
   Ambulance will continue to be billeted at Ferme du Roi until the
   move into their billeting area on the 22nd. instant.

5. The 6th. Field Ambulance will arrive on the 21st. instant and be
   billeted at Ecole Catorive that night, and will take over from the
   2/2nd East Lancs Field Ambulance, ANNEZIN, the M.D.S. and A.D.Ss, on
   the morning of the 22nd. instant. Handing over will be completed by
   5-0.pm. 22nd. instant.

6. The 2/2nd. East Lancs Field Ambulance will billet for the night of
   22/23rd. at Ecole Catorive, and will move into their billeting area
   on the 23rd instant, with their Brigade group.

7. Officers Commanding Field Ambulances to get into touch with Headquarters of their respective Brigades at once, namely.-

        2/1st. E. Lancs Field Ambulance.   197th. Inf Bde.
        2/2nd.   :   :   :   198th.   :   :
        2/3rd.   :   :   :   199th.   :   :

8. Each Field Ambulance site is to be handed over to the relieving
   unit as a going concern. Field Ambulances will move taking with
   them only their authorised mobilization equipment, handing over any
   surplus effects, fittings, equipment and stores to the relieving unit
   as part of the site. Each post has an inventory, and articles should
   be checked on handing over, and receipts obtained in triplicate, one
   copy of which will be forwarded to the A.D.M.S. 66th. Division.

9. Details to be arranged between Officers Commanding Field Ambulances
   concerned.

10. Completion of reliefs to be reported to A.D.M.S. 66th. Division.

11. Each Field Ambulance will be responsible for the Medical arrangements
    of their respective Brigade Groups whilst in billets, a small reception
    post will be opened, if necessary, and sick evacuated as usual to C.C.Ss.

12. Acknowledge.

D.H.Q.   (sd)   H.G. FALKNER. Colonel.
19-6-17.
                                         A.D.M.S. 66th. division.

SECRET.   199th. Infantry Brigade.   Copy. No. 12.
                      Operation Order No. 31.

Copy.
In so far as it effects the 2/3rd East Lancs Field Ambulance.

Reference.- Bethune (Combined Sheet) 1/40.000.

1. The 199th. inf Brigade will be relieved by the 99th. infantry Bde on June.21st. in the Cambrin Sector and move back into Billets.

6. Location Table attached.

10. The 2/3rd East Lancs Field Ambulance will be relieved by the 5th. Field Ambulance at Ferme du Roi (E.6.c.7,3) on 21st. June. They will proceed to Brigade Billet Area on 22nd. June as per attached Location table.

13. All Defence schemes, Secret maps, Aeroplane photos, Trench stores, etc, will be handed over to relieving units and receipts obtained.
    All 1/100000 -- 1/80000 --- 1/250000 maps now in possession of units will not be handed over but kept.

14. Brigade Headquarters. 199th. Infantry Bde will close at Chateau-des-Pres (F.27.d.1.6) at Midnight on 21st. June and reopen at same hour at BETHUNE.

15. The completion of reliefs will be reported at once to Brigade Headquarters by B.A.B. Code.

16. On arrival in billets in new area all units will at once send in a Strength and Location Return with Map References to Brigade Headquarters

18. Acknowledge.

                              (sd)   G.D. HICKMAN. Major.
20-6-17.   Brigade Major.

                    Location Table referred to above.

2/3rd East
Lancs Field
Ambulance........ From.- Ferme du Roi.......... to MARLES-LES-MINES.

199th. Infantry Brigade.   Copy. No. 13.

Copy of Administrative Order in so far as it effects 2/3rd East Lancs Field Ambulance.

Ref.- Bethune Combined Sheet 1/40.000.

1. Advance parties will move by 'bus at 7.am. Saturday, 23-6-17.

2. Units will detail the following.-

	Officer.	N.C.O's.	Men.
2/3rd. East Lancs Field Amb.	1	1	1

3. These parties will be at Brigade Headquarters MARLES-LES-MINES at 7-0.am. 23-6-17. (D.19.a.3.1)

4. Officers or N.C.O's in charge of parties will bring with them numbers of officers, other ranks, vehicles and horses to be accommodated.

5. Acknowledge.

(sd) A. HOWARD. Captain.
Staff Captain.

199th. Infantry Brigade.

SECRET.   Operation Order No. 32.   Copy No. 12.

1. The 199th. Infantry Briage and its affiliated units will entrain on the 25th. and 26th. June. 1917. Destination XV Corps Training Area.

2. The details for entraining have been sent out under this Office No. SQ/64 of to-days date.

3. The following officers are detailed to act as entraining officers during the whole period of the groups entraining, and will travel by the last train.-

        Capt King. 2/8th. Manchester Regt.   CHOCQUES.
        Capt Maxwell. 2/6th.   :   FOUQUEREUIL.

4. The Officer in charge of each train load will ensure that the station is reconnoitred and will be responsible that the train is loaded in accordance with the orders of the R.T.O. that he is supplied with the loading parties if demanded and gets the exact numbers of the train/1/ loads.

5. Transport will reach the station exactly three hours before the hour of departure. Dismounted personnel $1\frac{1}{4}$ hours.

6. The strictest discipline is to be maintained during the train journey and all instructions laid down in S.S.554 are to be carefully studied by O.C. Train.

7. Acknowledge.

                      (sd) G.D. HICKMAN. Major.
                              Brigade Major.

2/3rd East Lancashire Field Ambulance.

Programe of Training. Week commencing 29th.
June. 1917.

Daily Routine.

```
5-30.am. ................. Reveille.
6- 0.am. to 6-30.am. ...... Physical Drill.
6-30.am. to 7- 0.am. ...... Fatigue Duties.
9-15.am. ................. Commanding Officer's Parade.
```

Date.	Time.	Particulars.
Friday. June.29.	9-30.am.to 12-30.pm.	Route March and Instruction in new Tactical Scheme.
	2-0.pm. to 3-0.pm.	Instruction in First Aid by Section Commanders.
Saturday. June.30.	9-30.am. to 12-30.pm.	Kit Inspection.
Monday. July.2.	9-30.am.to 12-30.pm.	Instruction by Section Commanders on "The Formation of Bivouacs."
	2-0.pm.to 3-0.pm.	Instruction in First Aid by Section Commanders.
	3-0.pm.to 4-0.pm.	Discussion on the Medical Service in the Forward Area during an Attack.
Tuesday. July.3.	9-30.am, to 12-30.pm.	Instruction in new Tactical Scheme.
	2-0.pm.to 3-0.pm.	Instruction in First Aid by Section Commanders.
Wednesday. July.4.	9-30.am.to 12-30.pm.	Instruction by Section Commanders on the Medical Services in the Forward Area during an Attack.
	2-0.pm. to 3-0.pm.	Instruction by Section Commanders in First Aid.
	3-0.pm. to 4-0.pm.	Lecture by Commanding Officer on Military Law.
Thursday. July.5.	9-30.am.to 12-30.pm.	Company Drill & Gas Drill.
	2-0.pm.to 3-0.pm.	Instruction by Section Commanders on First Aid.

Lieut-Colonel.R.A.M.C.(T.F),
Commanding 2/3rd East Lancs Field Amb.

29-6-17.

ORIGINAL

Confidential

War Diary

of

2/3rd. East. Lancs. Field Ambulance.

From 1st July 1917   To 31st July 1917

(Volume 1.)

Army Form C. 2118.

Page 1.

WAR DIARY

INTELLIGENCE SUMMARY

(Erase heading not required.)

Instructions regarding War Diaries and Intelligence
Summaries are contained in F. S. Regs., Part II.
and the Staff Manual respectively. Title pages
will be prepared in manuscript.

Place	Date	Hour	Summary of Events and Information	Remarks and references to Appendices
Petite Synthe BEF (VIII Section) BELGIUMS (Sect -19)	July 1	1000	Routine – training –	SAR
"	2	1000	Routine – training –	SAR
"	3	1000	Routine – training –	SAR
"	4	1000	Routine – training –	SAR
"	5	1000	Routine – training –	SAR
"	6	1000	Routine – training –	SAR
"	7	1000	Routine – training – under orders from A.D.M.S. 6th Div., 50 n.c.o. & men reported to XV Corps M.D.S. for temporary duty. Two Cobatenabants are XV C Rest Stations for temporary duty. Statistics for the week ending the 7th – as litter sick 32 To C.C.S. 16 To duty 8	SAR

Army Form C. 2118.

WAR DIARY
or
INTELLIGENCE SUMMARY.
(Erase heading not required.)

Instructions regarding War Diaries and Intelligence Summaries are contained in F. S. Regs., Part II. and the Staff Manual respectively. Title pages will be prepared in manuscript.

Place	Date	Hour	Summary of Events and Information	Remarks and references to Appendices
Petit Saythly	July 8	1000	Routine training.	
~	~	1345	Operation order No: 34 received from 199th Infantry Brig.	A/ops : I
~	~	1400	On instructions received from A.D.M.S., 66th Div., One officer (Capt. R.C.S. Smith, R.A.M.C. (T.F.)) & one sergeant were detailed to proceed to Sraelo-les-Termes to open up the 66th Divisional Laundry.	S/A.C.
~	9	1015	Acting on Operation order No: 34, Motorist forward at 10 a.m. & at 1015 proceeded by road to Trouit's farm (Ref: Map 1/100,000 Sheet 19 — I.7.a.1.9.) Here the field ambulance went into billets & occupied 3 Shea Terrus — 4 farms altogether — in the immediate vicinity of Trouit's farm.	
Fataybin	10	1000	Routine training.	S/A.C.
~	~	9330	Telegram received from 199th Inf. Brig. to stand by & report as officer immediately if required.	A/ops : I
				S/A.C.

Army Form C. 2118.

Page 3.

WAR DIARY
INTELLIGENCE SUMMARY.
(Erase heading not required.)

Instructions regarding War Diaries and Intelligence Summaries are contained in F. S. Regs., Part II. and the Staff Manual respectively. Title pages will be prepared in manuscript.

Place	Date	Hour	Summary of Events and Information	Remarks and references to Appendices
Pittsfleur	July 11th	1000	The unit is still under orders to stand by.	
		1800	Capt. Chapman, M.C. (T-F) of this unit, on instructions received from A.D.M.S., reports to D.M.S., 4th Army, to act temporarily as O.C. 13th Sanitary Section.	
	"	2100	Operation order No: 36 received from 99th Infantry Brigade. Operation order No: 36 Cancelled. O.O. No37 received from 99th Infantry Brigade.	Appx iii SWC
	"	2330		
	12th	0630	In accordance with O.O. No 37, the unit travelled at 6:30am moved by road - the main Doulens-Amiens - to Glysville	
Glysville		0930	Arrival at billets at 9:30am. Location of Hqs: Sheet 19 - 4/40000, D. 27.6.19. The unit took over from a section of a field ambulance of the 32nd Division - 14th Inf. Brig.	
"	13th	1000	Routine	
		1500	46 Other ranks B.&tr. A.D.S./Forms/C-2118 5/15 H.D.&tr.A.D.S./Forms/C-2118 5/15 of ranks proceed 6th, 17th, 2 & 8th Batts. march Rif. for training	SWC

Army Form C. 2118.

Page 4.

WAR DIARY
or
INTELLIGENCE SUMMARY.
(Erase heading not required.)

Instructions regarding War Diaries and Intelligence
Summaries are contained in F.S. Regs., Part II.
and the Staff Manual respectively. Title pages
will be prepared in manuscript.

Place	Date	Hour	Summary of Events and Information	Remarks and references to Appendices
Thyvelde	Jul 13	23:30	Instructions received from A.D.M.S. to detail two Officers to report immediately to D.C. XV Corps M.D.S. (Capts. Rault & Gleeson were detailed.	
"	14	10:00	16 stretcher bearers reports from 2/1st wessex Fd. Fr. training	S.R.
"	"	13:00	Operation order No:28 received from A.D.M.S. 66th Div.	Appx IV
"	"	16:00	The Unit paraded in full marching order turned by road to Terrib' Farm, Tatyphine, hor: I.7.a.1.9. This was a former billet of this unit.	
"	"	22:15	Operation order No:29 received from A.D.M.S., 66th Div.; wishing in this order affects this unit.	S.R.
			Useful statistics: Sick as within Officers 3 O.R. 47.	
			To C.C.S. Officers 3 O.R. 36	
			To duty O.R. 10	

2353 Wt. W3114/1454 700,000 5/15 D. D. & L. A.D.S.S./Form/C. 2118.

Army Form C. 2118.

WAR DIARY
or
INTELLIGENCE SUMMARY.
(Erase heading not required.)

Instructions regarding War Diaries and Intelligence Summaries are contained in F. S. Regs., Part II. and the Staff Manual respectively. Title pages will be prepared in manuscript.

Place	Date	Hour	Summary of Events and Information	Remarks and references to Appendices
Tatlehurst	July 15	1000	Routine – training	SAR
"	16	1000	Routine – training	SAR
"	"	1800	Capt. Berry relieved Capt. Gleeson at XV Corps H.D.S. Capt. Gleeson ordered to relieve Capt. Sparrow at 2/4th Batt: Leinster. Reg. Capt. Sparrow reported to this unit for Duty.	
"	17	1000	Routine – training.	
"	18	0630	Lt. Col. E.K. Cox left for 10 days leave in England.	SAR

E.K.Cox, Lt.Col.
O.C. 1/3 F.A. Lancs 55 Devils

2353 Wt. W2544/1454 700,000 5/15 D. D. & L. A.D.S.S./Forms/C. 2118.

Army Form C. 2118.

WAR DIARY
or
INTELLIGENCE SUMMARY.

(Erase heading not required.)

Instructions regarding War Diaries and Intelligence Summaries are contained in F. S. Regs., Part II. and the Staff Manual respectively. Title pages will be prepared in manuscript.

Place	Date	Hour	Summary of Events and Information	Remarks and references to Appendices
TETEGHEM	30/7/17	4 pm	A.D.M.S. 66th Division visited & inspected the billets & transport of the unit.	App 67
"	21.7.17	9 a.m.	64 Stretcher bearers from 199th Infantry Brigade having completed a week's training were discharged to their units. Admissions & discharges for week ending 21-7-17 Admitted sick - 6 Discharged to duty - 0 to C.C.S. - 3	App 67

Army Form C. 2118.

WAR DIARY
or
INTELLIGENCE SUMMARY.
(Erase heading not required.)

Instructions regarding War Diaries and Intelligence Summaries are contained in F. S. Regs., Part II. and the Staff Manual respectively. Title pages will be prepared in manuscript.

Place	Date	Hour	Summary of Events and Information	Remarks and references to Appendices
Jetyrhem	22-7-19	11 a.m.	Under orders from A.D.M.S. 66th Division, Capt W.P. Ferguson - acting C.O - and Capt R.E.L. Smith & Lieut & Quartermaster J.H. Bounds, & 61 N.C.O's & men proceeded to XV Corps Rest Station - Bravdunes (D E a Central) as an advance party to take over the Rest Station from the 141st Field Ambulance	[full?]
Bravdunes	25-7-19	10.30 am	Details of this unit left Jetyphem under Capt W.H.M. White and were "Trainspt" arriving at XV Corps Rest Station at 10.30 a.m.	
		6 pm	Taking over of XV Corps Rest Station from 141st Field Ambulance completed. Report sent to D.D.M.S. XV Corps & A.D.M.S. 66th Div. that unit had taken over reported	[full?]
		8 pm	Capt A.W. Berry - Capt J.H. Paul and 50 N.C.O's & men reported from XV Corps Main Dressing Station. Patients remaining in hospital:- Sick { Officer - 1 / O.R. - 329 } Wounded { Officer - 0 / O.R. - 94 }	[full?]
	26-7-19	6 pm	D.D.M.S. XV Corps visited & inspected the Rest Station	[full?]

2353 Wt. W25H/1454 700,000 5/15 D. D. & L. A.D.S.S./Forms/C. 2118.

Army Form C. 2118.

WAR DIARY
or
INTELLIGENCE SUMMARY.
(Erase heading not required.)

Instructions regarding War Diaries and Intelligence Summaries are contained in F. S. Regs., Part II. and the Staff Manual respectively. Title pages will be prepared in manuscript.

Place	Date	Hour	Summary of Events and Information	Remarks and references to Appendices
BRAYDUNES	28/4/19	3 pm	D.M.S. Fourth Army and D.D.M.S. XV Corps visited IV Corps Rest Station	W.G.1
do	23/4/19	noon	Statistics for week ending 12 noon — 28/4/19. Admitted { Sick 260, Wounded 156 } Discharged { to CCS Sick 37, Wounded 294 } { to duty Sick 60, Wounded 38 } to No 1 Field Amb { Sick 21, Wounded 4 } to Queen Alexandra Military Hospital Sick – 3	W.G.3
do	29/4/19 11.45 am		Further order No 30 received from A.D.M.S. 66th Division then once made to forthcoming operations — only affecting this unit indirectly and no copy is appended. Nos Headquarters Café Roma	W.G.7

Army Form C. 2118.

WAR DIARY
or
INTELLIGENCE SUMMARY.
(Erase heading not required.)

Instructions regarding War Diaries and Intelligence Summaries are contained in F.S. Regs., Part II. and the Staff Manual respectively. Title pages will be prepared in manuscript.

Place	Date	Hour	Summary of Events and Information	Remarks and references to Appendices
3rd Depot	July 29th 1900		Lt.Col. E.H. Cox returned from 10 days leave in England.	S.M.
"	"	2030	Orders received from A.D.M.S. 66th Div., to detail Officers, being Paris to report to him immediately.	S.M.
"	30	Noon	D.D.M.S. XV Corps called at the Rest Station informed the unit that the Adjutant-General, B.E.F. France would inspect the camp on the following day.	S.M.
"	31	300	The Adjutant General, British Armies in France, accompanied by G.O.C. XV Corps, D.D.M.S. XV Corps, inspected the Camp.	
			Statistics for 29th, 30th, 31st.	
			A.D. with O.R. 330	
			To C.C.S. 268	
			To duty 66	
			5.	

S E C R E T.

Copy in so far as this Unit is concerned.

199th. Infantry Brigade.
Operation Order No. 34.

Ref.- Map. Sheet. 19.- 1/40000.

1. The 199th. Infantry Brigade will move (less 2/5th. Manchester Regt) on the 9th. July. 1917. to the E. of DUNKERQUE -- BERGUES Canal xxxxxxxxxx and billet in the area COUDERQUE BRANCHE -- LA MAISON ROUGE -- TETEGHEM. I.28.Central, with 1 Battalion in camp in squares C.15.d. and 16.a and b, otherwise all units will be south of the DUNKERQUE -- FURNESS Canal.

3. The Baggage wagons will be at Unit Headquarters from No.544.Co.A.S.C. at 7-0'am. 9th. July xxxxxxxx. and will return to Train on completion of Move.

4. (b) Billeting parties will meet their units as follows and conduct them to their billeting areas.-

   2/3rd. East Lancs Field Amb.   H.6.b.2.3.

5. All units will at one on arrival forward the location of their units to Brigade Headquarters.

7. Acknowledge.

                              (Sd)   C.D.HICKMAN. Major.
                                          Brigade Major.

Reference.- 199th. Infantry Bde.
B.M/343.

Copy.

TO. O.C.
2/3rd East Lancs Field Ambulance.

Telegramme from 199th. Infantry Brigade.

Battalions will be prepared to move at one hours notice. Lorries will pick up as follows, if move is ordered.-

2/5th. Details. X Roads C.25.c.9.5.
2/6th.   Road. C.21.c.5.7. to C.21.d.8.0.
2/7th.   I.15.a.9.9. to I.9.c.2.9.
2/8th.   Square in COUDEKERQUE BRANCHE. H.16.b.6.7.

Other units of your group stand fast, but be prepared to follow by march route if ordered.
Baggage wagon and one days supply will follow Battalions immediately to forward area.

Addressed 2/5th (Details) 2/6th. 2/7th. 2/8th. Manchesters. 204.M.G.C. 199th.L.T.M.B. 2/3rd.Field Ambulance. 544.Coy.A.S.C. repeated 66th.Division.

11-7-17.   199th. Infantry Brigade.

No.3.

Operation Order No: 37.

Copy. SECRET.
~~In so~~ far as this
Unit is concerned.
                          Copy. No. 12.
                          11-7-17.

Ref.- Map Sheet, 19. 1/40000.

1. Brigade Order No. 36. is cancelled.
   The 199th. Infantry Brigade will move to GHYVELDE tomorrow (less 2/5th. Manchester Regt) taking over billets from 14th. Infantry Brigade Group, 32nd. Division.

2. The starting point for the 2/3rd East Lancs Field Ambulance will be the Level Crossing. H.6.d.5.5. which will be passed at 6-38.am

5. Unit billeting representatives will meet the Staff Captain at PNT DE ZUYDCOOTE (D.13.b) at 5-30.am.

6. Completion of moves and location of Headquarters will be notified to Brigade Headquarters on completion.

                       (sd) R.L.BOND. Captain.

                             Brigade Major.

11-7-17.

No. 4.

Copy.   Copy. No. 5.

OPERATION ORDER No. 28.
BY
COLONEL H.G. FALKNER. T.D.
ASSISTANT DIRECTOR OF MEDICAL SERVICES.
66TH. DIVISION.

Reference. Map. Sheet. 19. Scale 1/40000.

1. The 2/1st. East Lancs Field Ambulance will move to D.27.b.1.9. on the 14th. July. 1917. and take over the site from the 2/3rd East Lancs Field Ambulance.

2. The 2/3rd East Lancs Field Ambulance will move to I.7.a.0.9. on the 14th. July. 1917. and take over the site from the 2/1st. East Lancs Field Ambulance.

3. The move will be arranged between the Officers Commanding ther respective Field Ambulances.

4. The main road S. of the Canal De DUNKERQUE -- FURNESS must not be used for the move. It will take place via TETEGHEM -- UXEM -- GHYVELDE Road.

5. The sick in each Field Ambulance will be evacuated to the Corps M.D.S.

6. Completion of the moves to be reported to this Office.

7. Acknowledge.

                                         (sd) W.H. ROWELL. Captain.
                                                       D.A.D.M.S.
14-7-17.   for A.D.M.S. 66th. Division.

Copy.

SECRET. A.D.M.S. 2/130/P.14.

TO: O.C.
2/3rd East Lancs Field Ambulance.

The 2/3rd East Lancs Field Ambulance will take over XV.Corps Rest Station at D.8.a.Central at a date to be notified later.

An Advance party consisting of the Officer Commanding this Field Ambulance, Captain R.C.S.Smith and the Quartermaster, with one section of the Field Ambulance (except transport and equipment) will report to O.C. Corps Rest Station this day.

The unexpended portion of this day's rations and rations for the following day to be taken.

Further orders will be issued regarding the move of the remainder of the Field Ambulance.

(sd) H.G.FLAKNER. Colonel. A.D.M.S.
D.H.Q,
22nd.July,1917.   66th.Division.

SECRET.

Copy.

A.D.M.S.66th.Div.Ref:- 2/130/P.14.

To: O.C.
2/3rd East Lancs Field Ambulance.

In continuation of my 2/130/P.14.dated 22nd.July.1917.

The 2/3rd East Lancs Field Ambulance will relieve the 141st.Field Ambulance, 1st.Division at the XV.Corps Rest Station (D.8.a.Central).

Relief to be completed by 6-0.pm.on the 25th.inst.

Details for this relief to be arranged between the Officers Commanding the Field Ambulances concerned.

(sd) H.G.FALKNER. Colonel,
A.D.M.S. 66th.Divn.

D.H.Q,
23-7-17.

Secret

War Diary
of
2/3rd. East Lancs. Field Ambulance
for the month of
August 1917
Volume No: 6

SECRET.

From Officer Commanding,
2/3rd. East Lancs. Field Ambulance.

To   Headquarters,
     66th. Division. "G".

I beg to enclose War Diary of the 2/3rd. East Lancs. Field Ambulance for the month of August 1917.

[signature]

Lieut. Colonel R.A.M.C. (T.F.)
Commanding 2/3rd. East Lancs. Field Ambulance.

1st. Sept. 1917.

Volume No. 6.

SECRET

Army Form C. 2118.

Instructions regarding War Diaries and Intelligence Summaries are contained in F. S. Regs., Part II. and the Staff Manual respectively. Title pages will be prepared in manuscript.

WAR DIARY
for AUGUST 1917.
INTELLIGENCE SUMMARY.
(Erase heading not required.)

Page 1.

Place	Date	Hour	Summary of Events and Information	Remarks and references to Appendices
BRAYDUNES	1-8-17	12.00	Routine. Heavy rain all day.	W.H.N.W.
"	2-8-17	12.00	Routine. Capt R.J. Chapman R.A.M.C. (T.F.) of 1/10 West reported for duty from 13th Sanitary Section. Special party of Artillery reported sick. 3 cases syphilitic rec'd — 8 Officers 128 other ranks. Above sent into hospital on A.& D. Book. Operation order No 26 issued. (Opening of 2nd A.C.S. Zuydcoote)	W.H.N.W.
	11.15		The D.D.M.S. XV Corps escorted & inspected Fort Mardyck. Many men not yet inoculated & constitution limited to Sheilus Hut; also of addition huts for convalescent troops. Bath orders are in NE corner of Camp.	
"	3-8-17	12.00	Routine.	W.H.N.W.
	15.00		Operation Order No 7039/2 issued. (Medical arrangements XV Corps during forthcoming operations). Heavy rain all day.	
"	4-8-17	12.00	Routine. Weather showery. Statistics from Aug 1 inclus. to Aug 4 inclus.	W.H.N.W.
			Sick Admitted	
			A.C.S. 237 87	
			68 28	
			Returned to duty 67 42	
"	5-8-17	12.00	Routine. Weather showery.	W.H.N.W.
"	6-8-17	12.00	Routine. Weather showery.	W.H.N.W.
"	7-8-17	12.00	Routine. Weather fine. Operation Order No 37 received from A.D.M.S. 66th Division. (R. Kent tapes). Statistics asked for. Communicated Army H.Q.	W.H.N.W.
"	8-8-17	12.00	Routine.	
"	9-8-17	12.00	Routine. Capt R.J Chapman R.A.M.C. (T.F.) reported to D.M.S. IV Army for duty.	W.H.N.W.
"	10-8-17	12.00	Routine.	
"	11-8-17	12.00	Routine. The D.D.M.S. & D.D.M.S. XV Corps inspected & inspected the Camp.	W.H.N.W.
			Statistics from Aug 6th incl. to Aug 11 incl.	
			Sick Admitted	
			A.C.S. 404 116	
			136 29	
			Returned to duty 224 207	

2353 Wt. W2544/1454 700,000 5/15 D. D. & L. A.D.S.S./Forms/C. 2118.

SECRET

WAR DIARY
or
INTELLIGENCE SUMMARY
(Erase heading not required.)

Army Form C. 2118.

PAGE 2.

Instructions regarding War Diaries and Intelligence Summaries are contained in F. S. Regs., Part II. and the Staff Manual respectively. Title pages will be prepared in manuscript.

Place	Date	Hour	Summary of Events and Information	Remarks and references to Appendices
BRAYDUNES	12-7-17	12.00	Routine	W.H.K.U.
"	13-7-17	12.00	Routine. The D.D.M.S. XV Corps inspected the troops. CAPT. F.A. MURRAY. R.A.M.C. (T.C.) promoted to A.D.M.S. 32nd Division for duty. CAPT. R.J. CHAPMAN R.A.M.C (T.F.) reported for duty from D.M.S. L'ARMY. LIEUT W.H. DOBSON U.S.A. M.O.R.C reported for duty from 2/1st EAST LANCS FIELD AMBULANCE	W.H.N.V.
"	14-7-17	12.00	Routine	W.H.N.V.
"	15-7-17	12.00	Routine	W.H.N.V.
"	16-7-17	12.00	Routine. The D.D.M.S. XV Corps inspected the Camp	W.H.N.V.
"	17-7-17	12.00	Routine. The D.D.M.S. XV Corps visited the Camp	W.H.N.V.
"	18-7-17	12.00	Routine. Statistics from Aug 1st 1917 to Aug 18th 1917 — Sick 340 {Admitted to C.C.S. 226. Evacuated 115. 13. Returned to duty. 254. 161	W.H.N.V.
"	19-7-17	12.00	Routine. Lt. L.W. SPARROW R.A.M.C. appointed to the 2/8th MANCHESTER REG CAPT A.W. BERRY R.A.M.C. (T.F.) reported for duty from 2/6th MANCHESTER REG.	W.H.N.V.
"	20-7-17	12.00	Routine	W.H.N.V.
"	21-7-17	12.00	Routine. D.D.M.S. XV Corps visited the Camp	W.H.N.V.
"	22-7-17	12.00	Routine. D.D.M.S. XV Corps visited the Camp	W.H.N.V.
"	23-7-17	12.00	Routine	W.H.N.V.

SECRET

Army Form C. 2118.

WAR DIARY
or
INTELLIGENCE SUMMARY.
(Erase heading not required.)

PAGE 3

Instructions regarding War Diaries and Intelligence Summaries are contained in F.S. Regs., Part II. and the Staff Manual respectively. Title pages will be prepared in manuscript.

Place	Date	Hour	Summary of Events and Information	Remarks and references to Appendices
BEAUDUNES	24-8-17	12.00	Routine. DDMS XI Corps visited the Camp	W/H of W
	25-8-17	12.00	Routine. Statistics from Aug 18 noon to Aug 25 noon. Admitted — Sick 322, Wounded 138 {Evacuated to F.C.S., Returned to duty}	
	26-8-17	12.00	Routine	W/H of W
	27-8-17	12.00	Routine. DDMS XI Corps visited the Camp. 23, 10, 249, 150	
	28-8-17	12.00	Routine. LIEUT W.A. SHARPIN R.A.M.C (T.C.) reported for temporary duty from XI Corps Main Dressing Station. LIEUT G. SUTTON U.S.A. M.O.R.C.	W/H of W
	29-8-17	12.00	Routine	W/H of W
	30-8-17	12.00	Routine. DDMS XI Corps visited the Camp	W/H of W
	31-8-17	12.00	Routine. Statistics from Aug 25 noon to Aug 31 noon. Admitted — Sick 392, Wounded 101 {Evacuated to C.C.S. 193, 133; Returned to Duty 293, 143}	W/H of W

E.W.O.B. Lt. Colonel
O.C. 2/3 West Lancs F.D. Ambce.

Original

War Diary
of
3rd East Lancs Field Ambulance
for the month of
September 1917
Volume No: I

COMMITTEE FOR THE
MEDICAL HISTORY OF THE WAR
Date -5 NOV. 1917

SECRET.

Army Form C. 2118.

WAR DIARY of 2/3rd East Lancs Field Amb.
for SEPTEMBER 1917.

INTELLIGENCE SUMMARY.

(Erase heading not required.)

PAGE 1.

Instructions regarding War Diaries and Intelligence Summaries are contained in F. S. Regs., Part II. and the Staff Manual respectively. Title pages will be prepared in manuscript.

Place	Date	Hour	Summary of Events and Information	Remarks and references to Appendices
BRAYDUNES	1-9-17	12.00	Routine. One O.R. of 1/1st West Riding Field Amb reported for duty. One Sergt & 2 O.R. of 1/3rd West Riding Field Amb. reported for duty.	M.H.W.W.
"	2-9-17	12.00	Routine. D.D.M.S. XV Corps visited the Station. Two O.R. of 2/2nd East Lancs Field Amb B. proceeded to XV Corps Main Dressing Station for duty. Ten O.R. (P.B.Men) reported to replace ten A.S.C. returned.	M.H.W.W.
"	3-9-17	12.00	Routine. D.D.M.S. XV Corps visited the Station.	M.H.W.W.
"	4-9-17	12.00	Routine. Ten A.S.C. returned proceeded to 544 Coy 66th Div. A.S.C. 1 Sergt & 24 O.R. of 4th Canadian Railway Troops reported for duty.	M.H.W.W.
"	5-9-17	12.00	Routine. D.D.M.S. XV Corps visited Station twice. No. 354247 L/Corp Eastwood L of 2/3rd East Lancs F.A. reported for duty from Base. 2 Sergts & 14 O.R. of 2/2nd East Lancs F.A. reported for duty. Capt H Foxton R.A.M.C. T.F. & 20 O.R. of 1/2nd West Riding F.A. reported for duty. Capt. C G Skinner R.A.M.C. T.C. & 20 O.R. of 90th F.A. reported for duty.	M.H.W.W.
"	6-9-17	12.00	Routine. Two Sergts & 73 O.R. of 92 F.A. reported for duty.	M.H.W.W.
"	7-9-17	12.00	Routine. Capt. J R E Russell R.A.M.C. T.F. of 2/2nd East Lancs F.A. reported for duty.	M.H.W.W.
"	8-9-17	12.00	Routine. Statistics from August 31st were to Sept 8th were: Admitted 158, Sick 558, C.C.S. 135, Returned to duty 267.	M.H.W.W.

2353. Wt. W2511/1454 700,000 5/15 D.D.&L. A.D.S.S./Form/C. 2118.

SECRET

WAR DIARY of 2/3rd EAST LANCS. FIELD AMB.
for SEPTEMBER
INTELLIGENCE SUMMARY

Army Form C. 2118.

PAGE 2

Place	Date	Hour	Summary of Events and Information	Remarks and references to Appendices
BRAY DUNES	9-9-17	12.00	Routine	A.D.M.S.W.
"	10-9-17	12.00	Routine. No. 354327 Pte Moyles G. of this Unit evacuated to No. 36 C.C.S.	A.D.M.S.W.
"	11-9-17	12.00	Routine	A.D.M.S.W.
"	12-9-17	12.00	Routine	A.D.M.S.W.
"	13-9-17	12.00	Routine. D.D.M.S. XV Corps visited the Station	A.D.M.S.W.
"	14-9-17	12.00	Routine. D.M.S. IV ARMY & D.D.M.S. XV Corps visited the Station. 1 Sergt & 9 O.R. of 2/2nd East Lancs Field Amb. returned to Unit. Special Medical Board Commission sat here.	A.D.M.S.W.
"	15-9-17	12.00	Routine. D.D.M.S. XV Corps visited the Station. Lt W.A. SHARPIN R.A.M.C. T.F. & 19 O.R. of 4th WEST RIDING FIELD AMB. returned to their Unit. Capt H. FOXTON R.A.M.C. T.F. & Sutton U.S.R. & 37 O.R of 1/2nd WEST RIDING FIELD AMB returned to their Unit. 1 Sergt & 2 O.R. of 1/3rd WEST RIDING F.A. returned to their Unit. Capt J.R.B. RUSSELL & 5 O.R of 2/2nd East Lancs F.A. returned to Unit. Statistics from 8th September to 15th Sept inclusive. Admitted Sick 719	A.D.M.S.W.
			C C S 189 269	
			Returned to Duty 220 155	
			3	
"	16-9-17	12.00	Routine. D.D.M.S. XV Corps visited the Station.	A.D.M.S.W.
"	17-9-17	12.00	Routine	A.D.M.S.W.
"	18-9-17	12.00	Routine. No. 354248 Pte BRADLEY W. & No. 354312 Pte MABBOT A. of this Unit evacuated to No. 36 C.C.S.	A.D.M.S.W.

SECRET.

WAR DIARY of 2/3rd EAST LANCS FIELD AMB.
for SEPTEMBER 1917

Army Form C. 2118.

INTELLIGENCE SUMMARY

(Erase heading not required.)

PAGE 3

Place	Date	Hour	Summary of Events and Information	Remarks and references to Appendices
BRAYDUNES	19-9-17	12.00	Routine. 2nd P.B. men proceeded to 66th DIV. EMPLOYMENT COY.	M.H.W.W.
"	20-9-17	12.00	DDMS XV CORPS visited the Station.	M.H.W.W.
"	21-9-17	12.00	No 354372 Pte A. DAY of this Unit evacuated to No 36th C.C.S.	M.H.W.W.
"	22-9-17	12.00	DDMS XV CORPS visited the Station. Statistics from 15th Sept. noon to 22nd Sept. noon: Sick 718, Admitted 190; C.C.S. 212, 115; Returned to Duty 337, 58.	M.H.W.W.
"	23-9-17	12.00	Routine. DDMS XV CORPS visited the Station. Operation Order No 32 received from ADMS. 66th DIV. Copy No 5.	See Appendix I. M.H.W.W.
"	24-9-17	12.00	DDMS XV CORPS visited the Station. No 354482 Pte HUTCHINSON Q.L. of this Unit evacuated to No 36 C.C.S.	M.H.W.W.
"	25-9-17	12.00	DDMS XV CORPS visited the Station. Operation Order No 58 received from 199 Infantry Bde. H.Q. Copy No 12. No 354373 Pte CAMM J.E. of this Unit reported for duty from DIV. SCHOOL. No 354249 Pte BEILBY F. of this Unit evacuated to No 36 C.C.S. ADMINISTRATION ORDER No 21 Copy No 9 received from 199 Infantry Bde. H.Q. THE 90th FIELD AMB. LT. COL. HALLOWES R.A.M.C. on command arrived at the REST STATION.	See Appendix II. See appendix III. M.H.W.W.
"	26-9-17	12.00	DDMS XV CORPS visited the Station. Operation Order No 37 Copy No 12 received from 199 Infantry Bde. H.Q.	See Appendix IV. M.H.W.W.

SECRET

WAR DIARY OF 2/3rd EAST LANCS. FIELD AMB.

Army Form C. 2118.

for SEPTEMBER. 1917.

INTELLIGENCE SUMMARY.

(Erase heading not required.)

PAGE 4.

Instructions regarding War Diaries and Intelligence Summaries are contained in F.S. Regs., Part II. and the Staff Manual respectively. Title pages will be prepared in manuscript.

Place	Date	Hour	Summary of Events and Information	Remarks and references to Appendices
BRAYDUNES	27-9-17	7.00	TRANSPORT, (consisting of 6 G.S. MARK X WAGON'S; 4 G.S. LIMBERS, 3 Ambulances, 3 Motor Carts, 1 Maltese Cart, 44 horses), proceeded by road to new destination. CAPT. BERRY R.A.M.C. T.F. i/c. Personnel - (APT. BERRY, CAPT WEBB, 1 WARRANT OFFICER, & 45 O.R.	
		8.00	XV Corps REST STATION handed over to 90th FIELD AMB.	M.H.H.W.
		14.00	ADVANCE PARTY, LT. J.H. BOUNDS. R.A.M.C. T.F. & 3 O.R. proceeded to WARDRECQUES.	
	28-9-17	10.30	MAIN BODY of Field Amb. CAPT. W.P. FERGUSON R.A.M.C. T/c. left REST STATION, proceeded to GHYVELDE & entrained at junction of DUNKERQUE - ADENKIRKE & GHYVELDE - BRAYDUNES Rds.	M.H.H.W.
		19.00	Detrained	
WARDRECQUES		20.00	Arrived at WARDRECQUES.	
	29-9-17	12.00	BRIGADE HOSPITAL opened. Statistics from 22nd Sept noon to 24th September {Submitted to C.C.S. / Returned to Duty} Sick 549. 216. 330. Wounded 110. 69. 42.	M.H.H.W.
	30-9-17	12.00	No 354162 P.L. HOLLAND J. of this Unit reported for duty from 203 M.G. Coy.	M.H.H.W.

W.W.B. Lt. Colonel
O.C. 2/3rd E. Lancs. F.D. Amb/-

SECRET.   APPENDIX I   Copy.No.5.

Operation Order No.32.
by
Colonel.H.G.FALKNER. T.D. A.D.M.S.
66th.Division.

The 66th.Division will be relieved by the 42nd.Divn in this sector of the line during the period Sept.24/25.th.1917.

1. ADVANCE PARTIES.   Advanced parties consisting of 1 Officer & a compliment of N.C.Os and men from 2 Field Ambulances from the 42nd.Divn will report to the Os.C. 2/1st & 2/2nd.Field Ambulances on Sept 24th.1917. Os.C.Field Ambulances will show the Officers in charge of Advanced Parties the A.D.Ss and R.A.Ps, and supply them with details of the Medical arrangements at present in force.

   Each Field Ambulance site is to be handed over as a going concern. All details of reliefs and exchanges of equipment will be arranged by Os.C.Field Ambulances.

2. EQUIPMENT.   All blankets, stretchers, Aid Post Stores, etc, previously taken over and equipment held as surplus to Mobilization Tables will be handed over and receipts forwarded to this Office in duplicate, as per enclosed pro forma. (pro forma to Field Ambulances only). B.R.C.S.Stores obtained whilst in this area by the Field Ambulances in the line Os.C. will only retain what is absolutely advisable, handing over the surplus to the incoming unit.

3. MEDICAL ARRANGEMENTS AFTER RELIEF.

   On relief the Field Ambulances will act and move in conjunction with their Brigade group, and be billeted in their Brigade area. As Field Ambulances may not be possible to move with their Brigade group, the Os C.66th.Div Train.A.S.C. will be advised when the Ambulance moves to rejoin its group.

   Each Field Ambulance will be responsible for the Medical arrangements of its group whilst in billets, a small reception post being opened if necessary, sick being evacuated as usual to the nearest C.C.S.

   Os.C.Field Ambulances are to get into immediate touch with their respective Brigade Headquarters.

4. ORDERS.   Further orders will be issued as required.

Acknowledge.

                              (sd)   H.G.FALKNER. Colonel.A.D.M.S.
                                        66th.Division.

D.H.Q.
23-9-17.

APPENDIX II

SECRET.   COPY. NO. 12.

199th. Infantry Brigade Order. (in so far as it effects this Unit)

Reference 1/40000
   Sheets 11 and 19
   COXYDE Sheet 1/20000

1.   The 199th Infantry Brigade Group will move from ST. IDESBALDE to GHIVELDE on Sept. 25th.

~~xxxxxxxxxxxxxxxxxxxxxxxxxx~~

3.   Distances of 200 yards between Field Companies, Infantry Coys., and Sections of transport of equivalent road space will be maintained on the march.

4.   (a) Administrative details are contained in Administrative Order No. 21 of 23/9/17.
     (b) Baggage and Supply wagons will march with units.

5.   Brigade Headquarters will close at ST. IDESBALDE and reopen at GHIVELDE at 4.0.p.m.

6.   The 199th. Infantry Brigade is to be prepared to leave the XV. Corps Area on Sept. 26th. Infantry will move by Bus. Transport will move by road one day previous to the personnel of its units.

7.   Acknowledge.

                            (sd) R.L.BOND. Captain.
                                 Brigade Major.
24-9-17.   199th. Infantry Bde.

APPENDIX III

199th. Infantry Brigade
Administrative Order No.21.   Copy.No.9.

(In so far as it effects this unit)   23-9-17.

1. Billeting Parties.   199th. Infantry Brigade group will move into Billets as follows. St Idesbalde 24-9-17, Ghyvelde 25-9-17.

Billeting Parties as follows will be sent forward on the 24th instant and arrangements will be made with area Commandants as to accommodation.

2/3rd East Lancs Field Ambulance. 1 Officer & 2 N.C.Os. The party will be at the area Commandants office, GHYVELDE at 4.pm. Representatives will take with them a roll of Officers, Other Ranks and Officers to be billeted.

2. Supply arrangements.   Rations for 199th. Infantry Brigade group for consumption on the 25th instant will be delivered to Q.M.Stores of Units at St Idesbalde. Units who are not billeted at St Idesbalde will send guides to the Refilling Point, 544 Co. A.S.C. at 7.30 am. on the 25th. inst.
Rations for consumption on the 26th. inst. will be issued as follows:-

199th. Infantry Bde group as at present.

3. Acknowledge.

(sd)   J.S.FOX. A/Staff Capt.

Appendix A.

1. Entraining will take place at the rail point at WHITE-DUNSMORE by 7.

2. Buses and lorries will assemble, including Judges, drivers, adjutant, all ranks, etc, and then proceed to embarking place to take up posn in early bringing personnel.

3. The personnel will be lined up on the right side of the road ready to entrain at 11.40 a.m. in groups of 25 or 50 (not as stated in Table A). Six transpt to go yards of road space. One bus takes 30 persons, one lorry takes 20 persons.

4. Allotment of buses is as follows:-

   A/878, 2/4 Inniskgs. L.I. ...... 10 lorries Nos. 70 - 79.

5. Transpt to Jon will meet Adjutants of all units or representatives (officers), who have no transport, at Postn on off-side of vehicle at 10.40 a.m. and issue any trans, any numbers with them that they may require.

6. All vehicles are numbered on the off-side, and numbers shown above must be strictly adhered to.

7. Units will march to the starting point in above order and will arrange to debouch into the start pnt in correct order.

APPENDIX IV

SECRET.   Copy. 12.

199th. Infantry Brigade Order No.57.
(in so far as it effects this unit)

Ref.- Sheet.11. S.E. 1/20.000. Ref.- Sheet.19. Ref.- Sheet.
HAZELBROUCK. 5a. 1/100000.

1. The 66th.divn (less Artillery) accompanied by one Divnl Supply Column and 10th.Batt.D.C.L.I. will be transferred from the XI.Corps Area to the 2nd.Anzac Corps.2nd.Army.

2. The 199th.Infantry Bde will move by Bus from Gnyvelde to Renescure area on Sept 27/28th.in accordance with attached table A.

3. Detailed arrangements for embussing units are given in appendix B.

4. Advance parties not exceeding 6 per Infantry Battalion and 2 from other units in the Bde group will proceed by Bus to Renescure area on the day previous to that on which their own units move.
   Advance parties of 2/5th and 2/6th.Manchesters,204th.M.G.C. & 2/3rd East Lancs Field Ambulance. Times and rendezvous of imbussing will be notified later.
   Advance parties will meet their units on arrival at the places of debussing in table A.and guide them to billeting areas.

6. Acknowledge.

                                        (sd)   R.L.BOND. Captain.
                                                 Brigade Major.
25-9-17.   199th.Inf Bde.

Table A.

27th. Sept. 1917.

2/3rd East Lancs Field Ambulance, from CHYVELDE to WORMHAUDT, by March Route. Route Time. Les Moeres--Krommel Hoeck--Cross Roads at P.4.a.0./7--Le Lonten-Burgh--West Capel--Wylder. Time.- To clear CHYVELDE by 10.am. Remarks.-

Billets on application to area Commandant, ZERNEZEELE. Captain Sunderland.O.C. 544.Co.A.S.C. will command the Bde Group Transport.

28th. Sept. 1917.

2/3rd East Lancs Field Ambulance from Chyvelde to Renescure area by Bus. Dunkirk--West out skirts of Bergues--Wornhoudt--Cassel. Troops to be drawn up ready to embus at 10.am. Unit will debus on Arques--Racquinghen Road, near the windmill (under C.in Compagne. Ref.- Map.Hazelbrouck.5.a). Billets on application to area Commandant, Arques.

Transport. 2/3rd East Lancs Field Ambulance. From Wormhouldt to Renescure area. Rout Time. Ledringhem--Arnecke--Dehdezeele. Time.- To be clear of Wormhoudt--Cassel Road by 8 am. To Rejoin personnel in Billeting areas. Guides from Units to meet transport at X Roads Le Nieppe.

Addendum No.1.
==================

Transport. Ref.- Table A. details from Sept.27th. Bde Transport will be formed up (closed up) on the Chyvelde-Les Moeres Road at 8.am. in the following order.- At 8.am the leading unit will march off followed by the remainder with an interval of 200 yards between units. 2/3rd East Lancs Field Ambulance (Horse Transport).

All cyclists will accompany their transport.
Os.C. will take steps to ensure that their transport debouches on to the main road in its correct position as regards other units.

Particular attention is to be paid to march discipline. Steel helmets will be worn.

Bde Group Transport will be timed not to enter Wormhoudt before 2-30.pm and must be clear of Wormhoudt by 3-30.pm.

Advance Parties. Ref para 4.a. Bde Group advance parties will be prepared to embus at 11-30.am. on the Chyvelde-Bray Dunes Road, between the 2/1st. Field Ambulance and 430th. Field Co.R.E. about 400 yds South of Pont De Chyvelde.

(sd) R.L.BOND. Capt,
Bde Major.
199th. Inf Bde.

25-9-17.

Confidential

War Diary

of

2/5th East Lancs Field Ambulance

From Oct 1st 1917.   To Oct 31st 1917.

(Volumn 1)

SECRET

Army Form C. 2118.

WAR DIARY of 2/3rd EAST LANCS. FIELD AMB.
for OCTOBER 1917

INTELLIGENCE SUMMARY.
(Erase heading not required.)

PAGE 1.

Place	Date	Hour	Summary of Events and Information	Remarks and references to Appendices
WARDRECQUES	1-10-17	9.00	LIEUT. W.M. DOBSON. M.O.R.C. U.S.A. proceeded for duty to 2nd ANZAC REINFORCEMENT CAMP	
Mid Y pres rec Shut 5a E4		12.00	No. 354203 L/Cpl HARPER T. of this Unit appointed A/Sergt. (unpaid) from 1-10-17.	
		14.00	Copy No 11 of Order No 58 received from 199 Infantry Brigade	See Appendix I.
		14.00	Copy No. 2 of Administration Order No 22 received from 199 Infantry Brigade	See Appendix II.
		15.00	No. 354445 Pte HOLLAND W. reported from 203 (ly) M.G.C.	
		18.00	(CAPT A W BERRY RAMC (TF) proceeded for duty to No 6 M.A.C.	M.N.H.W.
	2-10-17	6.00	Establishment of Clearing Station No 50 Offrs 13 received from 199 Infantry Batt.	See Appendix I.
		11.00	Transport moved by road to New Station (CAPT. E.P. WEDD RAMC (T.F.) in charge.	M.N.H.W.
BRANDHOEK	3-10-17	6.00	Front left Camp for ARQUES STATION. 7.00 Unit entrained	
M.Ref Sh. 28 I.7 & S5 No 6 a.d.s.		9.10	Unit arrived at BRANDHOEK	M.N.H.V.
		9.00	ANZAC CORPS Medical Arrangements No 4 Copy No 10 & 12 received from A.D.M.S. 56th Division	See Appendix III
		20.00	Unit Offrs arrived at BRANDHOEK	M.N.H.W.
			Main Tent	
	4-10-17	14.00	Sub Officers & 40 Other Ranks proceeded to YPRES PRISON. MAP REF Sheet 28 I.7 & S5	M.N.H.W.II.
YPRES PRISON		19.00	Remainder of R.A.M.C. Personnel proceeded to YPRES PRISON	
MAP REF SH. 28 I.7 & S.5	5-10-17	9.00	(CAPT A W BERRY RAMC (TF) reported for duty	
	6-10-17	10.00	Evacuated Sitters taken over from 9th Australian Field Amb 86 Other ranks, 6 H.V. horses, 4 G.S. Horse Ambulances reported for duty from 2/1st East Lancs F.A.	
			99	2/2
	7-10-17	17.00	No. 354445 Pte Holland W # Pte 354516 Pte OLDHAM J wounded.	M.N.H.W.

SECRET

Army Form C. 2118.

Instructions regarding War Diaries and Intelligence Summaries are contained in F. S. Regs., Part II. and the Staff Manual respectively. Title pages will be prepared in manuscript.

WAR DIARY of 2/3rd EAST LANCS. FIELD AMB.
for OCTOBER 1917.
INTELLIGENCE SUMMARY.
(Erase heading not required.)

PAGE 11.

Place	Date	Hour	Summary of Events and Information	Remarks and references to Appendices
YPRES PRISON.	7-10-17	10.00	Operation Order No. 34. Copy No. 12 received from A.D.M.S. 66th Division	See Appendix IV
		12.00	" " " 35. " " 15. " " " "	See Appendix V
		12.00	No. 354528 Pte. WILKINSON S. Killed, 9 No. 354073 Pte. RILEY H., No. 354256 Pte. PIERCY J.W. No. 354383 Pte. HUNTINGTON V., No. 354396 Pte. PURDY R.W., No. 354298 Pte. REID M., No. 354481 Pte. HAMPSON H. No. 352123 Pte. TODD H. & No. 352099 Pte. MARSHALL G.W. Wounded.	N.W.N.W.
"	8-10-17	12.00	Routine Evacuation of Wounded.	N.W.N.W.
"	9-10-17	12.00	Routine Evacuation of Wounded.	N.W.N.W.
"	10-10-17	12.00	Routine Evacuation of Wounded.	
		13.00	Operation Order No. 36 received from A.D.M.S. 66th Division	See Appendix VI
		15.10	No. 354476 Pte. WALL W. Wounded	See Appendix VI
		19.00	Addendum to Operation Order No. 36 received	N.W.N.W.
"	11-10-17	10.00	Ambulance Sites handed over to 9th Australian Field Amb.	
		12.00	No. 354476 Pte. WALLS W. died of Wounds received in action	
		14.30	Unit proceeded from YPRES PRISON to BRANDHOEK. Personnel of 2/2nd & 2/1st Field Ambulances rejoined their Units.	N.W.N.W.
BRANDHOEK	12-10-17	12.00	Operation Order No. 61 Copy No. 11 received from 199 Infantry Brigade	See Appendix VII
"		0.00	Unit entrained at BRANDHOEK for New Station	N.W.N.W.
		4.00	Unit detrained at ARQUES	
		8.00	(CAPT. R.J. CHAPMAN R.A.M.F.(T.F) proceeded for duty to 25th East Lancs Reg.	N.W.N.W.

SECRET

Army Form C. 2118.

Instructions regarding War Diaries and Intelligence Summaries are contained in F. S. Regs., Part II. and the Staff Manual respectively. Title pages will be prepared in manuscript.

WAR DIARY of 2/3rd EAST LANCS FIELD AMB.
for OCTOBER 1917.
INTELLIGENCE SUMMARY.
(Erase heading not required.)

PAGE III

Place	Date	Hour	Summary of Events and Information	Remarks and references to Appendices
ARQUES	14-10-17	12.00	LIEUT. W.M. DOBSON. M.O.R.C. U.S.A proceeded for duty to 2/9th Manchester Regiment. Routine.	M.H. & W.
"	15-10-17	10.00	No. T4/247461 Dvr GROOM H.W. proceeded to No. 544 Coy A.S.C.	See Appendix VIII
		12.00	Routine. Report on Recent Active Operations by LIEUT COLONEL E.H. COX sent to A.D.M.S. 66th Division	M.H. & W.
"	16-10-17	12.00	Routine	M.H. & W.
"	17-10-17	12.00	Routine	M.H. & W.
"	18-10-17	12.00	Routine	M.H. & W.
"	19-10-17	12.00	Routine. 6 Reinforcements reported from the Base.	M.H. & W.
"	20-10-17	12.00	Routine	M.H. & W.
"	21-10-17	12.00	Routine. CAPT R.J. CHAPMAN R.A.M.C. T.F. reported for duty from the 2/5th East Lancs Reg. No. 354208 Sergt. RHODES R. evacuated to No. 15 C.C.S.	M.H. & W.
"	22-10-17	12.00	Routine	M.H. & W.
"	23-10-17	12.00	Routine	M.H. & W.
"	24-10-17	12.00	Routine. No. 354340 Cpl MAGNALL E.E. evacuated to No. 15 C.C.S.	M.H. & W.
"	25-10-17	12.00	Routine. 6 Reinforcements reported for duty from the Base.	M.H. & W.
"	26-10-17	8.00	Routine. CAPT R.J. CHAPMAN R.A.M.C. T.F. proceeded to No. 2 C.C.S. for temporary duty.	M.H. & W.

Army Form C. 2118.

SECRET

WAR DIARY of 2/3rd EAST LANCS FIELD AMB
for OCTOBER 1917

INTELLIGENCE SUMMARY.

(Erase heading not required.)

PAGE IV

Instructions regarding War Diaries and Intelligence Summaries are contained in F. S. Regs., Part II. and the Staff Manual respectively. Title pages will be prepared in manuscript.

Place	Date	Hour	Summary of Events and Information	Remarks and references to Appendices
ARQUES	27-10-17	12.00	Routine	W.H.W.L.
"	28-10-17	6.00	Operation Order No. 62 Copy No. 11. received from 199th Infantry Brigade (details for capture by O.C.) by F.M. Sir Douglas Haig.	W.H.W.L
"	29-10-17	12.00	66th Division inspected by Field Marshal Sir Douglas Haig.	
"		10.00	Lieut W.M. Dobson M.O.R.C. U.S.A. returned from 2/9th Manchester Regiment	
"	30-10-17	12.00	Routine.	W.H.W.L.
"	31-10-17	11.00	Major-General The Hon. Sir H.A. Lawrence, K.C.B. presented the Military Medal to No. 354337 Sergt Lomax J } 18-11/10/17 No. 354246 Sergt Fox A.H } for gallantry in the Field } 19-10/10/17	W.H.W.L.

D.W.W., Lt Colonel.
O.C. 2/3rd E Lancs Field Amb

Appendix No. I

COPY.

ADDENDUM TO 199TH INFANTRY BRIGADE. OPERATION ORDER NO. 58.

1. The 199th Infantry Brigade will move as arranged tomorrow to the EECKE Area where it will entrain.

2. Billeting parties are to stand by pending further orders.

(Signed) GERALD UNSWORTH, Captain.
for Brigade Major.
199th Infantry Brigade.

B.H.Q.,
2.10.17.

(Copy).

No. 11.

C O R R E C T I O N
TO
199th BRIGADE ORDER NO.5o.

MARCH TABLE.

Brigade starting point Column 2 and Column 4 should read B.8.a.75.60 not A.8.a.75.60.

B.H.Q.
1-10-17.

R.W.Bond. Captain.
Brigade Major.
199th Infantry Brigade.

Distribution:-

To all recipients of OO.58.

COPY. SECRET. COPY NO. 11.

199th Infantry Brigade.
ORDER NO. 58.

Ref. Maps. HAZEBROUCK 5A.

Sheet 27)
" 36A) 1/40.000.

1. The 60th Division (less Artillery, R.E., and Pioneer Battalion) will move from the RENESCURE area to the EECKE area on the 1st 2nd and 3rd of October.

2. The 199th Infantry Brigade Group will move to the EECKE area (Western sub-area) on October 3rd.

3. A march table is attached.

4. Distances as laid down in 199th Infantry Brigade G.466,29.9.17, are to be observed on the march. There will be a distance of 100 yards in rear of L.T.M.B., and 100 yards in rear of M.G.Coy., and 500 yards in rear of 2/3rd Field Ambulance.

5. 1st Line Transport and 2nd Line Baggage wagons will march with Units. Supply wagons will march with the train Company.

6. Advance parties from all Units will proceed to the new area on October 2nd at least two members of each Battalion party will be mounted on bicycles. The whole of the advance parties will rendezvous at the Main Square WARDRECQUES at 8.0.a.m. on the 2nd October whence dismounted personnel will be marched under an Officer (to be detailed by O.C., 2/5th Manch.Regt) to ST. SYLVESTRE CAPPEL. This party will meet the Staff Captain at the road junction near the church P.23.c.70. on arrival.

7. Guides from advance parties will meet units at cross roads P.35.b.5.2. at 2.0.p.m. on 3.10.17.

8. Brigade Headquarters will close at WARDRECQUES at 7.45.a.m. on October 3rd and reopen at ST. SYLVESTER CAPPEL on arrival.

9. Units must send in map location of H.Q. immediately on arrival.

10. The Division will move to the WINNEZEELE area on October 4th. The 199th Brigade will move in the afternoon.

(Signed) R.W. BOND, Captain,
Brigade Major,
199th Infantry Brigade.

B.H.Q.,
1.10.17.

March Table to accompany 199th Infantry Bde.

Order no. 58.

Units in order of March	Starting Point	Time	Time at Bridge S.P.	Route	Remarks
2/3rd. Fld. Amb.	Ro-junction. A.8.a.75.60.	9.31. a.m.	A.8.a.75.60 / 9.31. a.m.	PONT ASQUIN - X roads B.2.b.90. - LYNDE - WALION CAPPEL - Road junction. U.24.c.2.8. - Level crossing at LA HTE LOGE - X roads V.21.d.5.2. - X roads V.22.b.0.1. - ST SYLVESTRE CAPPEL	Motor Amb. will move independently under orders of O.C. 2/3rd Field Amb.

Appendix No. II

COPY.　　　　　　　　　　　　　　　　COPY NO. 12.

　　　　　　　199th Infantry Brigade.
　　　　　　　Administration Order No.22.

　　　　　　　　　　　　　　　　　　　　1/10/17.

Ref: 199th Brigade Operation Order No.57.
　"　Maps.- HAZEBROUCK "A".
　　　　　Sheets 27)
　　　　　　　　 36a) 1/40.000.

BAGGAGE. 1.　Baggage Wagons will be sent to Units 18 hours before move, Horses and Drivers returning to Company Lines.

RATIONS. 2.　(i)　Rations for consumption for day of moves will be carried by Units.

　　　　　(ii).　Rations for consumption following day will be loaded on Supply Wagon, from present Dump, on the evening prior to respective moves. Loaded wagons will return to, and park in, Company Lines. Wagons will move with Company and will deliver Rations to Units upon arrival in EECKE Area.

TRANSPORT. 3.　The following additional transport has been allotted to Units for carrying Blankets, Surplus Kit, etc.-

　　　199th Brigade Headquarters.) 1 Lorry.
　　　2/3rd Field Ambulance.　　　)

　　　　　　　　　　(Signed) GERALD UNSWORTH, Captain,
　　　　　　　　　　　　　　　　　Staff Captain.
　　　　　　　　　　　　　　199th Infantry Brigade.

Appendix No. III

COPY.   SECRET.   D.D.M.S.
                                        II ANZAC CORPS.
                                        No. 18 12.
A.D.M.S., 66th Divn.   2/10/17.
No. 2/53/703-3.

II Anzac Corps.

Medical Arrangements No. 4.

Divisions are responsible for the evacuation from the first line, through the Regimental Aid Posts and Collecting posts to the Advanced Dressing Stations. Corps will arrange for the evacuation from the Advanced Dressing Station to the Main Dressing Station, Walking Wounded Collecting post and Casualty Clearing Stations.

The scheme of evacuations is based on Casualty Clearing Stations - to which both walking and stretcher cases will be sent - at NINE ELMS, No. 44 and 3rd Aust. C.C.S.
In the event of NINE ELMS becoming overcrowded, cases will be sent to REMY.

Regimental Aid Posts and Bearer Relay Posts will be established by divisions as required by the Military situation.

ADVANCED DRESSING STATION.-
                Right Division, PRISON, at YPRES.
                        Chateau at POTIJZE I.4.a.8.2.
            Advanced post at BAVARIA HOUSE, C.30.c.6.4.
                Left Division. MINE SHAFT at WIELTJE.
                                            (C.23.b.8.4.)

WALKING WOUNDED COLLECTING POST.   The Mill, VLAMERTINGHE.

MAIN DRESSING STATION.   Red Farm, G.5.d.7.3.

CORPS REST STATION.   HILLHOEK. =.L.20.b.6.4.

OFFICERS REST HOUSE.   LA MOTTE.

CENTRE FOR TREATMENT OF GASSED CASES.   BRANDHOEK. G.12.b.7.7.

SICK. Sick Collecting Stations will be formed under Divisional arrangements.
                Right Division. BRANDHOEK, G.12.b.8.7.
                Left Division. MOATED FARM, VLAMERTINGHE.
                                    (H.2.d.8.2.)

All sick from forward areas will be sent to these stations and there classified and disposed of.

MOTOR AMBULANCE CONVOY.   No. 6 M.A.C.

ADVANCED DEPOT OF MEDICAL STORES.   2nd Canadian, REMY.

EVACUATIONS.

WALKING WOUNDED.
            These cases will be directed along routes conspicuously flagged by Divisions to Collecting posts or Advanced Dressing Station. The Light Railway will provide trains from BAVARIA HOUSE, and WIELTJE, running back at regular intervals to CULLODEN (B.26.c.9.2.) From CULLODEN THEY WILL BE CONVEYED BY horse Ambulance wagons and Motor Lorries to THE MILL, VLAMERTINGHE, where they will be classified and despatched by motor lorries, to Corps Rest Station or Casualty Clearing Stations at NINE ELMS.

(2).

WALKING WOUNDED (Continued).

Should the Light Railway not be available a service of lorries will be run through WIELTJE by cross road to I.5.a.5.8.- where cases from Right Division will be picked up - and back to the MILL, VLAMERTINGHE.

The Officer Commanding Corps Walking Wounded Collecting post will be responsible for flagging the route from CULLODEN to VLAMERTINGHE.

LYING CASES. These will be collected and conveyed to Advanced Dressing Stations under Divisional arrangements. Use will be made of the Trench Tramway, wheeled stretchers, Ford Ambulances and Horse Ambulance wagons.

They will be conveyed to Main Dressing Station by M.A.C. and such Divisional cars as are available for pooling with the M.A.C.

All Gassed cases will be sent from Corps Main Dressing Station to be treated at the Gas Centre at BRANDHOEK. Officer Commanding M.A.C. will be responsible for all evacuations by Motor Ambulance and Motor Lorry.

Blankets, Stretchers and Splints will be returned from Casualty Clearing Station and Main Dressing Station to Advanced Dressing Stations by returning empty cars.
Special orderlies will be detailed for this duty at Corps Main Dressing Station and Corps Walking Wounded Collecting Posts.

Detailed instructions to be read in conjunction with II Anzac Medical arrangements will be issued to all concerned.

      (Signed) C.M. BEGG,
      Colonel, D.D.M.S.,
      II A.& N.Z.A.C.

2nd October,
1917.

COPY. SECRET O.O. 34 COPY 12.

Appendix No IV

OPERATION ORDER No.34
BY
COLONEL H.G. FALKNER T.D.
ASSISTANT DIRECTOR OF MEDICAL SERVICES,
66TH DIVISION.

1. The 66th Division will relieve the 3rd Australian Division in the line on the 5th, and night of the 5th/6th October 1917, relief to be completed by 10.0.a.m. 6th October 1917.

   MEDICAL ARRANGEMENTS FOR MOVE.

2. 2/3rd East Lancashire Field Ambulance.

   O.C., 2/3rd East Lancs. Field Ambulance will take over Medical charge of the Forward Area from O.C., 9th Australian Field Ambulance. Move to be completed by 10.0.a.m. October 6th 1917.

   He will detail an advanced party consisting of 4 Medical Officers, 1 tent sub-division, and the three bearer sub-divisions to report at THE PRISON, YPRES, at 6.0.p.m. 5th October 1917. The remainder of this Field Ambulance will report at the same place by 10.0.a.m. 6th October 1917.
   They will occupy the billets, transport lines etc. vacated by the outgoing Unit. Details of relief to be arranged between the respective Os.C. Units concerned.
   4 Daimler Ambulance Cars from this Unit will report to O.C., 6 M.A.C. RED FARM (C.5.d.7.3.) Sheet 28) by 10.0.a.m. 6th inst.

6. All moves to be completed by 10.a.m. (approximately) 6th October 1917.

   Completion of moves to be reported to A.D.M.S.,66th Division.

              (Signed) H.G. FALKNER,
              Colonel, A.D.M.S.,66th Division.

COPY.   S E C R E T.   O.O. 35 COPY 15.

Appendix No. V

OPERATION ORDER NO. 35.
BY
COLONEL H.C. FALKNER T.D.
ASSISTANT DIRECTOR OF MEDICAL SERVICES.
66TH DIVISION.

Medical arrangements for forthcoming operations by 66th Division.

Map Reference   Sheet 28 N.W. 1/40,000.

1. The O.C., 2/3rd East Lancashire Field Ambulance, will, under the direction of the A.D.M.S., 66th Division be responsible for the evacuation of wounded from the Forward Area. He will have at his disposal all bearer sub-divisions from the three Field Ambulances of this Division, all the Ford Motor Ambulance Cars, and Horsed Ambulance Wagons, also all additional stretcher bearer parties provided from this Division. The Headquarters of this Officer will be at THE PRISON, YPRES.

2. LOCATIONS.

    (a). Regimental Aid posts.

    For the left Sector.   BORDEAU FARM, D.15.d.6.7.

    For the right Sector. ALMA, D.22.a.2.4.

    Any alterations in positions of R.A.Ps. should be communicated at once to A.D.M.S., 66th Division, and to O.C., 2/3rd East Lancashire Field Ambulance.

    (b). Relay posts.

MITCHELL'S FARM.	D.20.c.2.2.
BREMEN HOUSE.	D.26.a.7.4.
FROST HOUSE.	D.25.a.6.1.
BAVARIA HOUSE.	C.30.c.6.5.

    (c) Divisional Walking Wounded Collecting post.

    MILL COT.   I.5.a.1.7.

    (d) Advanced Dressing Stations.

    CHATEAU AT POTIJZE.   I.4.c.2.3.
    THE PRISON at YPRES.   —

    (e) Corps Main Dressing Station.

    RED FARM.   C.5.d.7.3.

    (f) Corps Walking Wounded Collecting Station.

    THE MILL, VLAMERTINGHE.   H.8.a.9.9.

    (g) Corps Gas Treatment Centre.

    BRANDHOEK.   C.12.b.7.7.

    (h) Corps Rest Station.

    HILHOEK.   L.20.b.6.4.

(2)

Operation Order 35 (Contd).

3. ROUTES OF EVACUATION.

(a). Stretcher Cases.

Will be evacuated from the Regimental aid posts through RELAY POST at MITCHELL FARM, or BREMEN HOUSE to FROST HOUSE, to BAVARIA HOUSE, where they will be placed in Ford Motor Ambulance Cars or Horsed Ambulances and conveyed to Advanced Dressing Station POTIJZE CHATEAU, thence by M.A.C. transport, to CORPS MAIN DRESSING STATION.

(b) Walking Cases.

Will be directed to MILL COT I.5.a.1.7. From here they will be entrained and taken by Decauville Railway to Corps Walking Wounded Collecting Station at THE MILL, VLAMERTINGHE H.8.a.9.9.

If trains are not available they will be sent by busses' to this place.

If busses' are unable to get as far as MILL COT cases will be directed to MENIN GATE, from whence they will be conveyed by busses' to Corps Walking Wounded Station.

(c) Gassed Cases.

Same as above to Corps Gas Centre. All gassed cases are to be "Stretcher Cases."

4. MEDICAL STORES.

These will be drawn for Regimental Aid posts from Divisional Collecting Posts and Advanced Dressing Stations, who will draw direct from No.2 Canadian Advanced Depot Medical Stores, REMY SIDING.

The Officer Commanding the Field Ambulance in the Forward Area will ensure that a good stock of Drugs and Dressings is carried, including untouched stock in reserve.

5. MEDICAL COMFORTS.

These will be drawn in the usual way.

6. SPARE BLANKETS AND STRETCHERS.

A large number is kept at the Corps Main Dressing Station for use as required.

Dumps for stretchers will be at,-

```
MITCHELL FARM.      D.20.c.2.2.
BREMEN HOUSE.       D.26.a.7.4.
FROST HOUSE.        D.26.a.6.1.
BAVARIA HOUSE.      C.30.c.6.5.
POTIJZE CHATEAU.    I.4.c.2.0.
THE PRISON AT YPRES.
```

7. GENERAL.

(a) Stretcher Cases.

The responsibility for the conveyance of wounded to R.A.Ps. rests with Battalions and Brigades. At R.A.Ps. the medical personnel of the Field Ambulance will take over cases and convey them by hand carriage, wheeled stretchers, trench tramways, horse and motor ambulances etc., to the Advanced Dressing Station. Thence they are conveyed to Corps Main Dressing Station, Corps Walking Wounded Station, and Corps Gas Centre under Corps arrangements.

Operation Order No.35 Contd.

(b). Walking Cases.

These cases will be directed to Divisional Walking Wounded Collecting Posts, and must not be sent to A.D.Ss. They should be collected in parties and sent down with a guide.

(c). Sick Cases. All sick will be sent from A.D.Ss. to Divisional Sick Collecting Station at BRANDHOEK G.12.b.8.7., where they will be classified, and disposed of according to D.D.M.S. Instructions.

(d). Gassed Cases. Gassed Cases are sent to Corps Gas Centre through Corps M.D.S.

(e). Routes. All evacuation routes will be marked legibly.

(f). In the event of the A.D.S. POTIJZE being destroyed, cases will be sent to the A.D.S., at THE PRISON, YPRES.

(g). Records and anti-tetanic serum. All records will be kept and A.T. Serum administered at Corps Main Dressing Station, and Corps Walking Wounded Station.
No record will be kept at Advanced Dressing Stations except as follows:-
(a) Cases which have been dressed given A.T.S. and returned to duty.
(b) Deaths in Advanced Dressing Station.
In these cases particulars on A.F.W. 3210 will be taken at Advanced Dressing Stations and forwarded to Corps Main Dressing Station for entry in their A. and D. Book.

(h). Urgent Cases. Cases requiring urgent surgical attention such as abdominal, chest and fractured femur cases, are to be marked with a label "Special Cases" on the rear handle of stretcher.
No case with a fractured thigh will leave an A.D.S. without a Thomas Splint being applied.

(i). GASSED CASES. Gassed Cases should be labelled "gassed" and treated as Stretcher Cases.

(j). MORPHIA CASES. Cases to which Morphia has been administered should be marked "M" on forehead.

(k). TURNIQUETS. Only if absolutely necessary should a case proceed beyond an A.D.S. with a Turniquet.

(l). HAND GRENADES. Pockets of wounded will be searched and all grenades and ammunition carefully removed and collected in a place specially set aside for this purpose at A.D.Ss. and Walking Wounded posts.

(m). The R.A.M.C. Bearers must at all times keep in touch with Regimental Stretcher Bearers.

(n). A.D.M.S. must be kept informed of the situation in front by frequent messages - stating number of wounded (approximately) at A.D.Ss, number of wounded reported in front by Regimental Medical Officers and any breakdown in evacuation arrangements in order that he may make arrangements to detail more bearers.

(o). During active operations ordinary sick must be kept as low as possible and only urgent cases evacuated.

8. A.D.M.S. will be at Divisional Headquarters, BRANDHOEK H.7.c.0.7. (which is connected with the telephone) or at his Advanced Headquarters THE PRISON, YPRES.

9. ACKNOWLEDGE.

D.H.Q.,
Oct.7th, 1917.

(Signed) H.C. FALKNER, Colonel,
A.D.M.S., 60th Division.

Appendix No. VI

COPY.   SECRET.   O.O. 36.

TO, O.C.,
    2/3rd East Lancs. Field Ambulance.

ADDENDUM TO OPERATION ORDER
No. 36, Dated October 10th, 1917.

          Motor Ambulance Cars, Horsed Ambulance Wagons, Wheeled Stretchers etc., will return to their original Units upon relief taking place.

          (Signed) W.H. ROWELL, Capt., D.A.D.M.S.,
          for Colonel, A.D.M.S., 66th Division.

D.H.Q.,
Oct. 10th, 1917.

COPY.

SECRET   O.O. 36 Copy.

OPERATION ORDER NO. 36
BY
COLONEL H.G. FALKNER, T.D.
ASSISTANT DIRECTOR OF MEDICAL SERVICES,
66th DIVISION.

1.   The 66th Division (less Artillery, pioneers and R...) will be relieved in the line on the 10th October, and night 10/11th October 1917 by the 3rd Asutralian Division.

MEDICAL ARRANGEMENTS FOR MOVE.

2.   All Officers and Other Ranks attached to Corps Main Dressing Station, Corps Rest Station, and Corps Walking Wounded Collecting post will remain unchanged.

5.   2/3rd East Lancashire Field Ambulance.

   Upon relief by a Field Ambulance of the 3rd Australian Division the 2/3rd East Lancs. Field Ambulance (less all attached Medical Officers and Other Ranks who return to their Units) will move by Bus to BRANDHOEK No.2 Area, under arrangements made direct with Headquarters 199th Infantry Brigade.

6.   Officers Commanding Field Ambulances in making their arrangements with their affiliated Brigades will be careful to point out that they cannot move until all wounded have been evacuated, and their duties taken over by the relieving Field Ambulance.

                    (Signed), W.H. ROWELL, Capt., D.A.D.M.S.,
                        for Colonel, A.D.M.S., 66th Division.

D.H.Q.,
October 10th, 1917.

COPY.   SECRET.   COPY. No. 11.

199th Infantry Brigade.

ORDER NO. 61.

Appendix No VII

Ref: HAZEBROUCK 5A.
    Sheet 27) 1/40.000.
    Sheet 28)

1. (a) The 199th Infantry Brigade Group will move to the RENESCURE area on 13th October.

   (b) Personnel and a portion of transport will move by train from BRANDHOEK at 7.45.a.m. Remainder of transport will move by march route.

2. The Brigade will entrain at G.5.d.00. (the same place as that at which it detrained before) at 7.45.a.m.

3. Adjutants with markers and entraining states will meet the Brigade Major at G.5.d.00. at 7.30.a.m.

4. Units will arrive at G.5.d.00. in the following order and at the following times.-

       2/3rd Field Amb. ... 8.30.a.m.

5. To allow ample transport for units, blankets will be carried on the man to point of entrainment. At ARQUES blankets will be rolled in bundles of 10, and left at the station under a guard to be detailed by each Unit, and will be carried from there by transport under arrangements to be made by Staff Captain.

6. Location returns must be sent in immediately on arrival.

7. (a). The following 1st Line Transport will be ready to entrain at VLAMERTINGHE STATION at 8.0.a.m.

       2/3rd Field Amb. ... 1 Water Cart.
                                                  1 Cooks' Limber.

   (b) <u>Accommodation available.</u>

       17 flats   =   68 axles.
       21 covered
          wagons.   =   161 horses.

   Units may send riding and spare horses up to the following numbers by train.-

       Field Amb.   12 horses.

   (c) L.T.M.B. personnel will proceed by this train and will be responsible for loading all transport.

   (d) Brigade Transport Officer will be in charge of Transport in Transport Train and superintend loading and unloading.

8. Remainder of transport proceeds by road to RENESCURE area. It will billet on the night of 13/14th in the PANSGAT area (Q.1.c.) Report for billets to Area Commandant, STEENVOORDE.

       Route POPERINGHE - ABEELE - STEENVOORDE.

       Starting point Cross Roads G.17.c.6.9.

(2).

Continued.-

Order of march and time of passing starting point.-

Field Ambulance. ... 0.24.a.m.

N.B. Baggage waggons will be called for at 7.0.a.m. on 13th. It is essential that they should be ready at this time.

O.C., 544 Coy., A.S.C., will command the column.

9. The unexpended portion of the day's rations will be carried on the man.
Rations for the 14th. will be dumped in the new area by A.S.C. and drawn by units with limbers and mess carts on arrival.
Rations for the 15th will be drawn by the train Company on the afternoon of the 14th from railhead at EBBLINGHEM and delivered to Units.
The portion of transport proceeding by march route will carry rations for the 14th with it, in addition to unexpended portion of the day's ration.

10. Motor Lorries. 1 Lorry will be allotted to each Battalion (except 2/8th Manch.Regt. who will have 2 lorries) and 1 for L.T.M.B. and Manch Machine Gun Coy, together, and 1 for Brigade Laundry.
Time of arrival of lorries will be notified later.

11. Each unit must detail a billeting party of 1 Officer and 6 men to proceed by lorry.
544 Coy.,A.S.C., billeting party will report at B.H.Q.,(H.7.a.11.) at 8.0.a.m. to proceed by lorry.

12. All duties and working parties found by 2/8th Manch.Regt. will be taken over by 198th Infantry Brigade tomorrow.
Details relieved will probably proceed to BRANDHOEK on the 13th, continue to RENESCURE area on the 14th. Orders for this move will be issued later by 66th Division. (A).

B.H.Q.,
12.10.17.

(Signed) R.L. BOND, Captain,
Brigade Major,
199th Infantry Brigade.

Appendix No. VIII

REPORT ON RECENT ACTIVE OPERATIONS.

I beg to report that during the recent operations this Unit took over the Advanced Dressing Stations and Bearer posts from 9th Australians Field Ambulance on the 5th instant. 93 stretcher Bearers from the 1st Field Ambulance and 102 from the 2nd Field Ambulance reported for temporary duty in the line on the 6th instant.- The R.A.M.C. personnel were distributed as follows:-

    A.D.S., prison, YPRES.-   C.O.& 1 Officer, 46 N.C.O's and men.
    A.D.S. POTIJZE.-   2 Officers, 30 N.C.O's and men.
    Bearer posts.-   3 Officers, and 277 N.C.O's and men.

Six Ford Ambulances wagons and nine horse ambulances wagons worked between the A.D.S., POTIJZE, and Bavaria House in relays.
On the 9th, the day of the attack, the horse ambulance wagons went almost as far forward as Breman House.
92 men and one Sergeant were attached from the 197th and 198th Infantry Brigades on the 9th. These were immediately sent forward and distributed between the several Bearer posts.
On the 10th, 40 "Stragglers" were obtained from the A.P.M., 66th Division, and sent forward.

The general arrangements for evacuation from the R.A.Ps. worked well. Some difficulty was experienced owing to the change of position of the R.A.Ps. Some Medical Officers were apparently not always present with their battalions.
On the day of the attack, the ground over which the stretcher bearers had to work proved to be very heavy owing to rain.
All the stretcher bearers worked well, but were very exhausted.

So far as one could ascertain, the number of wounded evac evacuated on the 9th and 10th, was 1945 and sick 408.

                (sd)   E.H.COX.   Lt-Colonel.R.A.M.C.(T.F
15-10-17.   O.C. 2/3rd.East Lancs Field Amb.

SECRET.

I.

THE PRISON.

Two Tent Sub-divisions (one in reserve) acts as A.D.S., clears all wounded from Ypres and neighbourhood.

POTIJZE CHATEAU.
Sheet 28 I.4.a.58.2.

Run by one Tent-sub-division. Staff 4 Officers. Receives all wounded from Forward Area and 6th M.A.C. clears direct.

(All cases returned to duty fill in buff slip 3210 and send to Walking Wounded Collecting Post - men dying send 3210 to C.M.D.S.) Y.M.C.A. runs buffet here - place not absolutely shell proof - if destroyed send all cases to prison.

MILL COT.
(Divisional Collecting post for Walking Wounded)

This is a small dug-out with room for about three men. Walking wounded either :-
 (a) put on trains and run to CULLODEN (B.26.c.9.2.) and then to Corps W.W.CPP. (THE MILL VLAMERTINGHE)
 (b) By Motor Lorry under M.A.C. direct to C.W.W.C.P.
 (c) If trains and busses fail, cases are directed on to Cemetry just outside MENIN GATE (I.8.b.2.1.) just east of Ypres.

C.O., 9th A.F.A. considers Div. W.W.C.P. unnecessary except during battle.

II.

BAVARIA HOUSE.
Sheet 28.C.30.c.6.5.

One concrete pill-box and one sand-bagged elephant will accommodate 18 men.
Now useful as a Resting place for Bearers.

FROST HOUSE. (Derelict Tank opposite.)
Sheet 28.D.25.a.6.1.

Small pill-box, accommodate 8 men.
Two pill-boxes across road accommodate 20 men.
(1 motor cyclist here. 1 at POTIJZE. 1 at PRISON.)

MITCHELL'S FARM. Relay post.

Concrete gun emplacement requires sand-bagging.

BREMEN HOUSE.
D.26.a.7.4.

Shell-proof. Brigade H.Q. at present. Would make excellent A.D.S. The only place in advance of POTIJZE for A.D.S. Could hold 50 lying cases if racks put up by Engineers. Requires pumping out occasionally.

INSTRUCTIONS FOR THE DISPOSAL OF SICK AND WOUNDED
AT ADVANCED DRESSING STATION.

1. WOUNDED.

(a). Sitting and lying cases to Corps Main Dressing Station,
RED FARM. Particulars of these cases will NOT be taken.

(b). Walking cases to walking wounded post, THE MILL,
VLAMERTINGHE. Particulars of these cases will NOT be taken.

(c). Slight cases returning to duty to rejoin units.
Army Form W.3118 will be made out for these cases and clearly
marked "Wounded and at Duty." The dosage of A.T.S. and time
at which given will ALSO be shown on this form.

(d). Abdominal, Head, Chest, and Fracture Femur cases, will
be sent direct to Special Operating Centre (A.O.C. MENIN LINE)
Army Form W.3118 and W.3118 will be made out, full particulars
being stated (dosage of A.T.S. etc.) on both forms.
A.F.W.3118 will accompany patient, his name being printed in
BLOCK letters, as will also number of Field Ambulance.
A. Forms W.3118 will be signed by a Medical Officer.

In the case of head wounds, the time they were first
dressed will be stated on A.F.W.3118.

(e). DEATHS.
In the event of a death an A.F.W.3118 will be
completed, and time and date of death will be stated.
A.F.W.3118 will be collected by the Orderly Room
Clerk at A.D.M.S. and D.A.D.M.S. daily for despatch to Main
Dressing Station.

(f). Wounded prisoners of war will be dealt with in the same
manner as wounded British troops.

2. GASSED CASES.

Gassed cases will be sent to the Gas Treatment Centre -
BRANDHOEK.
As far as possible mixed loads of wounded cases and gassed
cases will be avoided. In the event of this being impossible
definite instructions in writing from the M.O. at A.D.S. will
be given to the driver of Motor Ambulances as to what he is to
do.
Motor Ambulances conveying mixed loads will stop at Brandhoek
to set down "Gassed" cases. A label with the word "GASSED"
plainly marked on it, will be tied to the near handle of
stretchers carrying gassed cases.
Particulars of these cases will NOT be taken.

3. N.Y.D.N. CASES.

All N.Y.D.N. cases will be sent to either walking wounded post,
or Main Dressing Station, according to their condition.
Particulars of these cases will NOT be taken.
The term "SHELL SHOCK" is NOT to be used.

Disposal of Cases - Continued.-

4. SICK.

All sick cases requiring at least 48 hours treatment will be sent to the sick collecting station, WINNEZEELE, where they will be classified and disposed of. Particulars will NOT be taken. No sick will be sent to either M.D.S. or A.D.S.

Cases of urgent sickness, which in the opinion of the O.C. Dressing Station, require evacuation, will be sent to C.C.S. taking in such cases. A Form W. 3118 and W.3118 will be made out in these cases.

5. INWALIDED CASES.

These will be sent to C.C.S. A Forms W. 3118 and W.3118 will be completed for these cases.

CONFIDENTIAL.

WAR DIARY OF

2/3RD EAST LANCS FIELD AMBULANCE

FROM. NOV. 1ST 1917 .TO. NOV. 30TH 1917.

VOL. I.

SECRET.

Instructions regarding War Diaries and Intelligence Summaries are contained in F.S. Regs., Part II. and the Staff Manual respectively. Title pages will be prepared in manuscript.

Army Form C. 2118.

WAR DIARY of 2/3rd EAST LANCS FIELD AMB.
for NOVEMBER 1917.
INTELLIGENCE SUMMARY.

(Erase heading not required.)

PAGE 1.

Place	Date	Hour	Summary of Events and Information	Remarks and references to Appendices
ARQUES	1-11-17	00.15	Administrative Order No. 23 Copy No. 18. received from 199th Infantry Brigade.	See Appendix I.
		12.00	Operation Order No. 64 Copy No. 14 received from 199th Infantry Brigade.	See Appendix II.
			No. 354233 Pte DIBB. W.E. & No. 354450 Pte WARNER. P.S. of this Unit evacuated to No. 15. C.C.S. No. 364340 Pte THOMAS. E.J. & No. 350241 Pte DAGGETT. C. of this Unit evacuated to NEW ZEALAND STATNRY. HPTL.	
		14.00	All R.A.M.C Personnel Horse Transport (Capt W.P. FERGUSON. R.A.M.C (T.F) i/c). left ARQUES for New Station journey starting point at 14.45. Route:- FORT ROUGE - Rd. JUNC. T 10 c 0 7 - CROSS ROADS T 10. c. 3 2. - STAPLE - QUEUE d' OXELAERE. O 34 & 67 (Sheet 27).	
QUEUE D' OXELAERE Map Ref. Sheet 27. O 34 & 67		19.00	Unit arrived at New Station.	
		20.00	No. 354521 Pte FRANCIS A.E.F 1/c to A/SERGT (unpaid).	M.N.N.H.
"	2-11-17	12.00	Routine. Small Hosp. started. Hospital of 16 Beds opened at Headquarters for Brigade sick	M.N.N.H.
"	3-11-17	12.00	Routine.	M.N.N.H.
"	4-11-17	12.00	Routine.	M.N.N.H.
"	5-11-17	12.00	Routine. Capt R C S SMITH R.A.M.C T.F & 3 men proceeded to Headquarters 66th Divisional Artillery for temporary duty. Two Men & One Motor Ambulance proceeded to 66th Divisional Ammunition Column for temporary duty.	M.N.N.H.
"	6-11-17	12.00	Routine.	M.N.N.H.

SECRET.

Instructions regarding War Diaries and Intelligence
Summaries are contained in F.S. Regs., Part II.
and the Staff Manual respectively. Title pages
will be prepared in manuscript.

Army Form C. 2118.

WAR DIARY of 2/3rd EAST LANCS. FIELD AMB.
for NOVEMBER 1917.

INTELLIGENCE SUMMARY.
(Erase heading not required.)

PAGE II.
16

Place	Date	Hour	Summary of Events and Information	Remarks and references to Appendices
QUEUE D' OXELAERE. MAP REF SHEET 27. O 34. & 6. 7.	7-11-17	12.00	199th Infantry Brigade Administrative Order No. 24 received. Operation Order No. 37 Copy No. 16. received from A.D.M.S. 66th Division Received.	See Appendix III. See Appendix IV. W.H. st W.
"	8-11-17.	12.00	CAPT R. & S. SMITH, & CAPT R. J. CHAPMAN & 2.O.R. of this Unit reported for duty. The Field Amb Transport — Capt. E P W WEDD in charge — proceeded the Unit by march to WESTOUTRE Addendum to Administrative Order No 24 received from 199th Infantry Brigade Order No 65. Copy No 12. received from 199th Infantry Brigade. Administration Order No 25. Copy No 12. received from 199th Infantry Brigade.	See Appendix V. See Appendix VI. See Appendix VII. W. H. st W.
"	9-11-17.	6.50.	CAPT R. & S SMITH & 20. O.R. proceeded as an Advance Party to Divisional Rest Station situated at WIPPENHOEK (Map. Ref. Sheet 27 V40,000 - L.28. d. 4. 5.).	
"	"	14.00	Remainder of Field Ambulance Personnel - (CAPT W P FERGUSON in charge - (CAPT W P FERGUSON in charge - marched to EBBLINGHEM, via STAPLES, 9 Ambulances at 17.00 o'clock. The Unit Bivouacked at 19.25 o'clock. not a front 4 miles from WESTOUTRE. to which place march was made. Bullets being received on Ascot Camp. at 20.50 o'clock. -(Map. Ref. Sheet-28 V40,000 M.9.c.2.7.)	W. H. st W.
WESTOUTRE. MAP REF SHEET 28 M.9. C. 2. 7.	10-11-17.	12.60	Routine. No 361340 Pte THOMAS E.J. Admitted Unit from Rest Zenboued Stationary Hospital	W. H. st W.
"	11-11-17	6.75	CAPT W. P. FERGUSON & 71. O.R. & 1 Ford Ambulance proceeded to 2/1st EAST LANCS. FIELD AMB. for Stretcher Bearing duties	

SECRET.

Instructions regarding War Diaries and Intelligence
Summaries are contained in F. S. Regs., Part II.
and the Staff Manual respectively. Title pages
will be prepared in manuscript.

Army Form C. 2118.

WAR DIARY of 2/3rd EAST LANCS FIELD AMB.
for NOVEMBER 1917

INTELLIGENCE SUMMARY.

(Erase heading not required.)

PAGE III

17

Place	Date	Hour	Summary of Events and Information	Remarks and references to Appendices
WIPPENHOEK M4 Ref Sheet 28 L 28 d & E	11-11-17 Cont.	10-50	Remainder of Field Ambulance personnel marched to WIPPENHOEK, & took over the 66th Divisional Rest Station from the 3rd Australian Field Ambulance.	
		12.30	Move completed. 147 Patients taken over. CAPT R J CHAPMAN & 2 O R proceeded for duty to Central Bearer. REMY SIDING. – CAPT CHAPMAN i/c.	M.H.N.W.
" "	12-11-17	12.00	One Motor Cyclist proceeded for temporary duty to Central Bearer. No 354283 Pte. DIBB W.E. rejoined Unit from No. 15. C.C.S. 2 O.R & one Ford Ambulance rejoined Unit from 66th D.A.C. 2. O.R & one Daimler " " " " Hqrs. 66th Div. Artillery	M.H.N.W.
" "	13-11-17	12.00	One Motor Cyclist rejoined Unit from Corps Central Bearer. Nt 352267 Pte Smith H.W + No 352486 Pte SKERRITT H attached 2/1 EAST LANCS F.A. wounded in action. (Pte Shell Poisoning) admitted to 66th Divisional Rest Station.	M.H.N.W.
" "	14-11-17	12.00	CAPT. E P W WEBB R.A.M.C (T.C) transferred to 53rd Heavy Artillery Group.	M.H.N.W.
" "	15-11-17	12.00	CAPT R C S SMITH proceeded to Corps Central Bearer for temp. duty vice CAPT. R J CHAPMAN who rejoined this Unit.	M.H.N.W.
" "	16-11-17	12.00	No 352491 Pte. DAVENPORT W J rejoined Unit from New Zealand Stationary Hospital No 354873 Pte TAMM J E evacuated to Lines of Communication. (Sick)	M.H.N.W.
" "	17-11-17	12.00	D.D.M.S. 2nd ANZAC CORPS inspected the Rest Station. Patients admitted during week ending 17-11-17. Sick 267, Wounded 16. Officers 8, Other Ranks 1. TOTAL 267 16	M.H.N.W.

SECRET.

Instructions regarding War Diaries and Intelligence Summaries are contained in F. S. Regs., Part II and the Staff Manual respectively. Title pages will be prepared in manuscript.

Army Form C. 2118.

18

WAR DIARY of 2/3rd EAST LANCS FIELD AMB.
FOR NOVEMBER 1917
INTELLIGENCE SUMMARY
(Erase heading not required.)

PAGE IV.

Place	Date	Hour	Summary of Events and Information	Remarks and references to Appendices
WIPPENHOEK Map Ref Sheet 27 L28 d 48	18-11-17	12.00	Routine	M.H.N.W.
"	19-11-17	12.00	Corps Control Bureau closed. Instructions received to render all correspondence & returns thro' A.D.M.S. 66th DIV. 2.O.R. received from Corps Control Bureau.	M.H.N.W.
"	20-11-17	12.00	CAPT. R.C.S. SMITH rejoined Unit from Corps Control Bureau. No 354494 Pte CHORLTON A.E. killed in action. No 354329 Pte FORSTER S.R. admitted on return.	M.H.N.W.
"	21-11-17	12.00	No 350257 Pte FITTON W } evacuated to C.C.S. No 354491 Pte DAVENPORT W.J No 15320 Pte CAMPBELL C (P.B.)	M.H.N.W.
"	22-11-17	12.00	S.S.M. FARNDALE J (A.S.C. attached). Promoted Temporary Warrant Officer Class I as from 2/5/17. No 354203 L/Cpl HARPER T promoted A/Sergeant as from 21/10/17. No 354835 A/Lance Cpl WHITTAKER P appointed Lance Cpl (paid) as from 23/11/17.	M.H.N.W.
"	23-11-17	12.00	Routine	M.H.N.W.
"	24-11-17	9.00	CAPT A.W. BERRY & 1.C. O.R. proceeded for temporary duty to 2/1st EAST LANCS F.A.	See Appendix VIII
"	"	12.00	Administration Order No 31 Copy No 10 received from 199th Infantry Brigade	M.H.N.W.
"	"	20.00	CAPT W.P. FERGUSON & 61 O.R. rejoined Unit from 2/1st EAST LANCS F.A.	
"	25-11-17	8.00	Advance Party proceeded to new stations at CAESTRE.	
"	"	12.00	Administration Order No 32 Copy No 18 received from 199th Infantry Brigade. Brigade Order No 70 Copy No 12 " " "	See Appendix IX See Appendix X
"	28-11-17	9.00	Field Ambulance, (CAPT W.H.N. WHITE 1/c), accompanied by Transport, proceeded by Road March via GODEWAERSVELDE, & KEMMELHOF, to East Billets at CAESTRE, arriving 13.00 o'clock.	M.H.N.W.

SECRET. Army Form C. 2118.

WAR DIARY of 2/3rd EAST LANCS. FIELD AMB.
for NOVEMBER 1917
INTELLIGENCE SUMMARY.

PAGE V
19

Place	Date	Hour	Summary of Events and Information	Remarks and references to Appendices
CAESTRE. MAP REF SHEET 27 Q33.C.24.	26-11-17 (cont)	16.00	No M 2/048789 Cpl Nash. C. evacuated to No. 15 C.C.S.	MH HH
	27-11-17	12.00	Routine	MH HH
"	28-11-17	12.00	Routine	MH HH
			No 354,216 Pte Wood H evacuated to No 15 C.C.S	
"	29-11-17	12.00	Routine	H H HW.
			Hospital opened for treatment of sick of 199th Infantry Brigade (No of Beds - 20)	
"	30-11-17	12.00	Routine	MH HH
			Lieut W M Dobson MORC USA proceeded for temporary duty as R.M.O to the 2/5th Manchester Reg.	

Major K Roland
O/C 2/3 E Lanc F Amb
29/12/20

Appendix I

COPY, in so far as it affects this Unit.

SECRET.   Copy No.18.

199th Infantry Brigade.
ADMINISTRATIVE ORDER.
No.23.

Ref: 199th Bde. Operation Order No.64.
Ref: Maps BELGIUM & FRANCE.
   Sheet 27, 1/40.000.

TRANSPORT. 1. First Line Transport will accompany units. The 544 Coy. A.S.C. will move independently and will be met by guides at T.11.d.8.7. at 12.noon. Second Line Baggage wagons will report at Q.M.Stores of 2/6th Manchr.Reg.at 7.a.m. and of other units at 7.30.a.m. They will march with the Train Coy. and be formed into a convoy on ARQUES-HAZEBROUCK road at road junction in S.17.c.75.70. by 10.a.m.

LORRIES. 2. Seven lorries have been allotted to the Brigade Group for the purpose of carrying blankets, surplus kits, stores etc. These lorries will each make two journeys. For the second journey lorries are allotted as follows:-

   2/3rd Field Amb.   1 lorry.   No.7.

   The 2/3rd Fld.Amb. will have a guide in the square at ARQUES at 2.0.p.m. to conduct lorry to their Q.M.Stores.

RATIONS. 3. Representatives of units will attend at Refilling point at 8.0.a.m. tomorrow Nov.1st. Rations for consumption on Nov.2nd will be loaded on to train wagons and delivered to units on arrival in new area.

BILLETING
PARTIES. 4. ....Units will send a party of at least an N.C.O. and four men on cycles to report to Staff Captain at Brigade Headquarters at 7.15.a.m. The 2/5th Manchr.Reg. will detail an Officer to take charge of this party, which will proceed to Area Commandant's Office, STAPLE and await the arrival of the remainder of the billeting party.

BILLETS. 5. The Brigadier-General hopes that all units will leave their billets and transport lines in the same clean and satisfactory condition as has always been the case in this Brigade.

6. ACKNOWLEDGE.

                           (Signed) GERALD UNSWORTH, Captain,
                                     Staff Captain,
                                     199th Infantry Brigade.

31.10.17.

COPY.
SECRET.

Appendix II

COPY No. 14.

199th Infantry Brigade.
ORDER No. 64.

Ref: Map Sheet 27. 1/40.000.

1. The 199th Infantry Brigade Group will move to the WALLON-CAPPEL area (STAPLE Sub-area) on Nov.1st, 1917.

2. A march table is attached.

3. Distances laid down in 66th Div. 520/1 G. 29.9.17, this Office No. G.466, 29.9.17. will be maintained on the march.

4. Officers and men belonging to Brigade Reinforcement School will move with their own units, and the School will be reopened in the new area under instructions which will be issued later.

5. Administrative instructions are being issued separately.

6. Brigade Headquarters will close at ARQUES at 1.30.p.m. and reopen at STAPLE at the same hour.

7. Units should take with them all training material in their possession, and not leave any dumped at ARQUES.

8. ACKNOWLEDGE.

(Signed) R.W.BOND, Captain,
Brigade Major,
199th Infantry Brigade.

31.10.17.

March Table to accompany 199th Infantry Bde.

Order No. 64.

UNIT	Starting Point.	Time of passing S.P.	Route.	Destination	Remarks.
2/3rd Field Ambulance	Rd. junction S. 17. c. 70. 75.	2.45 p.m.	FORT ROUGE – Rd June. T.10.c.0.7 – Cross Roads T.10.c.3.2 – STAPLE	STAPLE area	

Appendix III

COPY, in so far as it affects
the 2/3rd Field Ambulance.

199th Infantry Brigade Group.
Administrative Order No.24.-

Reference Map.- Belgium and France, Sheet 27 & 28, 1/40,000.

TRANSPORT. 1. The transport of the 199th Inf. Bde. Group will move from STAPLES to EECKE on the 8th inst. and to RENINGHELST Area on the 9th inst. Regimental Transport will be under the command of Lieut. THORPE, 2/7th Manchester Reg. who will act as Brigade Transport Officer to the transport other than 544 Coy. A.S.C.

STARTING POINT. 2. The starting point will be the Cross Roads at LONGUE CROIX, U.5.c.3.4. Reference Sheet 27.

ROUTE. 3. Cross Roads LA BREARDE, V.5.c.4.1.- Cross Roads P.30.a.1.3. Road junction Q.20.c.9.7.- Billets in EECKE Area.
On second day CAESTRE-BAILLEUL LOCRE WESTOUTRE, RENINGHELST Area.

TIME OF STARTING. 4. Units transport will past (?pass) the starting points at the following time on the 8th inst.-
2/3rd Field Amb. 11.45.
On the 9th inst. the transport will be clear of EECKE by 8.0.a.m., orders for time and place of starting will be issued by senior officer.

DISTANCES. 5. Distances as laid down in 199 Inf.Bde. G.466 of 29.9.17. are to be observed on the march.
The 544 Coy. will march at least 1,000 yds. at head of the Regtl. Transport.

ADVANCE PARTY FOR TRANSPORT. 6. Two mounted orderlies will be detailed by each unit as billeting party for transport, they will report to Officer to be detailed by 2/5th Manchr. Regt. at cross-roads LONGUE CROIX U.5.c.3.4. at 9.0.a.m. 8th inst. Billets will be allotted for the night of 8/9th on application to the Area Commandant EECKE.
Guides from Advanced Party will meet the transport at ROAD JUNCTION Q.20.c.9.7. at 2.0.p.m. on the 8th inst. On arrival in RENINGHELST area on the 9th inst. The Brigade Transport Officer will report at Bde. H.Q. the position of which will be notified to him before departure on the 8th inst.

TRAIN WAGON 7. The train wagon will be sent to units at 7.30.a.m. on the 8th inst. and will move with 1st line Transport to EECKE where they will join the 544 Coy. A.S.C. under arrangements to be made by the O.C., Coy., A.S.C. and the Brigade Transport Officer.

RATIONS. 8. The unexpended portions of the rations for the 8th inst., and rations for the 9th will be taken with the transport.

POSITION 9. Officers Commanding will take steps to ensure that their transport debauches on to the road in its correct position as regards other units.

MARCH DISCIPLINE. 10. Particular attention is to be paid to march discipline.

(2).

LOADING OF TRANSPORT. 11. The state of the roads cause for the greatest care in the loading of transport. O.Os. will be held responsible that wagons are not overloaded. A staff Officer will be detailed to inspect the Transport Column in the march and to note that loading has been properly carried out and that loads are not excessive.

MAPS. 12. Units are to ensure that their Transport Officers are provided with the necessary maps.

1/1st E.Lancs. Mobile Vet.Section. 13. will be attached to the Brigade Group and will move with the 544 Coy. A.S.C. The O.C., 544 Coy. A.S.C. will make the necessary arrangements for billets etc.

LORRYS. See this Office wire Q.7. of the 7th inst. Detailed instructions as to Guides and loading parties will be issued later.

BILLETING PARTY. 14. A bus will leave Brigade Headquarters for RENINGHELFT at 8.30.a.m. on the 8th inst. The following parties will be detailed by units and will report at these Brigade Headquarters at 8.15.a.m. to the Staff Captain.

    Each Batt. 4.
    204 M.G.C. 2:
    199 L.T.M.B. 2:
    544 Co.A.S.C. 2.
    Bde. Hqrs. 2.

(Signed) GERALD UNSWORTH, Captain,
Staff Captain, 199 Inf.Bde.

Appendix IV

SECRET.   COPY NO. 16.

Copy inso far as it affects
the 2/3rd E.Lancs. Field Amb.

Operation Order No.37.
by
Colonel H.G.Falkner T.D.,
Assistant Director of Medical Services.
66th Division.   7.11.17.

The 66th Division will relieve the 1st Asutralian Division in the line, relief to be completed by 10.0.a.m. November 11th 1917.

MEDICAL ARRANGEMENTS FOR MOVE.

2/3rd East Lancashire Field Ambulance.

The Officer Commanding this unit will take over the Divisional Rest Station, WIPPENHOEK from Officer Commanding 3rd Australian Field Ambulance, move to be completed by 10.0.a.m. November 11th, 1917.
All arrangements as regards numbers and composition of Advance Party and completion of move will be made direct between Officers Commanding the two Field Ambulances concerned.
The O.C. of this unit will detail the following:-
One Medical Officer and 70 bearers N.C.Os; and men to report to O.C., 2/1st East Lancs. Field Ambulance, at I.7.c.3.7. No.10 Bridge (Sheet 28) on the morning of the 11th November 1917.
Two clerks to the Corps Central Bureau at REMY Siding (opposite No.10 C.C.S.) to report by 10.0.a.m. 11th November 1917.

All the Field Ambulances will move with their Brigade Groups to WESTOUTRE area, and will move from thence to their respective posts as notified above.
All Bearers reporting to O.C., 2/1st East Lancs. Field Ambulance. will take with them the unexpended portion of the day's rations together with rations for the following day.   They will thencome upon the ration strength of the Unit to which they are attached.
Receipts for all stores taken over from the outgoing units will be forwarded to this Office as soon as possible.
Completion of moves to be reported to this office.

(Signed) H.G.FALKNER, Colonel,
A.D.M.S.,66th Division.

Appendix V

COPY, in so far as it
affects the 2/3rd Field Amb.-

199th Infantry Brigade.
Addendum to Administrative Order No.24.
================================

BILLETS	1. Billets for the 9th inst. will be allotted to units by Area Commandant WESTOUTRE. The location cannot yet be notified of the area to be allotted to this Brigade Group. It will not be the RENINGHELST area.
TRANSPORT.	2. The billets for the transport for the night of 8/9th inst. will be allotted by Area Commandant EECKE as already notified. The billets will however probably be at GODEWAERSWELDE.
ROUTE.	3. If the transport is billetted at GODEWAERSWELDE the route laid down in para. 3 of the above Brigade Order will not be adhered to. The Senior Officer will arrange with Brigade Transport Officer to have the more direct routes to WESTOUTRE reconnoitred in advance and will issue orders accordingly.
ADVANCE PARTY.	4. He will also detail an Advance party to report to Area Commandant WESTOUTRE who will allot billets for the transport for the 9th inst.
GUIDES.	5. He will issue Orders for Guides from advance party to meet transport at least a mile outside WESTOUTRE.

(Signed) GERALD UNSWORTH, Captain,
Staff Captain, 199 Inf. Bde.

B.H.Q.,
8.11.17.

Copy in so far as it   SECRET.   Copy No. 12.
affects 2/3rd Fld. Amb.-

Appendix VI

199th Infantry Brigade.
Order No. 65.

Ref: sheets 27 & 28.   1/40.000.
HAZEBROUCK 5A.

1. (a). The 66th Division (less Artillery and all Transport) will move by train on the 8th 9th and 10th Nov. to the WESTOUTRE AREA, and will relieve the 1st Australian Division on the front BROODSEINE TIBUR. Relief to be completed by Nov. 11th.

   (b). 66th Division will be under the tactical command of 1st ANZAC CORPS until Nov. 15th.

2. (a). The 199th Infantry Brigade Group (less transport) will entrain at EBBLINGHEM and detrain at OULERDOM (?) on Nov. 9th.

   (b). Entraining and March Table is attached.

   (c). Orders for move of transport have already been issued by Staff Captain.

3. After the relief in the line is complete the 199th Infantry Bde. Group will be disposed in the Canal Area, Brigade H.Q. BELGIAN CHATEAU in H.23. A location list is attached.

4. Code names and station code calls will be taken into use.

7. A list of H.Q. in the CANAL AREA to which the Brigade moves on 10.11.17. is attached.

8. Entrainment states will be prepared and handed to entraining officer (to be detailed by Brigade H.Q.) on the platform.

                                     (Signed) R.L. Bond, Captain,
                                         Brigade Major, 199th Infantry Bde.

B.H.Q.
8.11.17.

Copy sent as far as at
2/3rd Field Amb.

Move Table

Date	Unit	Route	Remarks
Nov. 9th	2/3rd Field Amb.	By train at 6.22 p.m. from EBBLINGHEM	2/3rd Field Amb. will march via STAPLE - U.7, V.1.2, EBBLINGHEM. All units to be in position ready at 3/45 p.m. at which hour entrainment commences. N.B. Guides meet all units at CUDERDOM (?) STATION.
Nov. 10th	199th Inf. Bde. Group (less 2/3rd Field Amb.)		2/3rd Field Ambulance convoy under orders of A.P.M. at WESTOUTRE.

Appendix VII

COPY.   SECRET.   199th Infantry Brigade Group.   Copy No. 12.

(Insofar as it affects
the 2/3rd Field Amb.-)   ADMINISTRATIVE ORDER NO. 25.

Reference:- 199th, Operation Order No.65.

LORRIES.   1. Seven lorries have been allotted to the Brigade Group for the purpose of carrying the remaining Stores, cooking utensils etc., which are not being carried on the Transport. One blanket per man is also to be carried on lorries. These lorries will each make two journeys.

They are allotted as follows:-

   204th M.G.Coy.   )
   2/3rd Field Amb.   )   1 lorry.

The lorry allotted to the 204th M.G.Coy. will return for the stores of the 2/3rd Field Ambulance.
The above units will send guides to Brigade H.Q. at 7.45.a.m. on the 9th inst. to conduct lorries to their Q.M. Stores.
An unloading party of an N.C.O. and 4 men will accompany each lorry.
N.C.Os. incharge of lorries will report to an Officer to be detailed by Brigade, at Cross Roads LONGUE CROIX, U.5.c.3.4. at 10.0.a.m. Lorries will proceed from this point as a convoy to the Area Commandant's Office, WESTOUTRE, where they will be met by guides from the advanced billeting party. Every effort should be made to get the lorries unloaded and returned without undue delay.

BLANKETS.   2. One blanket will be carried on the man.

RATIONS.   3. Rations for the 10th. will be delivered to units by Train wagons on the 9th inst. in the WESTOUTRE Area.

GUIDES.   4. Guides from the advanced billeting parties will meet units at the station CLUERUAM at the following times:-

   2/3rd Field Amb.   5.0.p.m.

Appendix VIII SECRET.

Copy in so far as it
affects the 2/3rd Field Amb.

Copy No. 18.

199th Infantry Brigade.
Administrative Order No.31 (Preliminary Order for move of
199th Brigade Group to CAESTRE area.)

Ref. Sheet 27. 1/40.000.

BILLETS. 1. On the 26th instant the 199th Infantry Brigade Group will move into Billets in the STAPLE No. 2 (Eastern) Area.
The approximate Areas allotted to Units will be as follows:-

Unit.	Area.	Headquarters.
2/3rd Field Ambulance.-	Q.33.c.	Q.33.c.2.4.

Sketch maps of approximate billeting Areas will be sent to Battalions tonight.

ADVANCE BILLETING PARTIES.
2. Billeting parties will be as set down in Administrative Order No.30 of 22.11.17. with the addition of 1 Officer and 2 other ranks of the 2/3rd Field Ambulance.
These parties will embus tomorrow the 25th inst. as follows :-

Unit.	Embus at.	Time.
2/3rd Field Ambulance.-	B.Hqrs. R.32.c.5.8.	8.0.a.m.

Unexpended portion of the day's rations and rations for the 26th inst. will be carried by these parties.
Officer in charge of billeting parties will carefully reconnoitre the best route to guide the personnel and Transport of their units from CAESTRE to the Areas allotted to them, prior to 10.0.a.m. on the 26th inst.

GUIDES. 3. Guides will meet units on the 26th inst. at the "X" Roads (W.3.a.6.5.) in CAESTRE at an hour to be notified later. Guides will also be detailed to meet lorries and the supply wagons of the train. All guides will be detailed Regimentally from the parties mentioned in para.2.

RATIONS. 4. Rations will be delivered to units by Supply wagons on 25th for consumption on 26th and on arrival in new Area on 26th for consumption on 27th.

(Signed) GERALD UNSWORTH. Captain,
Staff Captain, 199th Infy. Bde.

Appendix IX

SECRET.

COPY in so far as it affects
the 2/3rd Field Ambulance.

Copy No. 18.
25.11.17.

199th Infantry Brigade.
Administrative Order No. 32.

LORRIES. 1. Lorries will be allotted as follows for move on the 26th inst.:—

Bde. H.Q.	1 lorry.
2/7th Manch.R.	3 "
2/6th "	3 "
2/5th "	3 "
2/8th "	3 "
199th L.T.M.B.	1 "
204th M.G.C.	1 "
Total:—	15.

The above mentioned units will detail guides to report to an Officer at Brigade Headquarters at BERTHEN, R.32.c.5.3. at 8.a.m. on 26th inst. Commanding Officers will arrange for guides from advance parties to meet lorries at cross roads W.3.a.6.5. CAESTRE and will also arrange to send Officer with a map with leading lorry of their group. Lorries will be clear of BERTHEN area by 10.30.a.m.

LOADING PARTIES. 2. Units will detail a loading party of 1 N.C.O. and 4 men to accompany each lorry. These numbers are not to be exceeded (except for one Officer guide)

TRANSPORT. 3. First line transport and Train Baggage wagons will accompany units in the march. Distances as laid down in 199th Infantry Brigade Order G.46. of 29.9.17. will be adhered to. The Headquarters of the 544 Coy. A.S.C. and the Train Supply Wagons will move independently and will be clear of FLETRE by 9.30.a.m.
Guides for supply wagons to be at cross roads W.3.a.6.5. CAESTRE at 10.a.m. on the 26th.

(Signed) GERALD UNSWORTH, Captain,
Staff Captain, 199th Inf.Bde.

ADDENDUM TO 199TH INFANTRY BRIGADE Administrative Order No. 32.

Officers in charge of Advance parties have been informed that guides for units are to be at cross roads W.3.a.6.5. CAESTRE at 10.30.a.m. on 26th inst. for lorries at 10.a.m. and supply wagons at 10.a.m.
Train wagons will report to units at 8.a.m. on the 26th inst.

(Signed) GERALD UNSWORTH, Captain,
Staff Captain, 199th Infantry Brigade.

25.11.17.

Appendix X

COPY.   SECRET.   Copy No.12.

199th Infantry Brigade.
Order No.70.

Ref. Sheet 27. (Belgium & France)

1. The 199th Infantry Brigade Group will move from the BERTHEN Area on November 26th to STAPLE Sub-Area No.2.(Eastern).

2. March Table is attached.

3. Guides under arrangements made by Staff Captain will be ready to meet units at CAESTRE – Road junction N.6.a.6.5.

4. Brigade Headquarters will close at BERTHEN at 11.0.a.m. and re-open at CAESTRE at the same hour.

(signed) R.L.BOND, Captain,
Brigade Major, 199th Infantry BDE.

Copy in an [?] on it
attests 2/3rd Fld Amb.

March Table to accompany 199 Inf/By Order
Order No. 70.

Date	Units in Order of March	Detonaters	Route	Remarks
Nov 24th	2/3rd Field Ambulance	Q.33.c.		March independently via GODEWAERSVELDE and KEMMEL HCF (?E). Head of Column must to cross the roads junction Q.28.c.8.7. before 12.30 p.m.

Confidential

War Diary

of

2/3rd East Lancs Field Ambulance

From 1st Dec. 1917 to 31st Dec. 1917.

Vol I

SECRET

Army Form C. 2118.

WAR DIARY of 2/3rd East Lancs. Field Amb.
for DECEMBER 1917

INTELLIGENCE SUMMARY

PAGE 1.

Place	Date	Hour	Summary of Events and Information	Remarks and references to Appendices
CAESTRE Map Ref (Sheet 27) Q.33.c.2.4.	1-12-17	12.00	Capt A.W. Berry RAMC (TF) & 24 O.R. returned from 2/1st East Lancs Field Amb.	M.B.W.W.
"	2-12-17	12.00	No T4/247518 Dvr McCann.E returned for duty from 66th Divisional Train.	H.H.&W.
"	3-12-17	12.00	Capt R.J. Chapman, RAMC (TF) & 10 O.R. attached for temporary duty to 331st Bde RFA. No M2/265473 Pte Drayson attached for temporary duty to A.D.M.S. 66th Division. No DM9/207894 Pte McLean R. & one Ford Ambulance attached for temporary duty to 66th Divisional Laundry. No M2/12771 Pte Gaught S. } reported for duty. No M2/264568 Pte Steadman T.J. }	H.H.&W.
"	4-12-17	12.00	Routine	H.H.&W.
"	5-12-17	12.00	No 354216 Pte Wood H. rejoined Unit from No 15 C.C.S. No 354202 Pte Heaton R. evacuated to No 15 C.C.S.	H.H.&W.
"	6-12-17	12.00	Routine	H.H.&W.
"	7-12-17	12.00	No 354502 Pte Swanwick A.H. evacuated to No 15 C.C.S.	See Appendix I H.H.&W.
"	"	15.00	II Anzac Corps Medical Arrangements No 8 received.	H.H.&W.
"	8-12-17	12.00	Routine	H.H.&W.
"	9-12-17	12.00	No M2/265273 Cpl Caldecott A.B. reported for duty. No 354320 Pte Handley C. evacuated to No 15 C.C.S. 3 O.R. proceeded for temporary duty to Cantbaert # Ebblinghem. Capt W.P. Ferguson assumed Command of this Field Amb. during Lt Col Cox's absence on leave.	H.H.&W.
"	10-12-17	12.00	5 O.R. proceeded for temporary duty to D.A.D.O.S. 66th Div.	H.H.&W.

SECRET.

WAR DIARY of 2/3rd East Lancs Field Amb.
for DECEMBER 1917
INTELLIGENCE SUMMARY.

PAGE 11

Place	Date	Hour	Summary of Events and Information	Remarks and references to Appendices
CAESTRE Map Ref (Sheet 27) Q 33 c 24.	11-12-17	12.00	No. T4/247578 Dvr. McCann E) evacuated to No. 15 C.C.S. No. 368280 Pte Palmer R.H.)	A.N.N.H.
			One Daimler Ambulance with Driver & Orderly attached to 2/1st East Lancs. F.A. for temporary duty	
"	12-12-17	12.00	Routine	A.N.N.H.
"	13-12-17	12.00	Routine	A.N.N.H.
"	14-12-17	12.00	Routine	A.N.N.H.
"	15-12-17	12.00	Routine	A.N.N.H.
"	16-12-17	12.00	One Daimler Ambulance with Driver & Orderly reported for duty from 2/1st East Lancs F.A.	A.N.N.H.
"	17-12-17	10 pm	Capt R.C.S. Smith & 5 O.R. proceeded in Advance Party to 66th Divisional Rest Station, Hazebrouck. Map Ref Sheet 27. — V 27 d 1.2.	
		12.00	Two Daimler Ambulances with 2 Drivers & Orderlies attached for temporary duty to A.D.M.S. 49th Division.	A.N.N.H.
			Four O.R. attached for temporary duty to Officers Rest Home. La Motte	
"	18-12-17	10.00	Capt W.H.N. White & 7 O.R. proceeded to 66th Div Rest Station.	
		18.00	One N.C.O. proceeded for duty to 66th Div Laundry	A.N.N.H.
"	19-12-17	12.00	Xmas Celebrations held	
			No. 354821 W/A/Sergt Francis A.E. promoted to A/CpL (paid) from 24-10-17 & relieving W/A/L Corpl. Longbottom of Sergts form 1-11-17	A.N.N.H.
"	20-12-17	10.00	The Unit proceeded from CAESTRE by road (Capt. W.P. Ferguson R.C.) to 66th Div Rest Station, Hazebrouck.	
		12.00	Rest Station opened. Accommodation for 70 patients.	A.N.N.H.

SECRET.

WAR DIARY of 2/3rd EAST LANCS FIELD AMB.
for DECEMBER 1917

INTELLIGENCE SUMMARY
(Erase heading not required.)

Army Form C. 2118.

PAGE III

13

Place	Date	Hour	Summary of Events and Information	Remarks and references to Appendices
HAZEBROUCK Map Ref Sheet 27 V.27.d.1.2.	21-12-17	12.00	Routine	H.N.W.W.
"	22-12-17	12.00	Capt R.J. Chapman. 9.1.0.R. reported for duty from 331st Bde. R.F.A.	H.N.W.W.
"	23-12-17	12.00	№ 354,225 Pte Maltby T.W. evacuated to No. 15 C.C.S.	H.N.W.W.
"	24-12-17	12.00	Routine	H.N.W.W.
"	25-12-17	12.00	Routine	H.N.W.W.
"	26-12-17	12.00	Routine	H.N.W.W.
"	27-12-17	12.00	Routine	H.N.W.W.
"	28-12-17	12.00	№ 303187 Pte Ewing J.F. rejoined Unit from No. 50 C.C.S.	H.N.W.W.
"	29-12-17	12.00	Routine	H.N.W.W.
"	30-12-17	12.15	Routine	H.N.W.W.
"	31-12-17	12.00	Routine	H.N.W.W.

W.G. Ferguson Capt
O.C. 2/3rd East Lancs. Field Amb.

COPY.

Appendix I

II ANZAC CORPS.
Medical Arrangements No.3.

The Corps Area is divided into RIGHT and LEFT Sectors.

A.Ds.M.S. will be responsible for the evacuation of sick and wounded from all units in their respective sectors.

WOUNDED. RIGHT SECTOR :-

Regimental Aid posts.	J.15.a.9.9.
	J. 9.d.9.9.
	J.10.a.6.9.
Advanced Dressing Station.	I. 9.c.6.2. ECOLE.

LEFT SECTOR.-

Regimental Aid posts.	J. 4.c.7.5.
	D.29.a.3.2.
	D.22.c.1.0.
Advanced Dressing Station.	I. 9.c.6.6. MENIN ROAD.

In each case suitable Bearer Relay posts and Ambulance Loading posts will be established.

No.14 Motor Ambulance Convoy will evacuate wounded from the above Advanced Dressing Stations to the REMY Group of C.C.Ss.

An Ambulance Train leave YPRES daily at 1.30.p.m. Cases of Walking Wounded may be placed on this train.

SICK.

Sick will be dealt with at all Field Ambulance stations in accordance with C.R.O. 1437 dated 26.11.17.

Lying Cases will be transferred to C.C.S. at REMY Group by M.A.C.cars
Other Cases will be sent by Ambulance Train from No.10 Bridge YPRES at 1.30.p.m. daily. These cases will be marched to No.10 Bridge under a N.C.O. A nominal roll will accompany them.

D.D.M.S. VIII Corps has made arrangements for shelter in case of bad weather.

Parties should not arrive more than ten minutes before the train is due to depart.

CORPS REST STATION AND DIVISIONAL REST STATIONS.

No.3. Australian Casualty Clearing Station has been allotted to this Corps as a Corps Rest Station. This Station will take the severer cases of sickness, who are likely to be incapacitated from duty for about 14 days.

Cases likely to be fit to return to duty in 7 days will continue to be sent to Divisional Rest Stations for the present.

CORPS REST STATION.- 3rd Australian C.C.S. at NINE ELMS.

DIVISIONAL REST STATION.-

Right Division.	L.28.d.3.3.	WIPPENHOEK.
Left Division.	G.15.c.8.9.	WARATAN.
Resting Division.		HAZEBROUCK.

CORPS SCABIES AND INFECTIOUS HOSPITAL.   L.23.a.4.5.   REMY.

Scabies and Measles will be sent from all Divisions - including the Resting Division - to Corps Scabies and Infectious Hospital. This Hospital will be administered by A.D.M.S., right Division.

Suspected cases of infectious disease may be sent to this Hospital for observation.

EYE CASES.   TO No.50 C.C.S. MONT DE CATS.

(2);

DENTAL CASES.   Instructions will be issued later.

CORPS CENTRAL OFFICE FOR MEDICAL RETURNS has been established at

H.28.c.5.0.   DICKEBUSCH.

Full Instructions have already been issued.

CHINESE.   These are sent to No.4 Stationary Hospital by the Casualty Clearing Station admitting them.

FODEN DISINFECTOR.   These must be employed to travel round Units. All blankets to be treated as frequently as possible.

ADVANCED DEPOT OF MEDICAL STORES.   No. 2 Canadian, REMY.

SANITARY SECTIONS.   No. 82 Sanitary Section. R.4.c.5.4. BOESCHEPE.
This Section is allotted to the following Areas.-

BOESCHEPE
WIPPENHOEK
REMINGHELST
OUDERDOM.

New Zealand Sanitary Section. H.13.d.9.1.

HALIFAX
PIONEER
DICKEBUSCH
CANAL
SWAN
FORWARD AREA.

CORPS SANITARY SCHOOL.   BOESCHEPE.

OFFICERS REST HOUSE.   LA MOTTE CHATEAU.

MOBILE LABORATORY.   No.1 REMY.

As it is imperative that as much traffic as possible be kept off the roads A.Ds.M.S. will ensure that, as far as possible, all ambulance cars carry their full complement of cases. The fullest use must be made of the Ambulance Train from YPRES.

(Signed) C.M.BEGG, Colonel.
D.D.M.S., II A.&.N.Z.A.C.

5.12.17.

A.D.M.S., 68th Div. No. 3/36/821 d/ 7.12.17.

Second Anzac Medical Arrangements No.3.
A.D.M.S. Letter No.3/36/521 dated Dec.7th, 1917.-

The following amendment to be made to Section 1.
Evacuation of Wounded.-

From December 16th the local Ambulance Train will leave Bridge 10 at 3.0.p.m. daily instead of 1.30.p.m.-

A.D.M.S: No.3/36/521 d/16.12.17.-

COPY.

Second Anzac Corps Medical Arrangements No.8.

TO.- O.C.,
2/3rd East Lancs. Field Amb.-   FROM.- A.D.M.S.,
                                          66th Divn.

In continuation of my 3/36/881 dated 7.12.17.- Herewith Addendum to Second Anzac Corps Medical Arrangements No.8.-

GASSED CASES. These will be admitted to Gas Centre, at H.27.c.2.9. The Field Ambulance at this site will be responsible for the conduct of this Gas Centre.

All contaminated clothing will be removed, soaked in soda solution and returned to Salvage.

Arrangements will be made Divisionally, for replacement of clothing so withdrawn.

All cases, on admission, will be washed with solution of bi-carbonate of soda and eyes will be irrigated with diluted bi-carbonate solution, 10 per cent.

Cases, whose condition necessitates Hospital Treatment, will be evacuated to C.C.S. in the usual way.

If there is any doubt as to whether patients' condition is due to gas poisoning, casualty will be reported as N.Y.D. Gas. Nature of Casualty on Field Medical Card A.F.W.3118. will be left blank and patient will be sent to No.64 C.C.S. MENDINGHEM. On receipt of confirmation, or otherwise, from this C.C.S., records will be amended to shew "Battle Casualty", "Sick" etc., and D.A.G., 3rd Echelon notified.

(Signed) C.M.BEGG, Colonel,
D.D.M.S., 2nd Anzac.

7.12.17.

A.D.M.S., 66th Division No.3/36/881 d/9.12.17.

Confidential

War Diary

From Jan 1st to Jan. 31st 1918

2/3rd East Lancs Field Amb

Vol II

SECRET.

2/3rd EAST LANCASHIRE FIELD AMBULANCE

Army Form C. 2118.

Instructions regarding War Diaries and Intelligence Summaries are contained in F. S. Regs., Part II. and the Staff Manual respectively. Title pages will be prepared in manuscript.

WAR DIARY of 2/3rd EAST LANCS FIELD AMB.
for JANUARY 1918.
INTELLIGENCE SUMMARY.
(Erase heading not required.)

PAGE I

Place	Date	Hour	Summary of Events and Information	Remarks and references to Appendices
HAZEBROUCK SHEET 27. V 21. d. 1. 2.	1-1-18	12.00	Two O.R. detached for temporary duty at Railhead EBBLINGHEM. Appendix Unit.	W.H. N.W.
		17.00	LIEUT W.M. DOBSON. M.O.R.C. U.S.A. & Chairman detached for temporary duty to V Corps Schools.	
"	2-1-18	12.00	No. 341219 Cpl. ASHTON. H.) Reinforcement reported for duty & taken on the strength.	W.H. N.W.
			No. 352263 L/Cpl JONES. E.)	
		14.00	T4/241347 Pvt. HANCOCK. S. of 544 Coy A.S.C. attached unrolled, (remained on duty).	W.H. N.W.
"	3-1-18	12.00	Routine	W.H. N.W.
"	4-1-18	12.00	Routine	W.H. N.W.
"	5-1-18	20.00	Operation Order No 40 Copy No 5 Received from A.D.M.S. 66th Division.	See Appendix I.
		21.00	Preliminary Order Copy No 11 received from 199th Infantry Brigade	See Appendix II. W.H. N.W.
"	6-1-18	12.00	No 384505 Pte EMSLEY. S.C. evacuated to No 15 C.C.S.	
			(Capt R.J. CHAPMAN & Batman detached for temporary duty to 36th Batt Lancs Fusiliers	
		20.00	Corrigendum to Operation Order No 40 Copy No 5 received from A.D.M.S. 66th Division	See Appendix III. W.H. N.W.
"	7-1-18	12.00	One Chamber Amb Wagon & Orderly reported March on Return from temporary duty with A.D.M.S. 49th Division.	
			One Chamber Amb Wagon & Orderlies 2 Batmen detached for temporary duty to 2/2nd East Lancs F.A.	
			Operation Order No 73 Copy No. 11. Received from 199th Infantry Brigade	See Appendix IV. W.H. N.W.
"	8-1-18	12.00	Administrative Order No 34 Copy No 12 received from 199th Infantry Brigade	See Appendix V. W.H. N.W.
			Operation Order No 74 Copy No. 11. received from 199th Infantry Brigade	See Appendix VI. W.H. N.W.
			One Chamber Amb Wagon & Orderly reported March on return from 2/2nd East Lancs F.A.	
"	9-1-18	9.00	Capt R.C.S. SMITH, Capt J.H. BEARDS & 16 O.R. proceeded as Advance Party to WARATAH CAMP. (Sheet 28 G.15. C. 2. 9.)	See Appendix VII.
		12.00	Operation Order No 75 Copy No 12. received from 199th Infantry Brigade	

SECRET

Instructions regarding War Diaries and Intelligence Summaries are contained in F.S. Regs., Part II and the Staff Manual respectively. Title pages will be prepared in manuscript.

Army Form C. 2118.

WAR DIARY of 2/3rd EAST LANCS FIELD AMB.
for JANUARY 1918
INTELLIGENCE SUMMARY.

(Erase heading not required.)

PAGE 11

Place	Date	Hour	Summary of Events and Information	Remarks and references to Appendices
HAZEBROUCK Sheet 27 V27.d.1.2.	10-1-18 (cont)	17.00 24.00	One Bearer Sub Divn. & Bishop reported from A.D.M.S. 49th Division. LT COL. E.H. COX resumed command of Unit on return from leave.	M.H.W.W.
WARATAH CAMP Sheet 28 G.15.c.2.9.	11-1-18	8.00 9.00 13.00	The Transport proceeded by road to WARATAH CAMP. Remainder of Unit proceeded by train to WARATAH CAMP, arriving 11.00 Transport arrived at WARATAH CAMP. WARATAH CAMP taken over from West Riding Field Amb. 72 patients also taken over. There is accommodation for 240 patients.	M.H.W.V.
"	12-1-18	12.00	Routine	M.H.W.V.
"	13-1-18	12.00	Routine	M.H.W.V.
"	14-1-18	9.00 17.00	Two Serjts. & 20 men proceeded on Stretcher Bearers for temporary duty to 2/2nd East Lancs FA. Forty O.R. of 2/2nd East Lancs FA (Stretcher Bearers) arrived at this Camp for rest purposes. One Shoeing Smith & Saddler attached for temporary duty to 2/2nd East Lancs FA.	M.H.W.V.
"	15-1-18	12.00	Four O.R. reported third on termination of temporary duty with D.A.D.O.S. 66th Division. Lieut W.M. Dobson M.O.R.C. U.S.A. & Kinsman reported third from temporary duty at X Corps School	M.H.W.V.
"	16-1-18	9.00 17.00	Twenty nine O.R. attached for temporary duty to 2/2nd East Lancs FA. as Stretcher Bearers. Thirty one O.R. from 2/2nd East Lancs FA reported for rest purposes.	M.H.W.V.
"	17-1-18	12.00	Routine	M.H.W.V.
"	18-1-18	12.00	73/102972 Pte Tippin Bassett R. reported for study from 524 Coy A.S.C. & taken on strength.	M.H.W.V.

SECRET.

Army Form C. 2118.

Instructions regarding War Diaries and Intelligence
Summaries are contained in F. S. Regs., Part II.
and the Staff Manual respectively. Title pages
will be prepared in manuscript.

WAR DIARY of 2/3rd EAST LANCS FIELD AMB.
for JANUARY 1916.
INTELLIGENCE SUMMARY.
(Erase heading not required.)

PAGE III

Place	Date	Hour	Summary of Events and Information	Remarks and references to Appendices
VARATAH CAMP Map Ref Sheet 28 Sq. C.2.9.	19-1-18	9.00	Twenty-eight O.R. of 2/2nd East Lancs F.A. (Stretcher Bearers) attached to these units after resting.	
"	"	12.00	Patients admitted & evacuated for week ending 19-1-18. Admitted to D.R.S. 360 Returned to duty 17 Transferred to C.C.S. 205 Sick 6 10 3 Wounded	W.M.W.
"	20-1-18	12.00	Accommodation increased to 240 beds.	
"	"	13.00	Twenty-two O.R. of 2/2nd East Lancs F.A. reported for next purpose. Four O.R. reported these units from 2/6th Bttn MANCHESTER REG & taken on strength.	H.M.W.
"	21-1-18	12.00	No 6195 Pte HORTON (G) granted "1914 Star" No 1975 B. Pte MANNERS (W) granted "	H.M.W.
"	22-1-18	9.00	Twenty-nine O.R. rejoined 2/2nd EAST LANCS F.A. after resting.	
"	"	12.00	Two O.R. rejoined these units from 2/88 MANCHESTER REG & taken on strength.	H.M.W.
"	"	17.00	Thirty-three O.R. reported for next purpose from 2/2nd EAST LANCS F.A.	H.M.W.
"	23-1-18	9.00	CAPT R.C.S. SMITH & Batman proceeded for temporary duty to 2/6th MANCHESTER REG	
"	"	12.00	Three O.R. of 2/5th MANCHESTER REG rejoined these units & taken on strength.	H.M.W.
"	24-1-18	12.00	No 334.210 Pte RIDGES R.H. attached to No 3 Canadian C.C.S.	
"	"	19.00	CAPT R.J. CHAPMAN & Batman rejoined these units from 2/2 LANCS FUSILIERS.	W.M.W.
"	25-1-18	9.0	No 354,296 Cpl HARDMAN J. detached for temporary duty to 65th DIVISIONAL LAUNDRY	
"	26-1-18	9.00	Twenty-five O.R. proceeded to 2/2nd EAST LANCS F.A. for duty after resting.	H.M.W.
"	"	12.00	Patients admitted & evacuated for week ending 26-1-18. Admitted to D.R.S. 194 Returned to duty 14 Transferred to C.C.S. 87 Sick 6 1 4 Wounded	H.M.W.

SECRET.

WAR DIARY OF 2/3rd EAST LANCS FIELD AMB.
for JANUARY, 1918.

Army Form C. 2118.

INTELLIGENCE SUMMARY.
(Erase heading not required.)

PAGE IV

Place	Date	Hour	Summary of Events and Information	Remarks and references to Appendices
ARATAH CAMP Ref Sheet 28. 15. c 2 9	27-1-18	12.00	Three O.R rejoined Unit from 2/1st MANCHESTER REG, 9 taken on strength	W.West.W
	28-1-18	9.00	Capt A.W BERRY detached for duty to 2/2nd MANCHESTER REG, also taken	
			CAPT. R.S WEIR attached for duty from 2/1st MANCHESTER REG.	M.N.W.
		17.00	Thirty-one O.R proceeded to 2/2nd EAST LANCS F.A for duty after Training	M.H.P.W.
			Thirty-one O.R rejoined from " " for that purpose	M.H.P.W.
	29-1-18	12.00	Routine	
	30-1-18	12.00	Routine	
	31-1-18	12.00	Routine	
			Patients admitted & evacuated for week ending 31-1-18.	M.H.W.

Admitted to D.R.S. 83
Sick 40
Wounded 2 nil

Transferred to C.C.S. 28
nil

W.W.K.Lea.
O.C. 2/3rd S. Lancs. Field Amb.

COPY, in so far as it affects
2/3rd Field Ambulance.-   Copy No.5.

Appendix I

SECRET.   Operation Order No.40.
                                by
                     Colonel H.G. FALKNER T.D.
             Assistant Director of Medical Services, 66th Division.

Reference Map: Sheet 28. 1/40.000.   5th January, 1918.

1. The 66th Division (less Artillery) will relieve the 49th Division in the line, relief to be completed by the morning of Jan.13th.1918.

2. **MEDICAL ARRANGEMENTS FOR MOVE.**

3. 2/3rd East Lancs. Field Ambulance.- The O.C. this unit will take over the Divisional Rest Station, WARATAH CAMP. G.13.c.2.9½ from the O.C., 1/1st West Riding Field Ambulance. Move to be completed by the evening of the 11th inst.
   All arrangements as regards numbers and composition of advanced party and completion of move will be made direct between Os.C. the two Field Ambulances concerned.
   Two complete Bearer Sub-divisions (less Officers) of this Field Ambulance will be at the disposal of O.C., 2/2nd E.Lancs.Fld.Amb.- The time and place where these bearers will report will be arranged direct between the Os.C. concerned.
   This Field Ambulance will move direct to WARATAH CAMP independently of their affiliated Brigade, in busses or lorries provided by the Division.
   Nominal rolls with full particulars of patients remaining in the D.R.S. HAZEBROUCK, will be handed over to the relieving Field Amb. in accordance with the instructions contained in my letter 3/42/880 dated 3rd Jan. 1918. Similar rolls will be obtained from the 1/1st West Riding Field Ambulance when they are relieved.

5. All bearers reporting to the O.C., 2/2nd E.Lancs.Field Amb. will take with them the unexpended portion of the days' rations, together with rations for the following day. They will then come upon the ration strength, when in the forward area, of the 2/2nd E.Lancs.Field Amb., and when in rest at WARATAH CAMP, the 2/3rd East Lancs.Fld.Amb.-

6. TRANSPORT ARRANGEMENTS.

   2/3rd East Lancs. Field Amb.   Transport will move by road on the 10th inst. direct to WARATAH CAMP.

7. Receipts for all stores taken over from the outgoing units will be forwarded to this office by the 16th instant.

8. Completion of moves to be reported to this office by wire.

                              (Signed) H.G.FALKNER,
                         Colonel, A.D.M.S., 66th Division.
D.H.Q.

COPY, in so far as it affects
2/rd Field Ambulance.-

Appendix II

SECRET.   Copy No.11.

199th Infantry Brigade.
PRELIMINARY ORDER.
----

1. The 199th Infantry Brigade will move from the CAESTRE sub-area on Jan.11th. into the POTIJZE area, and will relieve the 146th Infantry Brigade in the line, Right Sub-sector, on the night 12/13th January, (see March table attached).

3. 2/3rd Field Ambulance move with Brigade Group on 11th, and relieve 1/1st W.R.Fld.Amb. at WARATAH CAMP near POPERINGHE.

D.H.Q.   (Signed) C.H.Fox, Captain,
5.1.18.   A/Brigade Major, 199th Infantry Brigade.

COPY, in so far as it affects   Copy No.5.
2/3rd Field Ambulance.-   SECRET.

Appendix III

          Corrigendum to Operation Order No. 40. of
          5.1.18. by A.D.M.S., 66th Division.-

MOVEMENTS OF 2/3rd E.LANCS.FLD.AMB.

Jan.10th.   Transport will move direct to WARATAH CAMP by road, independently of Brigade Group.

Jan.11th.   Personnel will move direct to WARATAH CAMP by bus, independently of Brigade Group.-

D.H.Q.,   (Signed)   H.G.FALKNER,
6th Jan.1918.   Colonel, A.D.M.S.,
                                       66th Division.-

Appendix IV

COPY, in so far as it affects
2/3rd Field Ambulance.-   Copy. No.11.

SECRET.   199th Infantry Brigade
                        OPERATION ORDER No.73.

                Ref: Sheets 27S.E. & 28. 1/40.000.

1. The 199th Infantry Brigade Group will move on January 10th and 11th as laid down in Brigade "Preliminary" Order of 5.1.18.

2. Movement ~~tabel~~ table to follow.

4. "Code Names" and "Station Code Calls" will be taken into use on arrival in the forward area.

5. Careful records with receipts will be kept of all documents, equipment and stores taken over.

6. Particular attention is called to Fourth Army GS.148 issued under this Office No.G.640 of 28.12.17.

7. Befpre leaving area units should arrange to collect and store as near the work as possible, all loose wood, corrugated iron and other materials which might be removed by the inhabitants during the time the area is unoccupied.

9. Brigade Headquarters will close at CAESTRE at 9.30.a.m. 11.1.18. and reopen on arrival at Infantry Barracks, YPRES.

                                (Signed) C.H.FOX, Captain,
D.H.Q.   A/Brigade Major, 199th Infantry Brigade.
7.1.18.

COPY, in so far as it affects
2/3rd Field Ambulance.-   Copy No. 12.

Appendix V

SECRET.   199th Infantry Brigade
                   ADMINISTRATIVE ORDER
                         No. 34.

                    Ref: Sheet 28 N.W.

MOVE.   The 199th Infantry Brigade Group will relieve the 146th Infantry
                Brigade Group as laid down in Brigade Preliminary Order of 5.1.18.

BILLETING   Billeting Parties will report at Brigade H.Q. at 7.45.a.m. on the
PARTIES.   10th inst. as under :-

                    2/3rd Field Ambulance.   3.

                Parties from the Field Ambulance and Machine Gun Coy. will report
                at WARATAH CAMP (1/1st W.R.Fld. Amb) G.15.c.2.9.

BAGGAGE &   Baggage & Supply Wagons will report to units on the day
SUPPLY WAGONS. previous to the move of Transport.

TRANSPORT LOCATIONS ON COMPLETION OF MOVES.-

Unit.	Locality.	Date of taking over.	Relieving.
2/3rd Field Amb. and transport.	G.15.c.2.9. (WARATAH CAMP POPERINGHE).	Jan.11th.	1/1 W.R.Fd.Amb

AREA STORES   All Area Stores on charge of units in the back area will be
IN BACK AREA.   collected together prior to departure and handed over to the
                Area Commandant, from whom receipts will be obtained.
                Copies of these receipts will be forwarded to D.H.Q. by the
                13th inst.

TRENCH FOOT.   (a). Attention is called to 66th Divn. letter No. 2451/A.
                dated 13th Decr. 1917.   It is most important that every
                man's feet are carefully washed and treated as laid down in
                the above quoted letter before going into the trenches.

                (b). Socks.   Every man going into the trenches must be in
                possession of two pairs of socks in addition to those he is
                wearing.   The 49th Divn. have agreed to units of this Divn.
                in the line exchanging socks at the 49th Divn. baths, YPRES,
                in a similar manner to there own units.
                The following procedure adopted by the 49th Divn. will be
                carried out by units of this division, until other arrangements
                can be made.
                Every day the socks of all men in the line will be changed,
                the discarded socks being put into sandbags - 1 sandbag to
                each platoon.
                One man per platoon (or an equivalent number of men per Battn)
                will carry the sandbags of dirty socks to the 49th Divn.Baths,
                YPRES, and there receive a similar number of clean dry socks.
                (c) Foot troughs.   In the camps occupied by the 4 Battalions
                of the Reserve Brigade and the Reserve Battalions of the
                Brigade in the line, there are two troughs for foot washing
                and two Soyer stoves.   These will be taken over and used.
                (d). Trench Foot Powder and Soap.   This will be drawn from
                Brigade Q.M.Stores on the 12th inst.

(2).

ORDNANCE.   On and after Jan.13th. Brigade will draw from D.A.D.O.S. Store, RENINGHELST.

SUPPLY ARRANGEMENTS. Refilling points for units on first arrival in the new area are being reconnoitred and will be notified direct to units by O.C., Div. Train.

B.H.Q.
8.1.18.

(Signed)   J.G. Fox, Captain,
Staff Captain, 199th Infantry Brigade.

COPY, in so far as it affects *Appendix 7*
2/3rd East Lancs. Field Ambulance.-   Copy No.11.

SECRET.   199th Infantry Brigade
                 Operation Order No.74.

         Ref: Sheets 27 S.E. and 28 - 1/40.000.

1. Attached is movement table referred to in Brigade Operation Order
    No. 73.

                          (signed) C.H.Fox, Captain,
                          A/Brigade Major, 199th Infantry Brigade.

8.1.18.-

MOVEMENT TABLE - 199TH INFANTRY BRIGADE

Date.	Unit.	Embussing Point.	Times ready to embus.	Column moves.	Debussing Point.	Destination.	No. of busses.	Remarks.
Jan.11th.	2/3rd Field Amb. (dismounted portion).	Rue d'Eglise HAZEBROUCK.	8.30.a.m.	9.0.am.	WARATAH CAMP. G.15.c.2.9.	WARATAH CAMP.	Six.	

Appendix VII

COPY, in so far as it affects
2/3rd East Lancs. Field Ambulance.-   Copy. Mo.12.

SECRET.   199th Infantry Brigade.
                        OPERATION ORDER No. 75.

1. The 199th Infantry Brigade will relieve the 146th Infantry Brigade in the line, right sub-sector on Jan. 12th.

6. Brigade Headquarters will close at Infantry Barracks, YPRES, at 3.0.p.m. and reopen at D.26.c.1.3. on arrival.

7. Completion of relief to be reported by code word "HAPPY".

10.1.18.   (Signed) C.H.Fox, Captain,
                                A/Brigade Major, 199th Infantry Brigade.

Confidential

War Diary

of

2/3rd East Lancashire Field Amb.

From 1st February 1918. To 28th February 1918.

(Volume II.)

SECRET.

WAR DIARY of 2/3rd EAST LANCS FIELD AMB.
Army Form C. 2118.
for FEBRUARY 1918.

INTELLIGENCE SUMMARY

PAGE 1.

Place	Date	Hour	Summary of Events and Information	Remarks and references to Appendices
WARATAH CAMP. POPERINGHE. SHEET 28. G.15.C.2.9	1-2-18	12-00	No. 457443. Pte Ponsford R.H. attached to No 3 Canadian C.C.S.	W.H.H.W.
	2-2-18	12.00	No. 354313. Pte Hollingworth J to be A/Lance Corporal (Unpaid)	W.H.H.W.
	3-2-18	12.00	No 493011 Sergt Leaney S. proceeded to 66th Divisional Laundry for temporary duty	
			Capt A.W. Berry & Fakman rejoined Unit from 2/8th Batt. Manchester Regt.	See Appendix I
			Capt W.P. Ferguson & Fakman proceeded to 2/8th Batt. Manchester Regt. for temporary duty	See Appendix II
			Medical Arrangements for 66th Division received from A.D.M.S.	
	4-2-18	12-00	Operation Order No 61 received from A.D.M.S. 66th Division	W.H.H.W.
			No. 64462 Pte Flanigan W. admitted from Base Depot & taken on strength.	
	5-2-18	12.00	No T4/093050 Dvr Bond H.G. of 544 Coy A.S.C. attached 2/3rd East Lancs F.A. attached to No.3 Canadian C.C.S.	See Appendix II
			Addendum to Operation Order No 61 received from A.D.M.S. 66th Division	See Appendix III
			Operation Order No 80. received from 198th Infantry Brigade. (Copy No 24.)	See Appendix IV
			Extracts from Administrative Instructions issued by "A" Branch, 66th Division. received from A.D.M.S.	W.H.H.W.
	6-2-18	12.00	No. T/260277 Dvr Langer R of 544 Coy A.S.C. attached 2/3rd East Lancs F.A. attached to No.2 Canadian C.C.S.	
			One Motor Ambulance, Dvr, & Orderly rejoined Unit from 2/2nd East Lancs F.A.	
			Administrative Order No 37 (Copy No 12. received from 198th Infantry Brigade	See Appendix V
	7-2-18	12-00	No. 354246 Sergt Fox A.H. (M.M.) attached to No.3 Canadian C.C.S.	W.H.H.W.
			Lieut W.M. Dobson M.O.R.C., U.S.A. Sworn D.R. & one Motor truck proceeded to the 198. Infantry Brigade for the purpose of studying work of that Brigade whilst in the Proven Area.	
	8-2-18	12.00	Notification received of Promotion of Hon Lieut & Quarter Master J.H. Bounds to be Captain from 14-12-17 (W.O. London Gazette. No. 30443 of 21-12-17 of 22-12-17)	W.H.H.W.
			32 Motor Ambulances, Drivers & Orderlies rejoined Unit from 2/2 East Lancs F.A.	
	9-2-18	12.00	Lieut E.R. Rejoined Unit from XXII Corps Officers Rest Home	W.H.H.W.
			(Capt R.S. Weir R.A.M.C. (T.F.) taken on strength of Unit.	

SECRET.

WAR DIARY OF 2/3 EAST LANCS FIELD AMB.
for February 1918.
INTELLIGENCE SUMMARY.

PAGE 11

Place	Date	Hour	Summary of Events and Information	Remarks and references to Appendices
WARATAH CAMP. POPERINGHE. SHEET 28. G.15.c.2.9	10-2-18	12.00	LIEUT W.M. DOBSON, 7 O.R. 9 1 Motor Mech. regimental Unit - joined 198 Inf. Bdge. CAPT J.H. BOUNDS, 2 D.R., 1 Motor Amb. 9 Orders proceeded on ADVANCE PARTY to New Station at (Manchester) School Camp (Map Ref. Sheet 27. — L.3 a E.4)	W.H.A.W.
	11-2-18	08.40	(CAPT. W.P. FERGUSON 9 Batman rejoined Unit - from 2/8th MANCHESTER REGT.	
		10.00	THE UNIT (CAPT. W.P. FERGUSON i/c) proceeded by road at 10 a.m. to SCHOOL CAMP. arriving at destination at 13.00.	W.H.A.W.
		16.00	No. 354050 Pte BOYD J.A. evacuated to No 64 R.C.S.	
		16.00	No. 354510 Pte MOSTYN A. rejoined Unit from 204 Machine Gun. Coy 9 taken on Strength.	W.H.A.W.
SCHOOL CAMP MAP REF. SHEET 27	12.2.18	12.00	Routine.	W.H.A.W.
(L.3 a.E.4)	13.2.18	12.00	Routine.	W.H.A.W.
	14.2.18	12.00	No. T3/029972 Dvr FARR DORSETT A. of 544 Coy A.S.C. attached to this Unit rejoined 544 Coy A.S.C. No T3/006205 Dvr FARR SCOTT A.W. " " posted to this Unit. No. 354300 Sergt GREGORY T.A. rejoined Unit from 66th DIVISIONAL LAUNDRY (CAPT. W.P FERGUSON 9 Batman proceeded to 2/2nd East Lancs F.A. for Temporary duty. CAPT A.W. BERRY. S.O.R. 9 2 Motor Ambulances proceeded for Temporary duty to 66th DIVISIONAL ARTILLERY. Secret Instructions to move to 5th ARMY AREA received from 199th Infantry Brigade.	See Appendix VI W.H.A.W. W.H.A.W. W.H.A.W.
	15.2.18	12.00	CAPT. R.C.S. SMITH 9 Batman rejoined Unit from 2/6th BATT. MANCHESTER REGT.	
	16.2.18	12.00	No. M/226367 Pte NAYLOR. (Motor Cyclist). rejoined Unit from A.D.M.S. 66th DIVISION.	W.H.A.W.
	17.2.18	22.00	The Unit (less Transport) (2nd Lt. E.H. in charge), entrained at PROVEN STATION at 10 pm. 9 proceeded by rail to New Station.	W.H.A.W.
HARBONNIERES Map Ref 62.D. W.11.d cent	18.2.18	06.00	The Unit detrained at Guillancourt-Station. 9 marched to HARBONNIERES. (Map Ref. Sheet 62D.— W.11.d. cent.) arriving at 12.45.	W.H.A.W.
			CAPT W.P FERGUSON 9 Batman rejoined Unit from 2/2nd EAST LANCS. F.A.	W.H.A.W.

SECRET.

WAR DIARY of 2/3 EAST LANCS FIELD AMB. Army Form C. 2118.
for FEBRUARY 1918

Instructions regarding War Diaries and Intelligence Summaries are contained in F. S. Regs., Part II. and the Staff Manual respectively. Title pages will be prepared in manuscript.

INTELLIGENCE SUMMARY.
(Erase heading not required.)

Page III

Place	Date	Hour	Summary of Events and Information	Remarks and references to Appendices
HARBONNIERES, 19.2.18 Map Ref Sheet 62 D N 11 d cent.	19.2.18	12.00	Uneventful.	W/H.W.W.
"	20.2.18	12.00	Capt A.W. BERRY, 5 O.R. & 2 Motor Ambulances reported Wnt from 66th DIVISIONAL ARTILLERY.	W/H.W.W.
"	21.2.18	12.00	No. 352265 L/Cpl. JONES E. posted to 2/2 EAST LANCS F.A. & struck off strength. Five O.R. reinforcements reported from BASE DEPOT & taken on strength.	W/H.W.W.
"	22.2.18	12.00	Capt R.S. WEIR & Badman proceeded to 197 Inf. Bde. for temporary duty under 2/2 LANCS FUS. No. 354335 Pte. (A/L/Cpl) WHITTAKER A.P. to be A/L/Cpl (Paid) dated 22.2.18.	W/H.W.W.
"	23.2.18	12.00	No. 354570 Pte RICHARDSON F. evacuated to No 41 STATIONARY HOSPITAL. Administrative Order No 30 received from 199th Inf Bde. Operation Order No 42 received from A.D.M.S. 66th Division.	1st Appendix VII 2nd Appendix VIII W/H.W.W.
"	24.2.18	12.00	Lieut W.M. DOBSON M.O.R.C. U.S.A. & Batman & Ford Car, proceeded to 330 Bde. R.F.A. for temporary duty. Secret Operation Order, amendment received from A.D.M.S. 66th Division.	1st Appendix IX 2nd Appendix X 3rd Appendix XI
"	25.2.18	12.00	Uneventful.	
"	26.2.18	12.00	Operation Order No 75 received from 197 Infantry Bde.	W/H.W.W.
"	27.2.18	12.00	No. 354821 Pte (act Sergt) FRANCIS A.E. (in Hospital) to be Acting Sergt (Paid) from 7.2.18 inclusive. Capt W.P. FERGUSON (US) & Capt RES SMITH R.A.S.C. O.R. proceeded as Advance Party to new station, at the SUGAR FACTORY, BERNES, Map Ref Sheet 62 C (Q4 a O 5)	W/H.W.W.
"	28.2.18	11.00	Remainder of Unit plus Transport, Lt Col COX in charge, marched to new area, arriving at Staging Camp near VILLERS CARBONNEL at 17.00.	W/H.W.W.

DWR
Lieut Colonel R.A.M.C. (T.F.)
Commanding 2/3rd East Lancs Field Amb.

SECRET.

TO.- O.C.
2/3rd East Lancs Field Ambulance.

3/75/K.1.

Reference A.D.M.S. O.O. No.41 dated 3.2.18.

The paragraph referring to 2/3rd East Lancs Field Amb remaining in Waratah Camp until the Division moves out of this area is cancelled.

O.C. this Field Ambulance will hand over Waratah Camp to an Ambulance of the 20th Division on the 11th inst and make all the necessary arrangements to move with their affiliated Brigade Group.

Cases admitted to Divisional Rest Station after this date 5th inst., will only be retained if likely to recover before this Division moves into Fifth Army Area. (Medical Arrangements previously issued with regard to the subject are cancelled.)

The O.C. 2/3rd East Lancs Field Ambulance should inform the O.C. Field Ambulance, 20th Division, taking over this D.R.S. of the location of the 197, 198 and 199 Infantry Brigades in order that patients remaining in the Divisional Rest Station On recovery may be returned by him to their respective units.

When the 66th Division moves into the 11 Corps Area all sick will be transferred to No.64 C.C.S. PROVEN.

D.H.Q.
5.2.18.

(Sgd) H.S. Faulkner.
Colonel, A.D.M.S.
66th Division.

SECRET. *Appendix I*   A.D.M.S.No.3/75/681-23.

Copy in so far as it affects 2/3rd Field Ambulance.

MEDICAL ARRANGEMENTS 66TH DIVISION.

1. Field Ambulances will be responsible for the evacuation of the sick of their own Brigade Group.

2. Whilst in this Corps Area the sick will be evacuated to the Divisional Rest Station whilst open, and after it is closed to Corps Rest Station or C.C.S. No Brigade Hospital will be opened.
When the new area is reached other arrangements will be issued.

6. The 2/3rd East Lancs Field Ambulance will evacuate sick of the 198 Brigade Group when they move into the HOUTKERRKE Area from the 6th to the 10th inst on which date their affiliated Field Ambulance joins.

D. H. Q.
February 3rd, 1918.

(Sgd) H.G.Faulkner.
Colonel. A.D.M.S.
66th Division.

SECRET.

Appendix II

OPERATION ORDER No. 41
BY
COLONEL H.G. FAULKNER T.D.,
ASSISTANT DIRECTOR OF MEDICAL SERVICES.
66th DIVISION.   3rd Feby, 1918.

Reference Maps - Sheets 27, 28 and 19. 1/40,000.

1.   The 66th Division will be relieved in the line by the 11th Feby, 1918, and will proceed to the HOUTKERQUE SNT. JAN - TER - BIEZEN - PROVEN Area.

2. MEDICAL ARRANGEMENTS FOR MOVE.

   2/3rd EAST LANCS FIELD AMBCE.

   This Field Ambulance will occupy their present station WARATAH CAMP until their affiliated Brigade Group moves out of XXll Corps Area to their final Area, when they will accompany them under Brigade arrangements. Care will be taken that all arrangements for the evacuation of patients to C.R.S., or C.C.S., handing over of area stores etc., are completed in time for this move.
   A Field Ambulance of the 20th Division will take over WARATAH CAMP, with equipment, stores etc.

3.   All Field Ambulance Commanders will get into touch with their affiliated Brigade Headquarters, and ascertain the date and manner of their move.

4.   All necessary handing over certificates will be completed and forwarded to this office in due course.

5.   Completion of move to the Brigade Group Area within XXll Corps Area, and also to final Area will be reported to A.D.M.S. Office, giving exact location of new station.

6.   Time, date and place of closing and re-opening of A.D.M.S. Office will be notified later.

                              (Sgd) H.G. Faulkner,
                                 Colonel. A.D.M.S.,
                                    66th Division.

SECRET.
Appendix III
Copy No.24.

Copy in so far as it affects 2/3rd Field Ambulance.

199th Infantry Brigade
OPERATION ORDER NO. 80.

Ref:- MAP sheet 27/28 1/40,000.
      28 N.E. 1/10,000.

MOVES. 8. (b). On Feby 11th the 199 Infantry Brigade Group (including 432 Field Coy and 2/3rd Field Ambulance) will move to School Camp L.3.d. (Sheet 27) in accordance with Table G. (to be issued later).

                    (Sgd) J.S.Fox Captain.
                      for Brigade Major,
                       199th Infantry Brigade.

5.2.18.

SECRET.   *Appendix IV*   3/75/K.1.

Copy in so far as it effects 2/3rd Field Ambulance.

TO.- O.C.
2/3rd East Lancs Field Ambulance.

The following extracts from Administrative Instructions issued by "A" Branch 66th Division, dated 4.2.18. are forwarded for information and necessary action.

SUPPLIES. Supply Arrangements during the move to the HOUTKERQUE + ST. JANTER - BIEZEN - PROVEN Area are shown below. The exact locations of Refilling points in the new areas will be notified to units direct by their affiliated Train Coy.

BAGGAGE WAGONS Baggage wagons will report to Unit's Transport lines on the evening before moving and will rejoin the respective Companies of the Divisional Train as soon as possible after arrival in the new area.

ARRANGEMENTS FOR REFILLING DURING MOVE.

Date. February.	Unit or Formation.	Refills.	For Consumption.	Remarks.
9th.	2/3rd E.L.F.A.	1.0.p.m.	11th.	as at present.
11th.	do	10.0.a.m.	12th.	Drawn from R.P. at School Camp by unit's own Transport and daily thereafter.

AREA AND TRENCH STORES.

All area and trench stores, ammunition, reserve rations and water will be handed over to relieving units or Area Commandant concerned and receipts obtained.
Certificates that no stores of any kind have been taken from the Corps Area except such stores as are allowed by War Establishment or Amending G.R.O's will be forwarded by Commanders of all units through the usual channels to reach these Headquarters not later than Feby 13th (this certificate will be forwarded so as to reach this office by 9.0.a.m.Feb 12th)
It should be noted that certificate to the above effect has to be rendered to XXII Corps by the G.O.C. on behalf of the Division.

LORRIES. Lorries will call at D.R.S.Waratah Camp to pick up Trench Foot cases.

D.H.Q.
5.2.18.

(Sgd) H.S.Faulkner,
Colonel. A.D.M.S.
66th Division.

SECRET. *Appendix No. V* Copy No.12.

Copy in so far as it affects 2/3rd Field Ambulance.
----

199 Infantry Brigade
ADMINISTRATIVE ORDER
No. 37.

Ref MAP Sheet 27 - 28.

Administrative instructions issued with reference to 199th Infantry Brigade Operation Order No. 80.

BILLETS. (a) The 2/3rd Field Ambulance will be billeted as shown below:-

Night 9/10th Feb.

Unit.	Billets.	Transport. Q.M.Stores.
2/3rd Fld Amb.	WARATAH CAMP.	Stands fast.

Night 10/11th Feb.

-do-	WARATAH CAMP.	Stands fast.

Night 11/12th Feb.

-do-	SCHOOL CAMP.	L. 3. d.

BILLETING PARTIES. (c) Rear Parties (including an officer) will in all cases be left behind to clean up camps and transport lines, and a signed statement will invariably be obtained from Area Commandants concerned to the effect that the camp has been left in a satisfactory condition.
Particular attention is to be paid to the incineration of all refuse.

(e) Billeting Parties consisting of 1 Officer 1 O.R. and 3 cyclists per unit for the School Camp L.3.d. will report to A/Stf Captain at 8.0.a.m. on the 10th at Reserve Brigade H.Q.,H.19.b.2.3. WINNIPEG CAMP. Rations will be carried for 11th.

SUPPLIES.
Arrangements during move will be as under.

Date.	Unit.	Refills.	For Consumption.	Remarks.
Feb. 9th.	2/3rd Fd.Amb.	1.0.p.m.	11th.	as at present.
Feb. 11th.	do	10.0.a.m.	12th.	Drawn from Refilling point School Camp by units own transport & daily thereafter.

Locations of Refilling point new area will be notified to units later.

MEDICAL. The 2/3rd Field Ambulance will be at SCHOOL CAMP.

(Sgd) J.S.Fox Captain
Staff Captain.
199th Infantry Brigade.

6th Feb, 1918.

SECRET. *Appendix VI* 66th Divn No.3902/7/Q.

Copy in so far as it affects 2/3rd Field Ambulance.

MOVE TO FIFTH ARMY AREA.

MOVES BY RAIL   **1.**   Units will proceed by rail in accordance with table issued under this office A.899 of 12.2.18
            Entraining Station for all units will be PROVEN.
            Detraining   "   "   "   "   "   " GUILLACOURT.
                                                        (15 miles E of AMIENS)

            Approximate length of journey 10 hours.
            All trains halt one hour for refreshment at TINCQUES.

INSTRUCTIONS WITH REGARD TO ENTRAINMENT.   **2.** (a) All trains consist of 1 Officers' carriage, 17 flat trucks, 30 covered trucks.
            Each flat truck will take an average of 4 axles.
            Each covered truck will take 6 H.D.horses, or 8 L.D. horses or mules, or 40 men.
            No personnel or stores will be allowed in the brake vans at each end of the train, or on the roofs of the trucks.
            No covered trucks are to be used for baggage or stores without the permission of the DIVISIONAL STAFF OFFICER superintending the entrainment.

NOTE.- 1.   Entraining parties will report to the R.T.O. at the entraining station 3 hours before the departure of the first train they are loading.

        2.   The officer in charge of each detraining party will report to the R.T.O. immediately on arrival at the detraining station.

              (c). All units other than infantry battalions will arrive complete at the entraining station three hours before the departure of the train.

              (d). A complete marching out state showing the numbers of men, horses, G.S, Limbered G.S, two wheeled carts, cycles, and truck load of surplus baggage, will be sent to the R.T.O. with the transport of every unit so that accommodation on the train can be checked by the R.T.O. at the beginning of the entraining.
              NOTE.- 1 truck load - 3 lorry loads.

              (e). Supply and baggage wagons will accompany their units in every case.

              (f). The entrainment of all units must be completed half an hour before the time of departure of the train.
              Detraining station must be cleared of all baggage transport and personnel $2\frac{1}{2}$ hours after arrival.

              (g). Breast ropes for horse trucks must be provided by units themselves; ropes for lashing vehicles on flat trucks will be provided by the R.T.O.

              (h). The Senior Office on the train will be responsible for the discipline of the troops and will picket both ends of the train at every stop to prevent troops leaving.

              (k). All doors of covered trucks and carriages on the right hand side of the train when on the main line will be kept closed.

              (l). Attention is called to S.S.544. "TRAINS MOVING WITH TROOPS" which has been circulated to Infantry Brigade Headquarters and Divisional Artillery.

BILLETING.   **3.**   On arrival the Division will occupy the PROYART Area. Billets are allotted as shown in para./3 of this Office A.899 of 13.2.18.

Contd (2).

LORRIES FOR BAGGAGE. 4. Lorries for conveyance of baggage to the entraining station will be detailed in accordance with the attached Table B.

Similar numbers of lorries will be detailed at the detraining station by the D.A.A.G.66th Division, from the pool of lorries at his disposal.

Loading and unloading of lorries will be carried out as expeditiously as possible and baggage must arrive at the entraining station three hours before the departure of the train and leave the detraining station 2½ hours after arrival.

In the new area lorries transporting baggage from the detraining station will not dump at individual billets.

Baggage will be dumped at one central Dump only in each village and lorries will return immediately to GUILLACOURT.

SUPPLIES. 5. The attached table A shows the Supply Arrangements for all units during the period of the move. Refilling points in the new area will be notified direct to units by the affiliated train company as soon as possible after arrival.

The S.S.O. or his representative will be found at GUILLAUCOURT Station from noon on the 15th inst until the morning of the 18th inst when Divisional Train Headquarters will be opened at HARBONNIERES.

MEDICAL. 7. Field Ambulances will be responsible for the collection and evacuation of sick from all units in their respective groups from the time of arrival in the new area.

As soon as possible after arrival in the new area the A.D.M.S. will arrange to open a Divisional Rest Station.

POST. 8. The Divisional Mail will be delivered in the present area for the last time on the 16th instant, and the postal lorries will proceed on that date to the new area with mails for units that depart on the 15th and 16th inst.

The Divisional Mail will be delivered in the PROYART area on and after the 17th and mails for units moving on and after that date will be detained at the Divisional Post Office until their arrival.

BATHS, ETC., 9. Arrangements with regard to Baths, Laundry, Canteens, Theatres, etc., in the PROYART Area will be notified later.

LEAVE. 10. Until further orders all leave vacancies will be via Boulogne as at present, and the present allotments will remain in force.

Units should arrange with the Area Commandants of their present areas to accommodate personnel proceeding on leave during the two days following the day of departure and such officers or men will proceed from POPERINGHE by the present leave train.

Care will be taken that men left behind in this manner are in possession of sufficient rations for their journey as well as of an advance of pay and the necessary certificates with regard to bathing, etc.

On arrival at GUILLAUCOURT Station O's.C.Units will ascertain leave arrangements from the Divisional Staff Officer, Superintending detrainment.

The Divisional Railhead Disbursing Officer will leave POPERINGHE on the morning of the 17th and travel with Divisional Headquarters.

AREA STORES. 11. All Area and Billet stores in charge of units in the present area will be collected together and handed over to the respective Area Commandants from whom receipts and certificates that camps and billets have been left in a satisfactory condition will be obtained.

REPORT OF LOCATIONS. 12. Detailed Location Lists will be forwarded to Brigade Headquarters as early as possible after arrival in the new area.

B.H.Q.
Feb 14th, 1918.

(Sgd) J.S.Fox, Captain.
Staff Captain
199th Infantry Brigade.

Appendix VII

Copy in so far as it effects 2/3rd East Lancs Field Ambulance.

SECRET.
197 INFANTRY BRIGADE
ADMINISTRATIVE ORDER NO.38.

Move of 199 Infantry Brigade Group (less 2/3rd Field Ambulance) from BERNES Area to the Line.

MEDICAL. 2/1st East Lancs Field Ambulance will attend sick of this Brigade until the 27th inst., when the 74th Field Ambulance will take over the sick until arrival of the 2/3rd Field Ambulance.

23.2.18.

(Sgd) J.S.Fox, Captain
Staff Captain.
199 Infantry Brigade.

Appendix XIII

Copy in so far as it affects 2/3rd East Lancs Field Ambulance.

SECRET.   OPERATION ORDER NO 42.
                        BY
            LIEUT COLONEL J.BRUCE. R.A.M.C.T.
            ACTING A.D.M.S. 66th DIVISION.

                                            23rd Feby 1918.

Reference Maps.   Sheets 62.d. 62.e. and 62.c. 1/40,000.

1.   The 66th Division will be transferred from the XIX Corps to the Cavalry Corps between the 24th Feby and 3rd March 1918 and will relieve 24th Division in the Line.

2.   Medical Arrangements for move.

   2/3rd East Lancs Field Ambulance.

      This Field Ambulance will move with the 197 Infantry Brigade Group from MARCELCAVE Sub- area on Feby 28th and will take over forward evacuation, the GAS TREATMENT CENTRE AND CENTRAL RECORDS OFFICE at BERNES and relieve the 73rd Field Ambulance.
      On arrival in the BERNES - HANCOURT Area the 2/3rd East Lancs Field Ambulance will move independently of their Brigade Group to the Sugar Factory BERNES. Advance Parties for the Gas Centre at BERNES, the A.D.S. at TEMPLEUX LE GUERRARD, Relay Posts, and evacuation from R.A.P's in the line to be sent in advance. Their strength and time of taking over to be arranged direct between O's.C.Field Ambulances concerned.
      Relief to be completed by noon on March 2nd.
      Two Daimler Ambulance Cars and one Ford will be sent in advance so that the drivers may make themselves thoroughly acquainted with the routes of evacuation.

3.   All Field Ambulance Commanders will get into touch with their affiliated Brigade Headquarters and ascertain the date and manner of their move.

4.   All necessary handing over certificates will be completed and forwarded to this office in due course.

5.   Completion of moves and map location will be reported to this office

6.   During movements of reliefs the sick of both Divisions from the line of march and from the Stageing Camp, 1½ Miles west of VILLERS CARBONNEL will be sent direct to CORPS REST STATION CAPPY or to D.R.S. DOINGT.

7.   A.D.M.S office will close at VILLERS BRETTONNEUX at 10.0.a.m. on March 3rd and re-open at MOBESCOURT FARM at the same hour.

                            (Sgd John Bruce.
                             Lieut Colonel,
                             A/A.D.M.S., 66th Division.

SECRET.   *Appendix IX*   3/76/K.2.

TO. O.C.
    2/3rd East Lancs Field Ambulance.

        Your unit will move with the 197 Infantry Brigade on the 28th Feby to the Staging Camp, 1 mile west of VILLERS CARBONNEL.
        On the 1st from Staging Camp to BERNES - HANCOURT Area.
        On the 2nd from BERNES - HANCOURT Area you will move independently of the Brigade to relieve the 73rd Field Ambulance.
        If agreeable to the Commander, 197 Infantry Brigade, you could move up to the Sugar Factory, BERNES, on the night of the 1st of March, making arrangements for the collection of the sick of the 197 Brigade who will stage in the BERNES - HANCOURT Area on the night of the 1st.

D.H.Q.
Feby 24th, 1918.
                                        (Sgd) John Bruce,
                                           Lieut- Colonel,
                                        A/A.D.M.S. 66th Division.

Appendix X

Copy in so far as it affects 2/3rd East Lancs Field Ambulance.

SECRET.   197 INFANTRY BRIGADE OPERATION ORDER NO 75.

Map Reference ROSIERES Combined Sheet 2/40000.
Sheet 62.c. .... 1/40,000.

26th Feb, 1918.

1. INTENTION.

The 66th Division will be transferred from the XIX Corps to the Cavalry Corps between the 24th Feby and the 3rd March and will relieve the 24th Division in the line.

2. DISPOSITION.

1. The 24th Division is the left Division in the line of the Cavalry Corps and holds the front of 4500 yards just east of HARGICOURT - VILLERET.
2. The Divisional front will be held with 3 Brigades in the line each on a one battalion front.

4. AMBULANCES.

The 2/3rd East Lancs Field Ambulance will move with the 197 Infantry Brigade Group and will take over forward evacuation relieving the 73rd Field Ambulance, at BERNES.

6. BAGGAGE WAGONS AND LORRIES.

Baggage wagons will report to units at 2.30.p.m. on 27th inst and will remain with units throughout the move.

Lorries for conveyance of baggage are allotted as under:-

2/3rd East Lancs Field Ambulance...... 1

To report to Brigade Headquarters at 6.0.a.m. 28th inst.
Units will send guide at that hour to conduct lorries to their Headquarters.

7. CLEANLINESS OF BILLETS.

Units will obtain a certificate that billets have been left clean, also that there are no claims for damage before leaving areas and copies of certificates will be forwarded to Brigade Headquarters.

11. ARRIVAL IN CAMP.

Units will notify to this Office their arrival in Camp.

Issued at 6.30.a.m.   (Sgd) J.M.Monk, Major.
                                              Brigade Major,
                                          197 Infantry Brigade.

TABLE "A" TO ACCOMPANY 197 INFANTRY BRIGADE OPERATION ORDER NO 75.

MARCH TABLE, FEBRUARY 28TH.

Unit.	From.	Starting Point.	Time.	Route.	Remarks.
2/3rd East Lancs Fld Amb.	HARBONNIERES.	Road Junction. W.11.B.6.7.	11.34.a.m.	Road Junction. Q.30.D.85.25.- as for 2/8th Lancs Fusiliers.	To follow 542 Coy, A.S.C. from Q.30.D.85.2

N.B.   2.   The Brigade Group will halt at 12.50.p.m. until 2.0.p.m. for dinner.

TABLE B.

L O R R I E S.

1. 11 Lorries to report at Brigade Headquarters, School Camp, L.3.d.2.8. (Sheet 27) at 4.0.p.m. February the 16th, are allotted as under:-

   Field Ambulance............. 1.

SECRET.

TABLE "G" (to accompany 199 Infantry Brigade Order No.80.)

March Table for February 11th, 1918.

Units in order of march.	From.	To.	Time at Bde starting point X roads G.6.d.5.1.	Subsidiary Starting Point.	Time.	Route.	Remarks.
2/3rd Field Amb.	WARATAH CAMP.	SCHOOL CAMP. L.3.d. (Sheet 27)	-	-	-		To proceed independently to arrive School Camp 1.0.p.m. after remainder of Brigade.

Vol 13

160/2900

COMMITTEE FOR THE
~~CAL HISTORY~~ ~~THE WAR~~
Date 6 JUN 1918

Vol II

From March 1st 1918 to March 31st 1918

2/3rd EAST LANCASHIRE FIELD AMBULANCE.

War Diary
of

Confidential

WAR DIARY

~~INTELLIGENCE SUMMARY~~ (Erase heading not required.)

2/3rd EAST LANCASHIRE FIELD AMBULANCE.

Army Form C. 2118.

In the field

Place	Date	Hour	Summary of Events and Information	Remarks and references to Appendices
BERNES	MARCH 1st, 1918		Unit moved from staging camp, Villen Carbonnel, at 8.30 a.m. proceeded to BERNES (Map Ref. Sheet 62 c Q 4 a 0.5") arriving at 3.30 p.m. relieving 43rd Field Ambce. Accommodation of Division Station 14 Officers - 86 O.R. comes a 8 a Centre 34 patients taken over from 1/3rd Field Ambulance. The unit also took over Templeux Advanced Dressing Station (Sheet 62 c L 2 c 9.6) the following bearer posts run from A.D.S. TEMPLEUX taken over The IGG L11 b 3.4 LEAVE TRAIN L11 b 2.9 HUSSAR ROAD F 22 d 9.5 HARGICOURT L5 c 7.6 HARDY BANK F 28 a 2.2 Sheet 62.c	S.W.E.
"	MARCH 2nd		5 DAIMLER motor ambulances reported for duty from 2/1st East Lancs. Field Ambulance 1 Daimler from No 16 M.A.C. 1 Ford " " 2/2nd East Lancashire Field Ambulance	S.W.E.
"	MARCH 3rd		1 Ford Ambulance with driver and orderly reported unit from 2/2nd 230th Bde R.F.A. 3 O.R. reported for duty from 2/1st East Lancs Field Ambulance 10 O.R. " " from 2/2nd " "	S.W.E.

WAR DIARY

INTELLIGENCE SUMMARY

2/3rd EAST LANCASHIRE FIELD AMBULANCE. In the field

Army Form C. 2118.

Place	Date	Hour	Summary of Events and Information	Remarks and references to Appendices
BERNES	4-3-18		D.D.M.S. XIX CORPS visited + inspected camp	EWR
do	9-3-18		No. 68399 Pte Major G. evacuated to C.C.S. No. 354,500 Pte Richardson rejoined unit from C.C.S.	EWR
do	10-3-18		1 Officer and 9 O.R. reported for duty from 2/2nd East Lancs Field Amb's. 2 Daimler motor Ambulances returned to 2/1st East Lancs Field Amb's. Captain W.M. Doheny + batman reported back to unit from 330 Bde R.F.A.	EWR
do	11-3-18		JEANCOURT A.D.S. taken on from 1st Cavalry Field Ambulance. 2 Daimler motor Ambulances with drivers and orderlies reported for duty from 2/2nd East Lancs Field Ambulance.	EWR
do	12-3-18		Captain R.G. Weir + batman reported for duty from 2/5th Batt'n "Kings" Fusiliers	EWR
do	13-3-18		No. 472 034 Pte Haven J & 7 evacuated to hospital and other off struck off. 2 Brit horse drawn motor Ambulance.	EWR
do	15-3-18		Captain J.C. Ruddiffe aspirant 2/1st East Lancs Field Ambulance. Captain W.M. Doheny + 2 O.R. proceeded to Cavalry Corps Gas School.	EWR
do	16-3-18		Capt R.G. Weir was to No 34 C.C.S. for duty. Capt R.C.C. Smith admitted to 4 fld Amb Convalescent Depot. Capt W.E. Knight & 1 O.R. reported for duty from 2/2nd East Lancs Field Ambulance. One Daimler motor Ambulance returned from 24th Division.	EWR

Army Form C. 2118.

WAR DIARY

INTELLIGENCE SUMMARY

(Erase heading not required.)

Instructions regarding War Diaries and Intelligence
Summaries are contained in F.S. Regs., Part II.
and the Staff Manual respectively. Title pages
will be prepared in manuscript. 2/3rd EAST LANCASHIRE FIELD AMBULANCE.

Place	Date	Hour	Summary of Events and Information	Remarks and references to Appendices
BERNES	18.3.18		2 O.R. reported from 430 Field Coy R.E. and other O.R. strength 1 Sergeant & 81 O.R. reported from 2/2nd East Lancs. Field Ambulance. 26 O.R. reported returned to 2/2nd East Lancs. Field Ambulance. 4 O.R. reported from 492nd Field Ambulance.	SR
BERNES	21/3/18	6.10 am	Order received from A.D.M.S. 66th Division "Prepare for battle". This was passed on to Officers in charge of A.D.S.'s TEMPLEUX & JEANCOURT, & the personnel at other dressing stations were reinforced. In addition twenty bearers were sent from 2/2nd East Lancs Field Ambulance to A.D.S. TEMPLEUX. Preparations were made to receive wounded & the Gas Centre was opened up. Walking Wounded Collecting Post was opened at MONTIGNY FARM under CAPT WHITE & CAPT BOUNDS, and was equipped with material stores & comforts.
		6.45 am	The casualties began to arrive shortly followed by battle casualties of all sorts, of which there was a steady stream of admissions throughout the day. These were mainly collected from HERVILLY HESBECOURT & from battery positions throughout the whole divisional area. The cars passing on the main Divisional Rotation were unarmed to the Corps Rest Station at DOINGT by horse ambulance.

Army Form C. 2118.

WAR DIARY

INTELLIGENCE SUMMARY.

(Erase heading not required.)

Instructions regarding War Diaries and Intelligence Summaries are contained in F. S. Regs., Part II. and the Staff Manual respectively. Title pages will be prepared in manuscript. 2/3rd EAST LANCASHIRE FIELD AMBULANCE.

In the field

Place	Date	Hour	Summary of Events and Information	Remarks and references to Appendices
BERNES	21-3-18		The neighbourhood of the A.D.S. TEMPLEUX was very heavily shelled and it was difficult to maintain communication with the posts in the forward area. Word from the M.O.'s attached to the 5th Border Regiment 1/4th East Lancashire Reg't and 2/5th East Lancs in Regiment fell back on TEMPLEUX A.D.S and the M.O.'s in charge of TEMPLEUX A.D.S opened up the Reserve A.D.S at the HESBECOURT - ROISEL-TEMPLEUX cross road. This was completed at 3.30 p.m. All equipment & medical stores were removed in two lorries. G.S wagons under Capt J.H. Reynolds Relays 1 stretcher bearers were left to maintain communication with TEMPLEUX. Later in the day the Advanced Dressing Station was withdrawn to a site in ROISEL recently vacated by the 2/2nd East Lancs Field Ambulance. From JEANCOURT A.D.S. all cars were evacuated by cars of the Field Ambulance direct to BERNES. This A.D.S. became untenable at 6.30 p.m and the M.O and personnel - with the bulk of the equipment was withdrawn to MONTIGNY FARM. where a new A.D.S was formed in conjunction with the Welbeck Wounded Post.	2

Army Form C. 2118.

WAR DIARY
INTELLIGENCE SUMMARY

(Erase heading not required.)

Instructions regarding War Diaries and Intelligence Summaries are contained in F.S. Regs., Part II. and the Staff Manual respectively. Title pages will be prepared in manuscript 2/3rd EAST LANCASHIRE FIELD AMBULANCE.

Place	Date	Hour	Summary of Events and Information	Remarks and references to Appendices
BERNES	21.3.18		Capt. Ashford R.A.M.C. att.d 66th Div. R.E. reported for duty. Capt. Spruson 2/6th Manch. Regt. reported to Officer in charge Walking Wounded Post for duty. 54 Officers of whom 6 were gassed cases were admitted during the day 969 O.R. 2498	3 W.D.
do	22.3.18		Casualties continued to be admitted. The first evacuations to C.C.S. were begun about 3 a.m. by M.A.C. cars & lorries obtained on urgent requisition from D.D.M.S. Corps. The A.D.S. and Walking Wounded Post had to be evacuated early in the morning the A.D.S. at ROISEL was rushed some hours later. At noon - all remaining casualties and an Advance party of the Field Ambulance were withdrawn to BEAUMETZ - one officer and 12 men were left behind to evacuate further admissions. About 3 p.m. the "pom" cars under shell fire were withdrawn with sheaves	
BEAUMETZ			to HANCOURT. All remaining casualties were evacuated by Motor Ambulance Cars to C.C.S.	

Army Form C. 2118.

WAR DIARY
INTELLIGENCE SUMMARY.
(Erase heading not required.)

Instructions regarding War Diaries and Intelligence Summaries are contained in F. S. Regs., Part II. and the Staff Manual respectively. Title pages will be prepared in manuscript. 2/3rd EAST LANCASHIRE FIELD AMBULANCE.

Place	Date	Hour	Summary of Events and Information	Remarks and references to Appendices
BEAUMETZ	22-3-18		By order of A.D.M.S. 66th Div'n the Field Ambulance was ordered to fall back on LE MESNIL-BRUNTEL. The parts at HANCOURT and BEAMETZ were taken over by the 3rd Field Ambulance of the 39th Cavalry Division. The Field Ambulance arrived at LE MESNIL about 8 p.m. & were accommodated in huts. No. of casualties admitted during the day — 46.	W.E.
LE MESNIL	23-3-18	10 a.m.	Orders received from A.D.M.S. 66th Division to retire to BARLEUX. Field Ambulance used transport provided by march route via BRIE and VILLERS CARBONNEL. The Headquarters of the Field Ambulance was established immediately West of the village and an Advanced Dressing Station in a quarry on the left hand side of the road between BARLEUX & the SOMME. Bearer posts were established on the main PERONNE road - between LA CHAPELETTE and ETERPIGNY, two posts in the right sector and on in the left sector.	
BARLEUX			All cases were evacuated from the A.D.S. to the Headquarters of the Field Ambulance, which had now moved to ASSEVILLERS	

Army Form C. 2118.

WAR DIARY

INTELLIGENCE SUMMARY.

9a/the Field
2/3rd EAST LANCASHIRE FIELD AMBULANCE

Instructions regarding War Diaries and Intelligence
Summaries are contained in F. S. Regs., Part II.
and the Staff Manual respectively. Title pages
will be prepared in manuscript.

Place	Date	Hour	Summary of Events and Information	Remarks and references to Appendices
ASSEVILLERS	25.3.18	6.pm	The A.D.S. in the quarry was moved back to a broken down house in the East side of BARLEUX known as the "Reuter's Shop" Relay posts were established on the road to the Somme. No of cases evacuated during the day — 224.	JMc.
do	26.3.18		During the night the 66th Division moved to form northwards 2,000 yards and a new line was established S.W. of the village of BIACHES and behind the 3rd Can. post. From this evacuation was executed direct to ASSEVILLERS from LA CHAPELETTE. Casualties were evacuated by lorries to the A.D.S. at BARLEUX, then by motor ambulance to ASSEVILLERS	
		4.pm	The BARLEUX A.D.S. came under a very heavy barrage. The personnel were withdrawn to ASSEVILLERS. A mean post was established in BARLEUX with relay posts between BARLEUX and ASSEVILLERS. No. of casualties admitted during the day — 231.	JMc.
CHUIGNES	5.3.18		During the night the Headquarters of the Field Ambulance withdrew to CHUIGNES. Bearer posts were established at ASSEVILLERS and HERBECOURT with a relay post at BELQUINCOURT	

Army Form C. 2118.

WAR DIARY
INTELLIGENCE SUMMARY

(Erase heading not required.)

Instructions regarding War Diaries and Intelligence Summaries are contained in F. S. Regs., Part II. and the Staff Manual respectively. Title pages will be prepared in manuscript. 2/3rd EAST LANCASHIRE FIELD AMBULANCE. In the Field

6

Place	Date	Hour	Summary of Events and Information	Remarks and references to Appendices
THIEBAULT	25/3/18	10 a.m.	The Headquarters of the Field Ambulance were moved forward to a advanced Bivouac of War Cage Con. to the new position East of DOMPIERRE. Casualties admitted during the day Officers - 12 O.R. 219	W.
CHIPILLES	26/3/18	1 a.m.	Headquarters of Field Ambulance moved back to CHIPILLY-LES - the Bivouac of War Cage being maintained as an advanced Dressing Station	
		8 a.m.	Orders received from A.D.M.S. 66th Division to hand over the evacuation of wounded from the forward area to the 2/3rd East Lancashire Field Ambulance, placing at their disposal personnel and ambulance cars as was necessary.	
LA MOTTE		at 3 p.m.	The Field Ambulance marched by road to LA MOTTE arriving there during the evening. Personnel were accommodated in billets. No. of Casualties admitted = 42	W.
	27/3/18	6.30 a.m.	Instructions received from A.D.M.S. 66th Division to return to	

Army Form C. 2118.

WAR DIARY

INTELLIGENCE SUMMARY

(Erase heading not required.)

Instructions regarding War Diaries and Intelligence Summaries are contained in F. S. Regs., Part II. and the Staff Manual respectively. Title pages will be prepared in manuscript. 2/3rd EAST LANCASHIRE FIELD AMBULANCE.

In the Field

Place	Date	Hour	Summary of Events and Information	Remarks and references to Appendices
GENTELLES	28.3.18		GENTELLES. when they arrived in billets	WR
do	29.3.18	3 pm	Orders received from A.D.M.S. 66th Division to proceed to THENNES. From there to COTTENCHY via CASTEL. HAILES and to arrive at 10 p.m. & were accommodated from there to COTTENCHY	WR
COTTENCHY	30.3.18		DOMMARTIN The Field Ambulance was seen installed in COTTENCHY until MARCH 30th 1918	WR
			Orders received to move from COTTENCHY & BOUTILLERIE — The Field Ambulance arrived there at 6 pm & was billeted. CAPT. W.H.N. WHITE evacuated to C.C.S. — wounded. 23 O.R. (2/3 East Lancs Field Ambulance) missing since 21/3/18.	WR
BOUTILLERIE	1.4.18		The Field Ambulance was ordered to move to PONT. DE. METZ arriving there at 12.30 a.m. on April 1st 1918.	WR W. Holt RMC OC 2/3 E. Lancs 3 Fd Ambs

Confidential

War Diary

of

2/3rd EAST LANCASHIRE FIELD AMBULANCE.

From April 1st to April 30th 1918

WAR DIARY
INTELLIGENCE SUMMARY.

In the Field

Army Form C. 2118.

Place	Date	Hour	Summary of Events and Information	Remarks and references to Appendices
PONT DE METZ	April 1st 1918		Capt. W M Dolan proceeded on Officer in medical charge to 2/1/4 Battalion French Regt and taken up the strength of this unit Capt A W Berry proceeded on Officer in medical charge for Temporary duty to 2/5th Batt Manchester Regt	Au61
"	April 2nd 1918	6:30 pm	Evacuated PONT DE METZ and proceeded by march to FLUY arriving at 9:45 pm	Au61
FLUY	April 3rd 1918	7:30 am	Lieut M.A. Fealy MORC USA reported for duty and was attached to SOLEUX dining at 6 pm — then marching by way of LONG & AILLY LE HAUT CLOCHER arriving in billets at 8 pm.	Au61 Au61
AILLY LE HAUT CLOCHER	April 4th 1918		Capt R.S. Weir reported and from No 34 CCS & proceeded on Officer in medical charge of 336th Brigade R.F.A. and taken up the strength of the unit No other rank casualties sick to C.C.S. taken up the strength of the unit	Au61

WAR DIARY or INTELLIGENCE SUMMARY

Army Form C. 2118.

(Erase heading not required.)

Place	Date	Hour	Summary of Events and Information	Remarks and references to Appendices
AILLY-LE-HAUT CLOCHER	April 1918		Capt A.W. Perry rejoined unit from 2/5th Batt. "Manchester Regt." and taken on the strength of the unit	Ref 3
		9 a.m.	Evacuated AILLY LE HAUT CLOCHER and proceeded to NEVILLE arriving at 11 p.m.	Ref 4
			The Brigadier General 199th Infantry Brigade inspected the unit en route	Ref 4
NEVILLE	6th May		On other ranks rejoined unit from C.C.S. and taken on the strength	Ref 4
CANDAS	1st [April]		Evacuated NEVILLE at 9.15 a.m. and arrived at CANDAS 4 p.m. Six other ranks rejoined unit from C.C.S. and taken on the strength	Ref 4
do	do		16 Other ranks evacuated to C.C.S. and taken off strength	Ref 4
DRUCAT	April 10th	9 a.m.	Unit moved from CANDAS by march route to DRUCAT arriving at 4 p.m.	Ref 3
			One other rank evacuated to C.C.S. and taken off strength	Ref 4

Army Form C. 2118.

WAR DIARY
or
INTELLIGENCE SUMMARY.

(Erase heading not required.)

Instructions regarding War Diaries and Intelligence Summaries are contained in F. S. Regs., Part II. and the Staff Manual respectively. Title pages will be prepared in manuscript.

Place	Date	Hour	Summary of Events and Information	Remarks and references to Appendices
BRUAY	April 13th		One Ford Ambulance and one Motor Cycle with driver attached to Offr i/c A.D.M.S. 66th Division	Duty
do	April 14th		One Other rank evacuated to C.C.S. and taken off the Strength	duty
do	April 15th		Capt A.W. Berry and 10 other ranks together with 2 Daimler Motor Ambulances proceeded for temporary duty to open a Sick Collecting Station at HUCHENVILLE under orders of XIX Corps. Two other ranks vaccinated to C.C.S. and taken off the Strength. One other rank of attached Motor Convoy returned to his company and taken off the strength.	Duty
do	April 16th		Capt R.J. Chapman and 6 other ranks proceeded for duty to XIX Corps Baths HALLENCOURT & HUPPY.	Duty
do	April 17th		One other rank of attached Horse Transport returned to his company and taken off the strength	duty

2353 Wt. W2544/1434 700,000 5/15 D. D. & L. A.D.S.S./Form/C. 2118.

Army Form C. 2118.

WAR DIARY
or
INTELLIGENCE SUMMARY.

(Erase heading not required.)

Instructions regarding War Diaries and Intelligence Summaries are contained in F. S. Regs., Part II. and the Staff Manual respectively. Title pages will be prepared in manuscript.

Place	Date	Hour	Summary of Events and Information	Remarks and references to Appendices
BAVERS	April 20th 1918		The following appointments made: 354.2819 Cpl Churchill To be U/A/ Sergeant 354 244 S/Sgt Weel A.D. to be U/A/ Corporal 356 325 S/Cpl Whittaker A.D. to be U/A/Corporal 194768 Private Newman to be U/A/ R/Cpl Horse 354 220 Private G. A. David " do 354 290 " Jederly R.W. " do 354 333 " Shaw G.H. " do 354 494 " Hudston H. " do 354 690 " Solater J. " do One other rank. Horse transport reported for duty and taken on the strength. Capt A.W. Perry reported from Sick Collecting Post XIV Corps and attached by him M.A. (Motor Ambulance Convoy) reported for duty and taken on the strength.	duty duty debt debt

Army Form C. 2118.

WAR DIARY
or
INTELLIGENCE SUMMARY.

(Erase heading not required.)

Instructions regarding War Diaries and Intelligence Summaries are contained in F.S. Regs., Part II. and the Staff Manual respectively. Title pages will be prepared in manuscript.

Place	Date	Hour	Summary of Events and Information	Remarks and references to Appendices
DRUCAT	April 22		No. 356709 v/A/Surgeon Markel promoted to rank A/Surgeon. No. 354054 S/Surgeon Dale G. awarded the Military Medal for gallantry on 21.3.18	
	April 23rd		Section DRUCAT at 7.45 pm proceeded by march rout to LONGPRE arriving at 2.5 am 23rd April 1918	
	April 23	12 noon	Detatched in LONGPRE arrived in WIZERNES at 12 noon. Now billetted at ETREHEM. Whole Ambulance Convoy proceeded from DRUCAT & ETREHEM by motor	
ETREHEM				
VIEIL MOUTIER	April 26		Evacuated ETREHEM at 9.30 a.m proceeded to VIEIL-MOUTIER arriving at 5 pm	
	April 29		Lieut M A Gosden, M.O.R.C. U.S.A. no. 3 other ranks reported for duty from XIX Corps Field Collecting Station	

Army Form C. 2118.

WAR DIARY
or
INTELLIGENCE SUMMARY.   In the Field.
(Erase heading not required.)

Place	Date	Hour	Summary of Events and Information	Remarks and references to Appendices
VIEIL MAISNIL	28th April		Hon. Capt. and Q.M. J.H. Brooks awarded the Military Cross for gallantry on 21-3-18	ref.
	30th April 1918		Capt. A.W. Berry proceeded to A.D.M.S. 6th Division for duty	ref.
			Lieut. M.A. Crosby M.O.R.C. U.S.A. proceeded to A.D.M.S. 33rd Division for duty	ref.

J. Watt Lt Col.
CO 1/3 2 Lancs Fd Amb

Confidential

War Diary

of

2/3rd EAST LANCASHIRE FIELD AMBULANCE.

From May 1st to May 31st 1918

(Volume II)

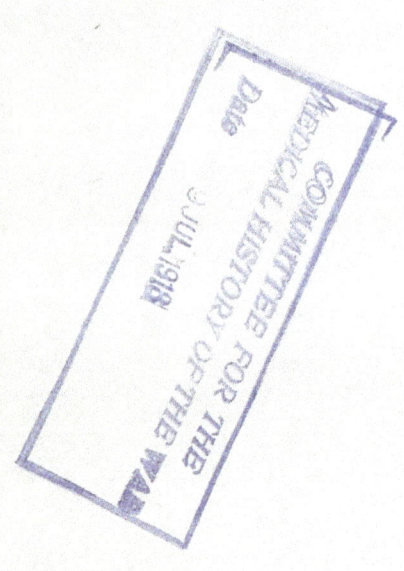

Army Form C. 2118.

Page 1.

WAR DIARY
INTELLIGENCE SUMMARY.
(Erase heading not required.)

Instructions regarding War Diaries and Intelligence Summaries are contained in F. S. Regs., Part II. and the Staff Manual respectively. Title pages will be prepared in manuscript.

Place	Date	Hour	Summary of Events and Information	Remarks and references to Appendices
Mobilisation	1915 May 1st	1 Day	Routine ordinary.	S.M.C
"	" 2nd	"	Routine ordinary.	S.M.C
VAUDRICOURT	" 3rd	"	The field ambulance entrained at Béenes at 4 A.M. & proceeded to NOYELLES, detraining at 10:30 A.M. The field marched to VAUDRICOURT, arriving in billets at 3:30 P.M. A divisional rest station was installed; fund for Divisional staff was taken from the division. The ambulance (nursing) which three field ambulances of the division passed at Vaudricourt in one convoy, reaching 17 other from R.S. at Vieil Moulin to billets in Vaudricourt.	S.M.C
"	" 4th	"	Routine ordinary.	S.M.C
"	" 5th	"	Routine ordinary.	S.M.C

Army Form C. 2118.

Page 2

WAR DIARY
or
INTELLIGENCE SUMMARY.
(Erase heading not required.)

Instructions regarding War Diaries and Intelligence Summaries are contained in F. S. Regs., Part II. and the Staff Manual respectively. Title pages will be prepared in manuscript.

Place	Date	Hour	Summary of Events and Information	Remarks and references to Appendices
VAUDRICOURT	1918. May 6	10 am	Routine O.D. in camp.	S.M.C
"	" 7	"	Routine O.D. in camp.	S.M.C
"	" 8	"	Two O.R. reported for duty from no. 544 Co. A.S.C.	S.M.C
"	" 9	"	2 O.R. proceeded to temporary staging camp at Eu for temporary duty with American personnel.	S.M.C
"	" 10	"	Routine O.D. in camp.	S.M.C
"	" 11	"	Routine O.D. in camp.	S.M.C
"	" 12	"	Routine O.D. in camp.	S.M.C
"	" 13	"	Routine O.D. in camp.	S.M.C

Army Form C. 2118.

Page 3

WAR DIARY
or
INTELLIGENCE SUMMARY.
(Erase heading not required.)

Instructions regarding War Diaries and Intelligence
Summaries are contained in F. S. Regs., Part II.
and the Staff Manual respectively. Title pages
will be prepared in manuscript.

Place	Date	Hour	Summary of Events and Information	Remarks and references to Appendices
VAUBRECOURT	1918 May 14	10 am	Routine Ordinary.	ME
"	" 15	"	Routine Ordinary.	ME
"	" 16	"	Routine Ordinary.	ME
"	" 17	"	Captain W.Y. MARTIN, R.A.M.C. (T.F.) reported for duty from 19th Infantry Brigade.	
"	" 18	"	Routine as usual.	ME
"	"	"	Routine Ordinary.	ME
"	" 19	"	Routine Ordinary.	ME
"	" 20	"	Routine Ordinary.	ME
"	" 21	"	Routine Ordinary.	ME

2353 Wt. W2544/1454 700,000 5/15 D. D. & L. A.D.S.S./Form/C. 2118.

Army Form C. 2118.

PSY4

WAR DIARY
or
INTELLIGENCE SUMMARY.
(Erase heading not required.)

Instructions regarding War Diaries and Intelligence Summaries are contained in F. S. Regs., Part II. and the Staff Manual respectively. Title pages will be prepared in manuscript.

Place	Date	Hour	Summary of Events and Information	Remarks and references to Appendices
Vandricourt	May 22	10 am	Routine Ordinary.	s/MC
"	23	"	Routine Ordinary.	s/MC
"	24	"	Routine Ordinary.	s/MC
"	25	"	Major W.P. Jefferson proceeds to England on 14 days special leave. Capt(?)Heath proceeds to A.D.M.S. Office for temporary duty.	
"	26	"	Routine Ordinary.	s/MC
"	27	"	Routine Ordinary.	s/MC
"	28	"	Routine Ordinary.	s/MC

2353 Wt. W2514/1454 700,000 5/15 D.D.& L. A.D.S.S./Forms/C. 2118.

Army Form C. 2118.

Page 5.

WAR DIARY
INTELLIGENCE SUMMARY.
(Erase heading not required.)

Place	Date	Hour	Summary of Events and Information	Remarks and references to Appendices
Hautrictourt	1918 May 29	10am	Routine O.D in camp.	SMO
"	30	"	Routine O.D in camp.	SMO
"	31	"	Routine O.D in camp.	SMO
			Hospital Statistics for month of May:—	
			Off. O.R.	
			No. of patients admitted 7 124	
			" " discharged to duty - 83	
			" " Evacuated to C.C.S. 7 15	
			average number of patients in D.R.S. for month of May	
			= O.R 36	

CONFIDENTIAL

WAR DIARY.

OF

2/3rd EAST LANCASHIRE FIELD AMBULANCE.

From June 1st to June 30th 1918

(Volume 2)

Army Form C. 2118.

Instructions regarding War Diaries and Intelligence
Summaries are contained in F. S. Regs., Part II.
and the Staff Manual respectively. Title pages
will be prepared in manuscript.

WAR DIARY
or
INTELLIGENCE SUMMARY.

2/3rd East Lanc. Field Ambulance
In the Field

(Erase heading not required.)

Place	Date	Hour	Summary of Events and Information	Remarks and references to Appendices
VAUDRICOURT	JUNE 1st		Map Ref Abbeville Sheet 14 1/1,000,000	Auth
OCHANCOURT	JUNE 3rd		Unit moved from VAUDRICOURT to OCHANCOURT (Map.Ref Sheet 14 (Abbeville) 1/1000) arriving in billets at 4 p.m.	Auth
			(a) O.R. evacuated to C.C.S. return off strength	
"	June 6th		3.54.2.10 AP/Cpl. Helling went & posted to Headquarters 66th Division	Auth
"	June 8th		3 Horse transport men & 3 G.S. wagons & 6 M.D. horses delivered for temporary duty to Emptoize Coy A.S.C.	Auth
			(a) O.R. returned unit from temporary duty with 198th Infantry Brigade	
			(a) O.R. with Motor Cycle returned unit from temporary duty with A.D.M.S. 66th Div	
"	June 9th 9 a.m		Major W.P. Ferguson reported for duty on return from leave	Auth
"	June 13th		two O.R.s Daimler Motor Ambulance wagon reported unit from Company duty at American Stationary Camp.	Auth

WAR DIARY
or
INTELLIGENCE SUMMARY.

(Erase heading not required.)

In the field

Army Form C. 2118.

Place	Date	Hour	Summary of Events and Information	Remarks and references to Appendices
CHARLOURT	June 14th 1918		One O.R. A.S.C. attached, evacuated to C.C.S. & struck off strength of unit.	
do	June 16th 1918		One Ford Car & driver attached to office of A.D.M.S. 66th Division for duty.	
PIERRÉGOT	June 21/18		Unit proceeded by motor lorries at 10 a.m. to PIERRÉGOT (Map Ref Sheet 11 lens 1/100000) arriving 5 pm. Horse transport moved separately arriving at 4 pm 22=6=18. Baths taken en route.	
			One O.R. (wireman) reported from strength.	
			One ambulance wagon (motor) + driver from 10th M.A.C. reported for duty.	
do	June 22nd		Major W.P. Harpur called as Liaison Officer to Divisional Surgeon, 33rd American Division.	

WAR DIARY
INTELLIGENCE SUMMARY

Army Form C. 2118.

Place	Date	Hour	Summary of Events and Information	Remarks and references to Appendices
PIERREGOT	Jun 25	11/8	Course of instruction by Lieut Col. E.H. COX. O/C. 2/3rd Eastern ca. Field Ambulance to medical officers of 131st & 132nd American Infantry Brigade, begun, and 48 men of Sanitary Detachment.	auft
"	June 26		Routine Ordinary. Training of American Troops	S.M.C.
"	" 27		Routine Ordinary	S.M.C
	" 28		"	S.M.C
	" 29		Routine Ordinary	S.M.C
	" 30		Routine Ordinary	S.M.C

S.Nisbet.McDonnel
Lt.Col. Comdg.
2/3 E.C.F.Amb.

War Diary
of
2/3rd East Lancs Field Amb

From July 1st to July 31st 1918

(Volumn 2)

July 1918

Army Form C. 2118.

Map ref: Lens, Sheet 11. 1/100,000.

WAR DIARY
or
INTELLIGENCE SUMMARY.
(Erase heading not required.)

Page 1.

Instructions regarding War Diaries and Intelligence Summaries are contained in F. S. Regs., Part II. and the Staff Manual respectively. Title pages will be prepared in manuscript.

Place	Date	Hour	Summary of Events and Information	Remarks and references to Appendices
Pirregot	1916 Feb 1st		Training of American Provisional Field Ambulance (they 66th American Field Ambulance) carried out. 8am. to 12 noon and 2 to 4 p.m. Training supervised by American medical Officers. Officers of Field Ambulance receive two lectures daily from Officers (newcomming 2/Lt S. Lewis 20 Feb.)	See.
	" 2		Routine ordinary - training ordinary.	See.
	" 3		Routine ordinary – do.	See.
	" 4		Routine ordinary – do.	See.
	" 5		Routine ordinary – do.	See.
	" 6		Routine ordinary – do.	See.

Army Form C. 2118.

WAR DIARY
INTELLIGENCE SUMMARY.
(Erase heading not required.)

Instructions regarding War Diaries and Intelligence Summaries are contained in F. S. Regs., Part II. and the Staff Manual respectively. Title pages will be prepared in manuscript.

Page 2.

Place	Date	Hour	Summary of Events and Information	Remarks and references to Appendices
Pierrefitte	1918 Feby 7	—	Routine ordinary. Training fresmen. Fld. amb. ordinary.	S/W
	" 8	—	Routine ordinary. do. do. do.	S/W
	" 9	—	Routine ordinary. — — —	S/W
	" 10	—	All equipment & stores, all horse wagons, all motor ambulance wagons, & all horse hauled over to the 130th Amer. Prov. Field ambulance, 33rd Amer. Div.	
			All hospital duties taken over by Amer. Field amb.	S/W
	" 11	—	Two "Training Cadres" formed & reported from personnel to Field ambulance. No: 1 cadre consisting of the following personnel — Lt. Commanding Quartermaster 7 Staff Sergts & Sergts. 15 O.R.s.	S/W

Army Form C. 2118.

Page 3.

WAR DIARY
INTELLIGENCE SUMMARY.
(Erase heading not required.)

Instructions regarding War Diaries and Intelligence Summaries are contained in F. S. Regs., Part II. and the Staff Manual respectively. Title pages will be prepared in manuscript.

Place	Date	Hour	Summary of Events and Information	Remarks and references to Appendices
Pierregot	1918 July 11	—	Routine Ordinary. 105 Other Ranks despatched to report Cyclists Base Depot, Rouen, to be held there intact pending further instructions from G.H.Q.	W.D.
	" 12	—	Routine Ordinary.	W.D.
	" 13	—	Routine Ordinary. Capt. Chapman, R.I., proceeded to No: 5 C.C.S. for temporary duty. D.A.D.M.S. Fourth Army.	W.D.
	" 14	—	Routine Ordinary.	W.D.
	" 15	—	Routine Ordinary. Capt. W.W.Y. Maurtin proceeded to 66th D.H.Q. for temporary duty.	W.D.
	" 16	—	Routine Ordinary. 3 O.R. proceeded to Cyclists Base Depot, Rouen.	W.D.

Army Form C. 2118.

p/c 4.

WAR DIARY

INTELLIGENCE SUMMARY

(Erase heading not required.)

Instructions regarding War Diaries and Intelligence Summaries are contained in F. S. Regs., Part II. and the Staff Manual respectively. Title pages will be prepared in manuscript.

Place	Date	Hour	Summary of Events and Information	Remarks and references to Appendices
Plenyft.	APR July 17	-	Routine Ordinary. Major W.P. Jerjuson, detached for temporary duty to 199th Inf. Brig. H.Q.	nil.
Pont Remy	" 19	-	The two training Cadres proceeded to Pont Remy in billets.	nil.
"	" 22	-	Routine Ordinary. Major W.P. Jerjuson rejoined unit from 199th Inf. Brig. H.Q.	nil.
"	" 25	-	Under instructions from Gen. S. Fourth Army, the two training Cadres attached for temporary duty to 41st Stationary Hospital.	nil.
"	" 27	-	Major W.P. Jerjuson proceeded from 41st Stationary Hosp. to No: 55 C.C.S. for temporary duty.	nil.

Army Form C. 2118.

Page 5

WAR DIARY
or
INTELLIGENCE SUMMARY.
(Erase heading not required.)

Place	Date	Hour	Summary of Events and Information	Remarks and references to Appendices
Port Remy	July 3rd 1918	—	14 Other Ranks proceeded from 41st Stationary Hospital to no: 12 C.C.S. for temporary duty.	

D.W.Wm. Lt Colonel.
O.C. 2/3rd 2nd Sanitary Sec.

Confidential

War Diary

of

2/3rd East Lancashire Field Ambulance.

from

1st August 1918 to
31st August 1918.

Volume II

WAR DIARY
INTELLIGENCE SUMMARY

Army Form C. 2118.
Page 1

Place	Date	Hour	Summary of Events and Information	Remarks and references to Appendices
Pont Remy (Somme)	1918 Aug 1		Map reference - Sheet 14 - Abbeville 1/100,000. The two "training Cadres" are on detached temp employment as follows:- 15 O.R. + 1 O.R. at No. 55 C.C.S. 1 " + 1 " " No. 5 C.C.S. 13 O.R. at No. 12 C.C.S. The remainder of Cadre at No. 41 Stationary Hospital.	
	Aug 28		This distribution remained until Aug 28. On this date all ranks, under instructions from D.M.S. Fourth Army, reassembled at No. 41 Stationary Hospital.	S/R
	Aug 30		Under instructions from D.G.M.S. through D.M.S. Fourth Army, the two training Cadres no	

D. D. & L., London, E.C.
(AF003) Wt. W1371/M2031 750,000 5/17 **Sch. 53** Forms C2118/4

Army Form C. 2118.

Page 2.

WAR DIARY
or
INTELLIGENCE SUMMARY.

(Erase heading not required.)

Place	Date	Hour	Summary of Events and Information	Remarks and references to Appendices
Port Henry	Aug 30		(cont.) proceeded to No. R.A.M.C. Base Depot at Etaples for disposal. The two cadres reported at 2.30 p.m.	see
	Aug. 31		The remaining personnel (R.A.M.C.) who were sent to No. Boys on July 11. 1916. were retaken on the strength of the unit. The unit is attached to the Depot for rations, accommodation & discipline.	

Ellis, Lieut.
O.C. No 3-31 (may?)
25 Army

Confidential

War Diary

of

2/3rd East Lancs Field Amb

from

Sep 1st to Sep 30th 1918

(Volume 2).

Army Form C. 2118.

WAR DIARY

2/3rd East Lancashire Field Ambulance

INTELLIGENCE SUMMARY

(Erase heading not required.)

page 1.

Place	Date	Hour	Summary of Events and Information	Remarks and references to Appendices
Étaples	1918 Sept. 1.		The Field Ambulance, consisting of R.A.M.C. personnel only, continues to be attached to the R.A.M.C. Base Depôt, Étaples, for rations & discipline — the unit remaining intact.	See
Abbeville	Sept 2nd	2.0pm	The Field Ambulance proceeded by train to ABBEVILLE.	App 91
	Sep/3rd		Equipment — consisting of medical & surgical stores, ordnance stores - horsed transport & 24 A.S.C. drivers supplied.	App 91
Grand Laviers			Unit proceeded to billets at GRAND LAVIERS (SOMME) by march route arriving at 6. p.m.	App 91
Prouville	Sep 24th		Unit rail from L of C. Field Ambulance proceeded by march route to PROUVILLE - starting at 2.30 pm & arriving billets at 10 pm (Lens Sheet 11 1/100,000)	App 91
Bouquemaison	Sep 25		Unit proceeded by march route to BOUQUEMAISON - arriving 5.30 pm (Lens Sheet 11 1/100,000)	App 91

Army Form C. 2118.

WAR DIARY
or
INTELLIGENCE SUMMARY.
(Erase heading not required.)

Instructions regarding War Diaries and Intelligence Summaries are contained in F. S. Regs., Part II. and the Staff Manual respectively. Title pages will be prepared in manuscript.

Place	Date 1918	Hour	Summary of Events and Information	Remarks and references to Appendices
IZEL-LÈS-HAMEAUX	Sept 26th	4pm	Unit proceeded by road route to IZEL-LÈS-HAMEAUX (Sheet 11. 1/100,000) - arriving at 6 p.m. 21 men joined the unit from 19th Infantry Brigade.	appx
	Sept 28th		11 A.S.C. M.T. men reported for duty	appx
		mid-day	15 Motor Ambulances & 2 Motor Cycles taken on charge of unit	
			Unit proceeded to TINQUES Station for entrainment to new area arriving at CORBIE at 8 p.m. (Amiens Sheet 1/100,000)	appx
CORBIE		mid-night		
PROYART	Sept 29th	5 pm	Unit proceeded by road route to PROYART - arriving in billets at 8 p.m. (Amiens Sheet 1/100,000)	appx

Wilson Lt Col.
O.C. 2/3 E. Lanc. Fd Amb.

Confidential

War Diary of

2/3rd EAST LANCASHIRE FIELD AMBULANCE.

Oct 1st to Oct. 31st 1918

(Volume 2).

WAR DIARY
or
INTELLIGENCE SUMMARY.

Army Form C. 2118.

2/3rd East Lancashire Field Ambulance In the Field

Place	Date	Hour	Summary of Events and Information	Remarks and references to Appendices
PROYART	OCT 3		The unit proceeded by march route to MARICOURT (Ref Sheet AMIENS 1/100,000 at 12.00 hours arriving in billets at 16.30 hours. A hospital to treat sick cases of the 199 Infantry Brigade was opened on the site of an old friendly Clearing Station.	W.63
MARICOURT	OCT 4		The unit proceeded by march route to MOISLAINS (Sheet 62c 1/40,000 C.18.c.33 arriving at 15.00 hours opening the sick of the 199 Infantry Brigade. A hospital to treat was opened in a large Nissen hut.	W.59
MOISLAINS			The Field Ambulance marched at 11.30 hours to TEMPLEUX-LA-FOSSE (Sheet 62c 1/40,000 D.22.c.03) arriving in billets at 13.45 hours	W.21
TEMPLEUX-LA-FOSSE	OCT 6		Major W. Martin + 20 O.R. proceeded to take over the Walhain Wounded Post at D.20.c. central (Sheet 62c) consisting of hospitals + marquees in a hospital for the treatment of the sick of the 66th Division	W.54

Army Form C. 2118.

WAR DIARY
or
INTELLIGENCE SUMMARY.

2/3rd East Lancashire Field Ambulance in the Field

(Erase heading not required.)

Place	Date	Hour	Summary of Events and Information	Remarks and references to Appendices
TEMPLEUX-LA-FOSSE	OCT 7		8 other ranks proceeded on stretcher bearer for temporary duty with the 9th Battalion Manchester Regiment. 6 O.R. similarly went to the 5th Battalion Connaught Rangers 6 O.R. similarly went to the 18th Battalion King's Liverpool Reg. Major R.J. Chapman & 66 O.R. proceeded for temporary duty as stretcher bearers with 1st South African field ambulance. One water cart, two large motor ambulances and three motor ambulances together with drivers and orderlies accompanied the party.	WM
	OCT 8		The unit proceeded by march route from TEMPLEUX-LA-FOSSE at 10.00 hrs. to RONSSOY (Sheet 62c 1/40000 F.20.B.25) arriving in camp at 13.25 hrs. 6 O.R. reported from R.A.M.C. Depot on return from leave. 6 O.R. proceeded to 66th Divisional Field Station for duty. MAJOR W.R. FERGUSON & 48 O.R. presumed as a stretcher bearer division for temporary duty with the 1st South African Field Ambulance.	WM
RONSSOY				

Army Form C. 2118.

WAR DIARY
or
INTELLIGENCE SUMMARY

2/3rd East Lancashire Field Ambulance

(Erase heading not required.)

Place	Date 1918	Hour	Summary of Events and Information	Remarks and references to Appendices
	OCT 9		The unit proceeded by march route from RONSSOY at 11.00 to camp at a point North of the main road between GOUY and BEAUREVOIR (Sheet 62c 1/40,000 B8 a 54) arriving at 14.30 hours.	W639
BEAUREVOIR	OCT 10		The unit moved by march route at 11.00 hours to SERAIN (Sheet 54l 1/40,000 V14 a 4.9.) arriving at 12.30 hours and a water cart reported unit from 30 C.R. Imperial African Field Ambulance.	W639
SERAIN	OCT 11		The following medical officers reported for duty. Lieut. J.J. Watson R.A.M.C. (S.R.) Lieut. J. Butterworth R.A.M.C. (T.C.) Lieut. R.L. Leighton M.O.R.C. U.S.A. Nos. 358 & 308 Pte. Richardson L. admitted to 66th Div. S.L. station suffering from Ja pneumonia (slight).	W639

WAR DIARY or INTELLIGENCE SUMMARY

Army Form C. 2118.

2/3rd East Lancashire Field Ambulance
in the Field

Place	Date	Hour	Summary of Events and Information	Remarks and references to Appendices
MARETZ	OCT 13		The unit moved by march route from SERAIN to MARETZ (Sheet 57c. 1/100000 V.1 & 16.D) at 10.00 hours arriving in billets at 14.15 hours. R.O.R rejoined unit from 2/2nd & 2nd Lancs Field Ambulance. Lieut J. Butterworth proceeded to 66th Divisional Rest Station for temporary duty. Number of patients admitted to 66th Div wounded Rest Station during the week = 312.	W67
	OCT 14		Major W.P. Stepman & Major R.J. Chapman rejoined unit from 2/2nd East Lancs. Field Ambulance.	W64
	OCT 15		The unit proceeded from MARETZ at 16.00 hours by march route to MAUROIS. (Sheet 57c. 1/100000 P22 & 56) arriving at Maulum	W14
MAUROIS			On arriving at MAUROIS the unit took over the Advanced	W67

Army Form C. 2118.

2/3rd East Lancashire Field Ambulance.
In the Field.

WAR DIARY
or
INTELLIGENCE SUMMARY.
(Erase heading not required.)

Instructions regarding War Diaries and Intelligence Summaries are contained in F. S. Regs., Part II. and the Staff Manual respectively. Title pages will be prepared in manuscript.

Place	Date	Hour	Summary of Events and Information	Remarks and references to Appendices
MAUROIS	1918 OCT 16th		Brewery Station. (situation is "easy" to the the sypress's in a hospital) – recently used by the 1st French African Field Ambulance. The unit became responsible for the evacuation of wounded from the forward area from 06.00 hours. We obtain from 2/1st East Lancs Field Amb. & 3 officers from 1st South African Field Amb. reported for temporary duty. One given Sub division (less equipment) from the 2/2nd East Lanc Field Amb. and 1 tent sub division from 1st South African Field Ambulance. reported for temporary duty. The Bearer Divisions, Motor Transport, & Horse ambulances of the 2/2nd East Lancs Field Amb. & 1st South African Field Amb. left came under control of this unit.	WM WM

Army Form C. 2118.

WAR DIARY
2/3rd Eastern
or
INTELLIGENCE SUMMARY.
Field Ambulance
(Erase heading not required.)

Place	Date	Hour	Summary of Events and Information	Remarks and references to Appendices
MAUROIS	OCT 16		Two route marches in town from the Convoy Corps came under orders of the unit	WM
	OCT 17		Pt. M. 954,243. Pte Wainwright W.R. evacuated to No 20 C.C.S. (S) No. 50,442 Pte Brompton to reporting to duty. "other non strength".	WM
	OCT 18		No. 354,519 Pte Willis H. Transferred to 2/1st East Lancs Field Amb. (sick) Lieut R.L. Teupter M.S.R.C. U.S.A. proceeded to Camp Hopetier No 52. A.E.F.	WM
	OCT 19		The following personal vehicles - re-reported 2/3rd East Lancs Field Amb. 2. Large Motor Ambulances. 3. Armed Ambulances. 1st O.R. The following reported to 1st South African Field Amb. 2. Large Motor Ambulances. 3. Horsed Ambulances. 1 G.P.R.	WM

WAR DIARY
or
INTELLIGENCE SUMMARY.
(Erase heading not required.)

Army Form C. 2118.

2/3rd Lowland Field Ambulance
In the Field

Place	Date	Hour	Summary of Events and Information	Remarks and references to Appendices
MAUROIS	Oct 19		1 O.R. reported for duty from 1st South African Field Amb.	inst.
			The Field Ambulance was called upon to treat & evacuate all Field sickness wounded & sick in LE CATEAU. 18 Cases were collected, treated & evacuated through XIII Corps M.D.S. to C.C.S. for disposal	
	Oct 20		Lieut J.S. Watson proceeded to duty as Medical Officer i/c 6th Battalion Royal Dublin Fusiliers. 5 travelled from LE CATEAU suffering from Gas Shell Poisoning were treated & evacuated to C.C.S. 1 O.R. admitted to hospital, sick & taken off the strength of the unit	left

Army Form C. 2118.

2/3rd East Lancashire Field Ambulance
In the Field

WAR DIARY
or
INTELLIGENCE SUMMARY
(Erase heading not required.)

Place	Date	Hour	Summary of Events and Information	Remarks and references to Appendices
MAVROS	OCT 1918 21		At 06.00 hours, the unit ceases to function as a Advanced Dressing Station. The title of the A.D.S. was this morning at - Corps main Dressing Station & the XIII corps a - Corps main Dressing Station & the unit took charge from 06.00 hours. The following personnel reported for duty 1 Officer & 1 O.R. from No. 54 Field Ambulance 1 " & 8 O.R. " No. 56 " 2 " & 6 O.R. from 2/2nd North'umbrian " 2 " 0. R. " 1/1st " " 2 " 0. R. Amb. 76. " 1 " 0. R. from No. 44 " 1 " 0. R. from No. 45 " 2 motor lorries & drivers from 2nd Cavalry Division requisition these until the remainder of the personnel attached to this unit from the 2/2nd East Lanc. Field Amb. & 1/1st North'umbrian Field Amb. - rejoined their units.	W.F.T.

WAR DIARY
INTELLIGENCE SUMMARY

Army Form C. 2118.

2/3rd East Lancs. Field Ambulance.
In the Field.

Place	Date	Hour	Summary of Events and Information	Remarks and references to Appendices
MAUROIS	Oct 21		2 O.R. returned to duty from R.A.M.C. Base Depot & taken on the strength.	
			28 wounded & gassed French civilians were treated & evacuated to C.C.S.	WM
	Oct 22		10 wounded & gassed French civilians were treated & evacuated to C.C.S.	WM
			3 O.R. reJoined unit from 66th Div: Rich Station	
	Oct 23		6 wounded & gassed French civilians were treated & evacuated to C.C.S. 2 O.R. posted to unit from L [paid] Corp. 66th Div: taken on the strength	WM
	Oct 24		Lieut J.T. Watson R.A.M.C (S.R.) taken off the strength of the unit. 15 wounded & gassed French civilians treated & evacuated to C.C.S.	WM
	Oct 25		Major General O'R FFFE D.M.S. 4th Army. inspected the C.M.D.S. at 12.30 hours.	WM

Army Form C. 2118.

WAR DIARY
or
INTELLIGENCE SUMMARY.
(Erase heading not required.)

2/1st Lanarkshire Field Amb.
by Lt. Col.

Place	Date	Hour	Summary of Events and Information	Remarks and references to Appendices
MAUROIS	Oct 25		The unit received a communication through the 66th Division from Brigadier General B.L. Williams, Commanding 199 Infantry Brigade thanking the unit for the prompt manner in which wounded were evacuated from the forward area during operations Oct 18-20 1918. 11 wounded but by own troops civilians were treated & evacuated to CCS & ambs.	copy
	Oct 26		do do do do Chas. of patients admitted for week ending 26th October 1918. Wounded 2, 194. Sick 443. Patients returned to duty 43. Wounded prisoners of war 16.2. ——— 3,132.	
	Oct 27		1 Ambulance Motor Ambulance driver reported for duty. 1 O.R. discharged from hospital & rejoined unit. 5 O.R. rejoined unit from 66th Div. Rest Station.	copy

WAR DIARY or INTELLIGENCE SUMMARY

Army Form C. 2118.

2/3rd East Lancashire Field Ambulance
In the Field

Place	Date 1918	Hour	Summary of Events and Information	Remarks and references to Appendices
MAUROIS	OCT 24		1 Officer & 10 P. rejoined No. 76 Field Ambulance. 8 "P.B" A.S.C men reported for duty men taken in through night. Any wounded drunk civilians evacuated to C.C.S.	W.O.Y
	OCT 31		The unit proceeded under orders 1 D.D.M.S XIII Corps to open a new Corps Main Dressing Station in LE CATEAU. The journey was completed at 11.30 hours. The new C.M.D.S was situated in a large factory - partially destroyed by fire & shell fire - & recently used by the Germans as a hospital. Within came 3 stabler care were established. One accommodation for wounded rank and files awaiting for a large number of wounded whilst awaiting evacuation.	W.O.Y

E.W.Wall
LIEUT. COLONEL, R.A.M.C. (T.F.),
COMMANDING
2/3rd EAST LANCS FIELD AMBULANCE.

Army Form C. 2118.

WAR DIARY
or
INTELLIGENCE SUMMARY.

(Erase heading not required.)

CONFIDENTIAL

WAR DIARY

of

2/2nd East Lancs Field Ambulance

VOL II

14
Army Form C. 2118.

War Diary
2/3 East Lancs Field Ambulance
November 1918.

WAR DIARY or INTELLIGENCE SUMMARY.
(Erase heading not required.)

Instructions regarding War Diaries and Intelligence Summaries are contained in F.S. Regs., Part II. and the Staff Manual respectively. Title pages will be prepared in manuscript.

Place	Date	Hour	Summary of Events and Information	Remarks and references to Appendices
LE CATEAU (Sheet 57b K 34 a & b)	Nov 1st		Unit functioned XIII Corps M.D.S. from 06.00. a side of all field duty. One O.R. returned unit from duty from XIII Corps Signal Exchange One O.R. returned from duty from Base Mechanical Transport 3 O.R. returned for temporary duty throughout Depot (N) 2 O.R. returned for temporary duty from 1/5 Field Ambulance 5 O.R. returned from temporary duty from No 55 Field Ambulance	W 3/4
	2nd		One O.R. returned unit from Hospital (2/2 East Lancs Fd Amb) 2 O.R. returned for temporary duty from No 56 Fd Ambulance 2 O.R. returned to 1/5 Fd Ambulance	W 4/4
	3rd		14 French Civilians (wounded & sick) treated & evacuated to C.C.S. Motor Ambulance received to A.D.M.S. 66 Division for temporary duty 10 O.R. reported for duty from Rouen Base Depot One Motor Cyclist received to A.D.M.S. 66 Division temporary duty The following personnel reported for duty: 2/1 Northumbrian Fd Ambulance 1 Officer, 16 other Ranks 1/2 " " " " 22 " " 1/1 " " " " 23 " " 1/2 " " " " " " 1/3 " " " " 19 " " R.E. 18th Division 1/2 Northumbrian Fd Amb. 1 " " " One Officer reported 2/2 Northumbrian Fd Ambulance	W 3/4

Army Form C. 2118.

War Diary
2/3rd South Lancs Field Ambulance
November 1915.

WAR DIARY
or
INTELLIGENCE SUMMARY.
(Erase heading not required.)

Instructions regarding War Diaries and Intelligence Summaries are contained in F. S. Regs. Part II. and the Staff Manual respectively. Title pages will be prepared in manuscript.

Place	Date	Hour	Summary of Events and Information	Remarks and references to Appendices
LE CATEAU (Sheet 54 b K34 a 83)	1st to 4th		During period 24 hours ending midnight these passed through 1st heads :— Wounded Officers 82, Other Ranks 1511. Sick Officers 7, Other Ranks 298. French Civilians ...	
	5th		53 Other Ranks detached to temporary duty with 1st South African Field Ambulance with Motor Transport and 3 Horse Ambulances. 1 Sergeant proceeded to 18/11/15 to 6 RE 66th Division for transport of Fathers twice in forward area. 1 Officer rejoined No 56 Field Ambulance.	W.J.H.
	6		The following reported for duty :— No 55 Field Ambulance 10 Other Ranks, No 56 „ „ 20 „ „ 2/2 N. Midland 111 Amb. 3 „ „	W.J.H.
	7th		One Other Rank admitted to Hospital (2/2 Sh Lancs Field Amb).	W.J.H.
	8		One O.R. rejoined unit from Hospital (2/2 South Lancs Field Amb).	W.J.H.
	9		No 354306 Pte Thornton J.W. sounded 2 c.c.s.	W.J.H.

War Diary
2/3 East Lancs Field Ambulance
3
16

Army Form C. 2118.

WAR DIARY
or
INTELLIGENCE SUMMARY.
(Erase heading not required.)

Instructions regarding War Diaries and Intelligence Summaries are contained in F. S. Regs., Part II. and the Staff Manual respectively. Title pages will be prepared in manuscript.

November 1915.

Place	Date	Hour	Summary of Events and Information	Remarks and references to Appendices
TAISNIERES (Shd. NAMUR)	Nov 9	14.00	Unit moved by hedge lorries etc to TAISNIERES arriving at 19.00. Transport moved by road arriving at 02.00 on 10th November 1915	W.911
ST HILAIRE SUR-HELPE	10th	10.00 12.00	Unit moved to ST HILAIRE-SUR-HELPE Unit detached ST HILAIRE	
(Shd. NAMUR)	11		9 other Ranks reported for duty from Base Mechanical Transport Depot Taken on strength of unit	W.912
	13		10 Ditto Ditto Base Mechanical Transport Depot Taken on strength of unit	3
SOLRE-LE-CHATEAU (Shd. NAMUR)	14	10.30 14.00	Unit moved by road to SOLRE-LE-CHATEAU Unit arrived at SOLRE-LE-CHATEAU 2nd O.R. (handed to Capt 207 A.S.C. for temporary duty	W.913 W.914
	15		Lieut P.A.Z. Stafford R.A.M.C.(T.C.) reported for duty, taken on strength (T.O)	
	16	14.00 15.00	Unit moved by march Route to MONTRLIART Unit arrived at MONTRLIART	
MONTRLIART	17		5 O.R. moved to 65th Divisional Reception Camp Lieut J. Buttersworth R.A.M.C (T.C.) proceeded to 331 Bde R.F.A. for duty and relieves of strength of unit	W.915 W.916

Army Form C. 2118.

WAR DIARY
or
INTELLIGENCE SUMMARY.
War Diary 2/3rd East Lancs Field Ambulance
November 1916

(Erase heading not required.)

Instructions regarding War Diaries and Intelligence Summaries are contained in F. S. Regs., Part II. and the Staff Manual respectively. Title pages will be prepared in manuscript.

Place	Date	Hour	Summary of Events and Information	Remarks and references to Appendices
MONTRLIART	Nov 18	07.30	Unit moved by Brigade march to CERFONTAINE	
		11.30	Unit arrived at CERFONTAINE	
CERFONTAINE			One O.R. reported for duty from C.R.E. 61st Division	1. yn
			5 Motor Ambulances, drivers and 1 motor cyclist reported for duty from No 30 M.A.C.	
	20		Capt A. C. Murray R.A.M.C. (T.F.) reported for duty from No 75 Field Ambulance and taken on strength	2. yn
			Lieut P. A. G. Shepherd joined 1/9th Bn Manchester Regt and taken off strength of this unit	
	21		Captain E. H. Coyne R.A.M.C.(T.F.) reported for duty from 9th Bn Manchester Regt and is taken on strength of this unit	3. yn
	22		Major W. P. Evison R.A.M.C.(T.F.) proceeded on leave to England	3. yn
	23		One O.R. attached to Headquarters 191st Infantry Bde for temporary duty	4. yn
			4 O.R's reported for duty from Base Mechanical Transport Depot and taken on strength	
			1 O.R. reported from Headquarters 66th Division	
MORVILLE	24	04.20	Unit moved by Brigade march to MORVILLE	4. yn
		17.00	Unit arrived at MORVILLE	

Army Form C. 2118.

WAR DIARY
or
INTELLIGENCE SUMMARY.

2/3 East Lancs Field Ambulance   November 1915

(Erase heading not required.)

Place	Date	Hour	Summary of Events and Information	Remarks and references to Appendices
MERVILLE	Nov 25th		One O.R. and Ford Motor Ambulance proceeded to Temporary duty with 9th RGA	W.34
	26		Captain G.C. Murray attached to 12 provisional Bn 1/0 1/6 18th Bn (L.H.Y.) Kings L'pool Regt No 254106 Capt Hollinworth proceeded to Army Remount Depot and returned Transfer Debit and return of Strength	W.34
	28		3 O.R's proceeded to Base Mechanical Transport Details 1st Aux Petrol Co Rouen	W.76
	29		One O.R. rejoined unit from Headquarters Royals	

W.J. Monk Lt/Col 29/11/15

for O.C. LIEUT. COLONEL R.A.M.C. T.F.,
COMMANDING
2/3RD EAST LANCS FIELD AMBULANCE.

Confidential

War Diary

of

2/3rd East Lancashire Field Ambulance

from

December 1st 1918

to

December 31st 1918

(Volume II)

WAR DIARY
INTELLIGENCE SUMMARY.
(Erase heading not required.)

Army Form C. 2118.

Page 1.

2/3RD EAST LANCASHIRE FIELD AMBULANCE.

Instructions regarding War Diaries and Intelligence Summaries are contained in F. S. Regs., Part II. and the Staff Manual respectively. Title pages will be prepared in manuscript.

Place	Date	Hour	Summary of Events and Information	Remarks and references to Appendices
Morville	1916 Dec. 1		Map reference: 8 Namur 1/100,000. I.4.9.8. Routine ordinary. Major W.J. Martin rejoined unit from temporary duty at D.D.M.S. 5th Army, 66 Div.	see
	Dec. 2		Routine ordinary.	see
	" 3		Routine ordinary. Captain & Qnr. J.H. Bowles evacuated sick to 20 C.C.S.	see
	" 4		Routine ordinary.	see
	" 5		Routine ordinary.	see
	" 6		Routine ordinary.	see
	" 7		Routine ordinary.	see

Army Form C. 2118.

Page 2.

WAR DIARY
INTELLIGENCE SUMMARY.
(Erase heading not required.)

Instructions regarding War Diaries and Intelligence Summaries are contained in F. S. Regs., Part II. and the Staff Manual respectively. Title pages will be prepared in manuscript.

Place	Date	Hour	Summary of Events and Information	Remarks and references to Appendices
Acheville	1916 Dec. 8.		Routine ordinary.	see
	" 9.		Routine ordinary.	see
	" 10.		Routine ordinary.	
			Horse Transport inspected by G.O.C. 199th Infantry Brigade.	
	" 11		Routine ordinary.	see
	" 12		Routine ordinary.	see
	" 13		Routine ordinary. Captain Owen J.A. Bownds rejoined from C.C.S.	see
			Field Ambulance moved by march route to Divicourt. Passed Starting Point at 9 p.m.	
			(cont.)	

WAR DIARY

INTELLIGENCE SUMMARY

Army Form C. 2118.

Page 3

Place	Date 1918	Hour	Summary of Events and Information	Remarks and references to Appendices
hierville	Dec. 13	(cont.)	G.O.C. Fourth Army inspected Field Ambulances on line of march. Prior billets in Dinant.	WC
Dinant	Dec. 14.		Field Ambulance moved by route to Champion arriving in billets at 2:30 p.m.	WC
Champion	"	15	Field Ambulance moved by route march to Huy on river Meuse, arriving in billets at 16:00 hours. Billets in Tihange, 1½ kilos east of Huy.	WC
Huy	"	16	Routine ordinary. Hospital for sick of 99th Infantry Brigade established in Tihange.	WC
"	"	17	Routine ordinary.	WC

Army Form C. 2118.

WAR DIARY
INTELLIGENCE SUMMARY.
(Erase heading not required.)

Instructions regarding War Diaries and Intelligence Summaries are contained in F. S. Regs., Part II. and the Staff Manual respectively. Title pages will be prepared in manuscript.

Page 4

Place	Date	Hour	Summary of Events and Information	Remarks and references to Appendices
Huy	1918 Dec 18		} Routine ordinary.	
	" 19			
	" 20			SDK
	" 21			
	" 22		Routine ordinary. 2 craftsmen & 1 lay service man proceed to X Corps concentration camp to disposal.	SDK
	" 23		} Routine ordinary.	SDK
	" 24			
	" 25			
	" 26		Routine ordinary. Captain A. E. Murray rejoined unit from 8th King's 1 post 2.	SDK
	" 27		} Routine ordinary.	
	" 28			
	" 29			
	" 30			
	" 31			

S.D.Kerr, Lt. Col.
o.c. 173rd Lt. Div. Amn. Sub. Park.

66th DIV
Box 3018

2/3RD EAST LANCASHIRE FIELD AMBULANCE

Confidential

War Diary — original

of

2/3rd East Lancashire Field Ambulance

from

1st Jany. 1919 to 31st Jany. 1919

(Volume III)

2/3RD
EAST LANCASHIRE
FIELD AMBULANCE

Army Form C. 2118.

WAR DIARY
or
INTELLIGENCE SUMMARY. 2/3rd Eastern Field Ambulance

Instructions regarding War Diaries and Intelligence Summaries are contained in F.S. Regs., Part II. and the Staff Manual respectively. Title pages in the field will be prepared in manuscript.

(Erase heading not required).

Place	Date 1919	Hour	Summary of Events and Information	Remarks and references to Appendices
HUY (LIEGE MAP)	JAN 1		Lieut Col F.H Cox awarded D.S.O Sergt Mayo E J W Langford awarded D.C.M London Gazette 1-1-19.	App4
	2		No O.R detached to 66th Divisional H.Q for temporary duty	App4
	3		Capt. R J Chapman proceeded on leave to England.	App4
	4		Capt. O.C. Murray proceeded to 84th Brigade R.G.A to duty, am taken off the strength.	App4
	6		Capt. E.H Bryan reported for duty on return from leave.	App4
	7		1 O.R proceeded to X Corps Conceal for disposal. 1 O.R taken on the strength	App4
	8		1 O.R demobilized at WIMBLEDON	App4
	10		1 O.R forwarded to No 49 Sanitary Section, BOSSOGNE for temporary duty	App4

Army Form C. 2118.

WAR DIARY
or
INTELLIGENCE SUMMARY. 2/3rd East Lanc. Field Ambulance
(Erase heading not required.)

Instructions regarding War Diaries and Intelligence Summaries are contained in F. S. Regs., Part II. and the Staff Manual respectively. Title pages will be prepared in manuscript. In the field

Place	Date	Hour	Summary of Events and Information	Remarks and references to Appendices
HUY S MEUSE	1916 JAN 11		4 O.R. proceeded to X Corps Concent. for dispersal	ap67
			1 O.R. rejoined unit from 66th D.H.Q	
	13		Unit transport inspected by Divisional Commander.	ap67
			6 O.R. proceeded to X Corps Concent. for dispersal to C.C.S. & taken off strength	
	14		1 O.R.	
			1 O.R. rejoined unit from 66th D.H.Q	ap67
			1 O.R. proceeded to 66 D.H.Q for temporary duty	
	16		7 O.R. proceeded to X Corps Concent for dispersal	ap67
			4 O.R. rejoined unit from M.	
	20		4 O.R. proceeded to V Corps Concent for dispersal	ap67
			1 O.R. rejoined unit from 66 D.H.Q.	
	22		1 O.R (A.S.C. M.T) evacuated to C.C.S. & taken off strength	ap67

Army Form C. 2118.

WAR DIARY
or
INTELLIGENCE SUMMARY.

(Erase heading not required.)

Instructions regarding War Diaries and Intelligence Summaries are contained in F. S. Regs., Part II. and the Staff Manual respectively. Title pages will be prepared in manuscript.

2/3rd East Lancashire Field Ambulance

Place	Date	Hour	Summary of Events and Information	Remarks and references to Appendices
HUY·S· MEUSE	1919 JAN 26		Lt Col E. H. Cox. proceeded to England on leave.	Aut?
	27.		1 O.R. rejoined unit from X Corps baths	Aut?
			Capt E. H. Cope detailed for temporary duty to 9th Batt. Gloucester Reg.	Aut?
	28		Capt R. J. Chapman & Capt J. H. Bowen reported for duty from leave in England	Aut?

W. G. Ferguson Maj. R.A.M.C.
OC 2/3rd EAST LANCASHIRE FIELD AMBULANCE.

Army Form C. 2118

WAR DIARY
or
INTELLIGENCE SUMMARY.
(Erase heading not required.)

Place	Date	Hour	Summary of Events and Information	Remarks and references to Appendices

Wor Diary — returned

21/3 Sent home

Field Marshal

28 February 1919

WO 95 III

Army Form C. 2118.

2/3RD EAST LANCASHIRE FIELD AMBULANCE

Page 1.

WAR DIARY
INTELLIGENCE SUMMARY.
(Erase heading not required.)

Instructions regarding War Diaries and Intelligence Summaries are contained in F.S. Regs., Part II. and the Staff Manual respectively. Title pages will be prepared in manuscript.

Place	Date	Hour	Summary of Events and Information	Remarks and references to Appendices
Hny.	1919 Feb. 1.		Help reference march 1/100,000 sheet no: 9. 1 O.R. proceeds to 14th. Bn. R.F.A. for temporary duty.	rile
	" 2.		Ordinary Routine.	rile
	" 3.		Ordinary Routine. Capt. E.M. Coyne M.C., reports for duty from 9th. Batt. Gloucester Reg.	rile
	" 4.		Ordinary Routine. Capt. R.J. Chapman proceeds to Reception Hospital Liney for temporary duty.	rile
	" 5.		Ordinary Routine. 18 O.Rs. proceed to 66th. Fd. Reception Hospital Liney for temporary duty.	rile
	" 6.		Ordinary Routine.	rile
	" 7.		Ordinary Routine. 4 O.Rs. R.Trave proceed to concentration Camp for dispersal.	rile
	" 8.		Ordinary Routine. 1 O.R. R.D.S.S. proceed to concentration Camp for dispersal.	rile

Army Form C. 2118.

2/3RD
EAST LANCASHIRE
FIELD AMBULANCE.

WAR DIARY
INTELLIGENCE SUMMARY
(Erase heading not required.)

Place	Date	Hour	Summary of Events and Information	Remarks and references to Appendices
Itap.	1918. Aug 9.		Routine Ordinary. 3 O.Rs. proceeded to concentration camp for dispersal.	2DC
	"10.		Routine Ordinary. Lieut. Col. E.H. Cox for duty on return from leave to England.	2DC
	"11.		Routine Ordinary. Captain E.H. Coyne reported to 2nd Conn. Rangers for temporary duty.	2DC
	"12.		Routine Ordinary.	2DC
	"13.		Routine Ordinary.	2DC
	"14.		Routine Ordinary. 1 O.R. proceeded to station of D.G.M.S. for temporary duty.	2DC
	"15.		Routine Ordinary.	2DC
	"16.		Routine Ordinary. 1 O.R. R.A.S.C. attached proceeded to concentration camp for dispersal.	2DC

WAR DIARY
INTELLIGENCE SUMMARY

Army Form C. 2118.

2/3RD EAST LANCASHIRE FIELD AMBULANCE.

Place	Date	Hour	Summary of Events and Information	Remarks and references to Appendices
Hug	1919 Feb. 17.		Field Ambulance moved by Rt hand route to Sorieure la Longue, arriving and billets at 1300 hours.	a/c
Sorieure la Longue	" 18.		Routine Ordinary.	a/c
"	" 19.		Routine Ordinary. 3 O.Rs. R.A.M.C. proceed to concentration camp for dispersal.	a/c
"	" 20.		Routine Ordinary. Major —— left Seymour + 15 O.Rs. proceeded to 48 C.C.S. for temporary duty.	a/c
"	" 21.		Routine Ordinary. Capt. E.H. Coy m proceeded to 331 Inf. Bn. R.E.B.	a/c
"	" 22.		Routine Ordinary.	a/c
"	" 23.		Routine Ordinary. 9 O.Rs. proceed to concentration camp for dispersal.	a/c

Army Form C. 2118.

WAR DIARY
INTELLIGENCE SUMMARY
(Erase heading not required.)

Instructions regarding War Diaries and Intelligence Summaries are contained in F. S. Regs., Part II. and the Staff Manual respectively. Title pages will be prepared in manuscript.

2/3RD EAST LANCASHIRE FIELD AMBULANCE

Place	Date	Hour	Summary of Events and Information	Remarks and references to Appendices
Soissons la Longue	1919 4th 4		Routine ordinary.	2ILO.
	" 5.		Routine ordinary.	2ILO.
	" 6.		Routine ordinary.	2ILO.
	" 7.		Routine ordinary. 1 O.R. R.A.S.C.(M.T) proceeded to Troyes return camp for dispersal.	2ILO.
	" 8.		Routine ordinary.	2ILO.

Sd/Wm St-PSC
O.C. 2/3rd E. Lanc: F.
Amb.

169/3559

Confidential
19
No. 19

Original
Vol 25

West Diary
2/3 Scott leaves trees Andrews
November 1919
Vol III

17 JUL 1918

2/3RD
EAST LANCASHIRE
FIELD AMBULANCE.

Army Form C.2118 & C.E.

WAR DIARY
or
INTELLIGENCE SUMMARY.
(Erase heading not required.)

Instructions regarding War Diaries and Intelligence Summaries are contained in F. S. Regs., Part II. and the Staff Manual respectively. Title pages will be prepared in manuscript.

Place	Date	Hour	Summary of Events and Information	Remarks and references to Appendices
Somme – la – Longue	March 1st		Routine	WR
	2.		Routine	WWE
	3.		1 O.R. reports for leave to U.K.	WWA
HALLOY	4.		Unit moved to HALLOY, arriving at bases at 12.30 p.m. 1 O.R. reports for duty on returning from leave to U.K. 1 O.R. R.A.S.C. H.T. proceeded to Reinforcement Depot. Base unit from Y H.D. proceeds with 1 Returned O.R. R.A.S.C. H.T. proceeds leave to U.K.	WWE
	5.			WWE
	6.		2 O.R. reports trains as reinforcements. Lt. P.H. McCaffrey M.C. U.S.A. taken on strength for wine. Major W.P. Ferguson proceeds to England for dispersal. G.O.R. proceeded to Concentration Camp. Capt (act Major) W.P. Ferguson relinquishes his acting rank on proceeding to England	WWE
	7.		1 O.R. Rivers Frances Special leave to U.K. Capt. P.H. Cayne M.C. struck off strength prine. Lt. P.H. Cayne M.C. S.H.L. C.A.M.C. taken off strength of this unit	WWE

2/3RD
1ST LANCASHIRE
Army Form C.2118.

WAR DIARY
or
INTELLIGENCE SUMMARY.

(Erase heading not required.)

*Instructions regarding War Diaries and Intelligence Summaries are contained in F.S. Regs., Part II. and the Staff Manual respectively. Title pages will be prepared in manuscript.

Place	Date	Hour	Summary of Events and Information	Remarks and references to Appendices
HALLOY	March 8		2 O.R. Base M.T. awarded 1914-15 Star	W.T.R.
	9.		2 O.R. Returnable Base H.T. prsnls leave U.K.	
			1 O.R. Base H.T. reports for duty from Personnel Depot, Base	
			1 O.R. Base prsnls spec. leave U.K.	
			5 O.R. Base H.T. prsnls war bonus as "returnable for army of occupation" from Feb 1st '19.	
			The remaining Base H.T. personnel prsnls war bonus as "required for military machinery of demobilization" from Feb 1st '19.	
			3 O.R. Base prsnls war bonus as "returnable for army of occupation" all other Base personnel prsnls war bonus as required for military machinery of demobilization.	
			5 O.R. Base M.T. prsnls war bonus as returnable for army of occupation. Notification received of 3 O.R. having been demobilized whilst on leave U.K.	
	10.		1 O.R. reports for duty from T.J. Sanders Sect.	
			1 O.R. " " from leave in France	
	11		Capt R.J. Chapman prsnls spec. leave to U.K.	W.T.R.

23RD EAST LANCASHIRE FIELD AMBULANCE

WAR DIARY or INTELLIGENCE SUMMARY

Place	Date	Hour	Summary of Events and Information	Remarks and references to Appendices
HALLOY	March 12		1 O.R. Rede MT reported 54L Coy Rede and one struck off strength of the unit. 1 O.R. No 7 P.B. Sot Coy reported 52L Coy Rede O/s " " " " Capt R.B Stewart M.C taken on strength of the unit	note
	13		24 O.R. reported for duty from 66 Div Recept Hospt. 14 O.R. proceeded to Convent Camp for dispersal. 2 O.R. rejoined this unit as reinforcements. Major (act Lt Col) P.H Cox DSO relinquished acting rank on proceeding to UK. Capt R.B Stewart M.C took over Command of unit	note
	14		9 O.R. proceeded to 48 C.C.S. for temporary duty. 1 O.R. died from S.I. injuries at 48 C.C.S. 1 LtSgn promoted to Sgt. from 24/11/18	note
	15			
	16		8 O.R. reported for duty from 48 C.C.S. 10 O.R. proceeded to 53 C.C.S. for temporary duty. 9 O.R. proceeded to Concentration Camp for dispersal	note

WAR DIARY
or
INTELLIGENCE SUMMARY
(Erase heading not required.)

Army Form C. 2118

2/3RD EAST LANCASHIRE FIELD AMBULANCE

Place	Date	Hour	Summary of Events and Information	Remarks and references to Appendices
HALLOY	March 17		Pte McCaffery M.C. R.S.A. reports for duty from 18 Kings Liverpool Regt.	WPR
	18		Pte McCaffery inclusa proceeds home to Colsyne.	WPR
	19		Capt J. H. Bounds M.O. travels Spec leave to U.K.	WPR
			1 O.R. proceeds spec leave to U.K.	
			3 O.R. Returnals, transferred to 77 Saunders, died	WPR
	20		1 O.R. reports for duty from 544 Coy R.A.S.C.	WPR
	21		1 O.R. " " " " 48 C.C.S.	
			1 "B" O.R. R.A.S.C. H.T. reports for duty from 2/2 E.L.F.A.	
	22		Capt P. H. Coyne M.C. reports " " - - 331 Pole R.F.C. & both men	WPR
			Command Quints	
	23		13 O.R. proceeded to Convalescent Camp for disposal.	WPR
			Lt McCaffery M.C. U.S.A. reports for duty on return from leave	WPR
			Capt R. B. Stewart M.C. left unit for disposal	
	24		2 O.R. proceeded to 9 Bn Manch R. for temporary duty	WPR
	25		Capt P.H. McCaffery M.C. U.S.A. struck off strength of unit	WPR
			1 O.R. reports for duty from 4 F.C.A.S.	
	26		Actg Cpln White R.a.d.c. att. promoted Temp. C.Jun. from 27/9/18.	WPR
			Capt J. H. Bounds M.O. reports for duty on return from leave	WPR

2/3rd
EAST LANCASHIRE
Army Form C. 2118.

WAR DIARY
or
INTELLIGENCE SUMMARY.
(Erase heading not required.)

Instructions regarding War Diaries and Intelligence Summaries are contained in F. S. Regs., Part II. and the Staff Manual respectively. Title pages will be prepared in manuscript.

Place	Date	Hour	Summary of Events and Information	Remarks and references to Appendices
HALLOY	March 27		2.O.R. Rd C. H.T. started for duty on return from leave	nil
	28		Unit moved to TAVIET arriving at billets 12.30 pm	
TAVIET.			10.R Rd C. H.T. rejoined his unit for disposal	nil
			Capt. W.R. Brown Reeve (T.C.) taken on strength of the unit	
			Capt. W.R. Brown Reeve (T.C.) att. g Bn Warwick R.	
	29.		10R reported for duty from 48 C.C.S.	nil
			2.O.R " " " " 53 C.C.S	nil
			2.O.R " " " " g Bn Warwick R	
	30.		8.O.R proceeded Trementhe Camp for disposal	nil
			2.O.R Reese. Nil. rejoined steam unit for disposal	
	31		Routine	nil

Major Capt. Reeve T.
O.C. 2/3rd EAST LANCASHIRE FIELD AMBULANCE.

Confidential.

140/3000.
M 26

April 1919.

War Diary.

2/3rd East Lancashire Field Ambulance.

April. 1919.

Vol. III.

Army Form C. 2118.

WAR DIARY
or
INTELLIGENCE SUMMARY
(Erase heading not required.)

2/3RD EAST LANCASHIRE FIELD AMBULANCE

Instructions regarding War Diaries and Intelligence Summaries are contained in F. S. Regs., Part II. and the Staff Manual respectively. Title pages will be prepared in manuscript.

Place	Date 1919 April	Hour	Summary of Events and Information	Remarks and references to Appendices
Taviet	1	—	4 Riders & 2 heavy draught horses evacuated to Remount Depot. 31.3.19	RR
"	2	—	5 O.R's R.A.M.C. proceeded to 66th B.H.Q for temporary duty	RR
"	3	—	1 O.R. reported for duty on return from leave 1 O.R. reported for duty as reinforcement	RR
"	4	—	1 O.R's reported for duty from 48 C.C.S. 1 O.R reported for duty from 53 C.C.S. One N.C.O struck off the strength of Unit.	RR RR RR
"	5	—	1 O.R. R.A.S.C (M.T) granted 14 days Special Leave to U.K.	RR
"	6	—	Routine duties	RR
"	7	—	1 O.R. reported for duty on return from leave to U.K.	RR
"	8	—	Routine duties	RR
"	9	—	1 O.R. R.A.S.C (H.T) reported for duty on return from leave to U.K. 1 O.R. R.A.S.C. (H.T) granted leave to U.K. 6 O.R. proceed for temporary duty to Tower Major Camp.	RR RR RR
"	10	—	1 O.R. proceed to Convalescent Camp for Dispersal	RR
"	11	—	1 O.R. granted Special Leave to U.K. 1 O.R. reported for duty on return from Leave to U.K.	RR

WAR DIARY
or
INTELLIGENCE SUMMARY.
(Erase heading not required.)

Army Form C. 2118.

2/3RD EAST LANCASHIRE FIELD AMBULANCE

Instructions regarding War Diaries and Intelligence Summaries are contained in F. S. Regs., Part II. and the Staff Manual respectively. Title pages will be prepared in manuscript.

Place	Date 1919 April	Hour	Summary of Events and Information	Remarks and references to Appendices
Taurit	12	—	1. O.R. R.A.S.C (MT) Struck off Strength of Unit.	
"	13	—	Routine Duties.	
"	14	—	1. O.R. reported for duty from 53rd C.C.S. 1 O.R. reported for duty from 25th Div. Employment Coy. 1 "returnable" O.R. transferred to 48 C.C.S.	
"	15	—	1. O.R. R.A.S.C. (HT) granted Leave to U.K. 1 O.R. reported for duty from Town Major's Office.	
"	16	—	4. O.R. Proceeded to Kantantara Camp for inspection.	
"	17	—	Routine Duties.	
"	18	—	Routine Duties.	
"	19	—	Routine Duties.	
"	20	—	Routine Duties.	
"	21	—	Routine Duties.	
"	22	—	Routine Duties.	
"	23	—	1. O.R. R.A.S.C. (MT) reported for duty from Leave to U.K. Captain R. W. Brown R.A.M.C. (T.F.) proceeded for duty to 48 C.C.S.	

WAR DIARY or INTELLIGENCE SUMMARY

2/3RD EAST LANCASHIRE FIELD AMBULANCE

Army Form C. 2118.

Place	Date 1919	Hour	Summary of Events and Information	Remarks and references to Appendices
Tartel	April 24	-	1 O.R. reported for duty on return from special leave to U.K.	A
"	25	-	Captain J.H. Rounds MC RAMC(TF) proceeded to U.K. for dispersal. 3 Nominals O.R. RAS.C.(MT) proceeded to E.D. & Army anx Horse Dep and struck off the strength of the Unit.	A
"	26	-	Routine Duties	A
"	27	-	Routine Duties	A
"	28	-	Routine Duties	A
"	29	-	1 O.R. RASC (MT) reported to this Unit for dispersal. 1 O.R. RAS.C.(MT) reported this Unit from 2/2nd East Lancs. Field Ambulance. 1 O.R. RAS.C.(MT) joined this Unit as reinforcement when 66th Div MT Coy 1 O.R. RAS.C.(MT) proceeded to 2/2nd East Lancs Field Ambulance for temporary duty. 1 O.R. RASC(MT) reported for duty from Office of ADMS 66th Div. Battn.	
"	30	-	One "nominal" O.R. RASC (MT) granted leave to U.K. One O.R. RASC(MT) proceeded to office of ADMS for temporary duty.	A

Capt. F. RAMC(TF)
2/3rd EAST LANCASHIRE FIELD AMBULANCE

Confidential

War Diary —
2/3rd East Lancashire Field Ambl.

Vol. III

May 1919.

2/3RD
EAST LANCASHIRE
FIELD AMBULANCE.

Army Form C. 2118.

WAR DIARY

~~INTELLIGENCE SUMMARY~~
(Erase heading not required.)

Place	Date	Hour	Summary of Events and Information	Remarks and references to Appendices
Taziet	May 1st		Routine duties	1174/19
	2nd		Captain R.W.Chapman M.C., R.A.M.C.(T.F), demobilized whilst on leave and struck off strength of this Unit from 25/3/19. (Auth. G.O. letter XC.88/19 A.M.D) D/10/4/19	1174/19 1173/19
	3rd		Routine duties	1173/19
	4th		Routine duties	1173/19
	5th		One other rank R.N.S.C. (M.T.), proceeded to Concentration Camp for dispersal and is struck off the strength of this Unit. Two other ranks reported for duty from Town Major, Ciney. One other rank reported for duty from 2/2nd East Lancs Field Ambulance. One other rank reported for duty from 66th Divisional Lorries H.Q.	1173/19 1173/19 1173/19 1173/19
Ciney	6th		Unit moved into Ciney, arriving in billets 13 o'clock. Fourteen other ranks proceeded to Concentration Camp for dispersal and is struck off the strength of this Unit.	1173/19 1173/19
	7th		One other rank reported for duty from 66th Divisional Lorries H.Q.	1173/19
	8th		Routine duties	1173/19
	9th		One other rank reported for duty from 544 Coy R.A.S.C.	1173/19

WAR DIARY

INTELLIGENCE SUMMARY

Army Form C. 2118.

2/3RD EAST LANCASHIRE FIELD AMBULANCE

Place	Date	Hour	Summary of Events and Information	Remarks and references to Appendices
Ciney	May 10th		Routine duties.	
	11th	–	Captain W.B. Wallman, M.C., R.A.M.C. (T.C), reported for duty from No 20 C.C.S.	
	12th		Captain E. McGuyne, M.C., R.A.M.C. (T.F), proceeded to No 48 C.C.S., for duty.	
			Captain W.B. Wallman, M.C., R.A.M.C. (T.C), took over command of this Unit.	
	13th		Routine duties.	
	14th		Routine duties.	
	15th		One Other Rank reported for duty from 66th Divisional Cadres' Canteen.	
			Two Other Ranks reported for duty from 66° Divisional Cadres' Baths.	
	16th		One Other Rank evacuated Sick to No. 55 C.C.S.	
	17th		Routine duties.	
	18th		Routine duties	
	19th		Routine duties.	
	20th		One other rank R.A.S.C. (H.T.) reported for duty on return from leave to U.K.	
	21st		Three other ranks reported for duty from Camp Commandant, Ciney.	
			One other rank reported for duty from S.M.O. 66° Divisional Cadres.	

2/3RD EAST LANCASHIRE FIELD AMBULANCE

Army Form C. 2118.

WAR DIARY
or
INTELLIGENCE SUMMARY
(Erase heading not required.)

Place	Date	Hour	Summary of Events and Information	Remarks and references to Appendices
Convoy	April 21st		One other rank evacuated sick to 55 C.C.S.	W.D.I. W.D.II.
			Five other ranks R.A.S.C. (M.T.) returned to 66th Divisional M.T. Coy.	
		18.00hrs	Unit embarked, embarked for Antwerp.	W.D.II.
Antwerp	" 22nd		Unit arrived Cadre Embarkation Camp, Antwerp, 10.00 hrs.	W.D.II.
	" 23rd		Routine duties	W.D.II.
	" 24th		Routine duties	W.D.III.
	" 25th		Routine duties	W.D.II.
	" 26th		Cadre of Unit Embarked for United Kingdom s.s. "Sicilian".	W.D.II. W.D.III.

W B Hallinan, Captain, R.A.M.C.(T.C.)
Commanding.

2/3rd EAST LANCASHIRE FIELD AMBULANCE (T.F.)

www.ingramcontent.com/pod-product-compliance
Lightning Source LLC
Chambersburg PA
CBHW080914230426
43667CB00015B/2676